Audience Participation in Theatre

**University**Campus
Oldham

**A partnership between**
the University of Huddersfield & Oldham College

Library & Computing Centre: 0161 344 8888
UCO Main Reception: 0161 344 8800
Cromwell Street, Oldham, OL1 1BB

**Text renewals: text `renew' and your UCO ID number to
07950 081389.**

THIS BOOK IS FOR
<u>REFERENCE ONLY</u>
AND MUST NOT BE TAKEN OUT
OF THE LIBRARY

# Audience Participation in Theatre

## Aesthetics of the Invitation

Gareth White

First published 2013 by
PALGRAVE MACMILLAN

Palgrave Macmillan in the UK is an imprint of Macmillan Publishers Limited,
registered in England, company number 785998, of Houndmills, Basingstoke,
Hampshire RG21 6XS.

Palgrave Macmillan in the US is a division of St Martin's Press LLC,
175 Fifth Avenue, New York, NY 10010.

Palgrave Macmillan is the global academic imprint of the above companies
and has companies and representatives throughout the world.

Palgrave® and Macmillan® are registered trademarks in the United States,
the United Kingdom, Europe and other countries.

ISBN 978–1–137–01073–5   hardback
ISBN 978–1–137–35463–1   paperback

This book is printed on paper suitable for recycling and made from fully
managed and sustained forest sources. Logging, pulping and manufacturing
processes are expected to conform to the environmental regulations of the
country of origin.

A catalogue record for this book is available from the British Library.

A catalog record for this book is available from the Library of Congress.

Typeset by MPS Limited, Chennai, India.

*This is for all the Armadillos...*

# Contents

# Acknowledgements

Like many first books, I imagine, this has taken a very long time to emerge, and thus has gathered inspiration and assistance from many more people than I will be able to acknowledge here. It originated as an academic enquiry when I started a part-time PhD at Goldsmiths College in 1999, but the germ of an idea that there was something more to audience participation than a means to an end occurred to me earlier than that. Armadillo Theatre's work between 1993 and 1996 is described and critiqued in the chapters that follow, but the people who devised and performed it with me, and set me on the path to the peculiar obsessions of this text, deserve the first thanks. To the original Armadillos, David Gilligan, Nina Anderson and Tim Dowan, and the second wave, including Tracey Emerson and Will Meddis: thank you.

For help and support during a long and meandering PhD studentship, which provided the foundation of the first half of the book, I would like to thank my supervisor, Brian Roberts, and Katja Hilevaara, Alex Mermikides and other members of the Drama@Goldsmiths research posse. Thanks to the Research Office at Central School of Speech and Drama for financing invaluable sabbatical leave and to my colleagues for taking up the slack. Particular thanks to Stephen Farrier, Katherine Low, Sheila Preston, Josh Edelman, Kelly Vassie and the Lynnes Kendrick and McCarthy, for giving their time and generous attention to early drafts of these chapters, to Jane Munro and The Visitors, for some stimulating PaR. Thanks to the students of BA Drama, Applied Theatre and Education, guinea pigs for these ideas in lectures and devised performances over the years; and also to the Performance, Community and Identity working group at TaPRA for listening and asking the difficult questions. And thanks to Pichon Baldinu and others in the De La Guarda company of 2000 (Jim, Helen, Claire); and to Jonathan Kay and Tim Crouch, at either end of a decade, unaware of me stalking them around the country. Thanks to Paula Kennedy at Palgrave for being into it, guiding me through the process, and finding a sympathetic and insightful (and still anonymous) peer reviewer. Thanks to my mother Peggy and my sister Paula for encouragement and sustenance, and to Sam Evans for putting up with me, for a while.

And thanks to you, Dear Reader. If there is to be hope for a book to mean anything, it depends on you. I have found it helpful at points to speculate how 'we' react to performances and their invitations to participate. I don't mean to assume that everyone feels as I do, or ought to. I hope you are not offended.

# Introduction

## Audience participation

There are few things in the theatre that are more despised than audience participation. The prospect of audience participation makes people fearful; the use of audience participation makes people embarrassed, not only for themselves but for the theatre makers who choose to inflict it on their audiences.

This is true not only among theatre's traditionalists, but also among those with broad horizons, aficionados of theatre informed by a century of experiments with theatre form, by the influence of 'performance' practices originating in fine art, and by an understanding of non-western theatre traditions. Audience participation is still often seen as one of the most misconceived, unproductive and excruciating of the avant-garde's blind alleys, or otherwise as evidence of the childish crassness of popular performance.

Meanwhile techniques, practices and innovations that ask for the activity of audience members and that alter the conventions of performance and audience relationships proliferate and garner critical and popular support. What is it that makes participation exciting to some audiences, and horrifying to others? Or, perhaps, what makes some kinds of audience participation seem trivial and embarrassing, and others substantial, seductive and effective? In what ways are the additional activities (additional to the activity that usually adheres to the role of 'audience member', that is) of audience members meaningful? What kind of conceptual vocabulary do we need in order to answer these questions? Unpicking and exploring some of the difficulties and potentials of audience participation is the purpose of this book.

This is not, however, a defence of audience participation, nor is it an attempt to re-define or re-describe the relationship between

1

performers and audiences. I do not aim to convince you that 'conventional' audience–performer relationships are bankrupt (I shall return to that 'conventional' shortly), or that participatory performance has the special capacity to liberate audiences or to make spectators more human. Audience participation has many passionate advocates already, and I am inclined to side with them on occasion, but my aim here is to articulate some important things about audience participation that have not been clearly articulated before, and to do so in a systematic way that can be applied to audience participation of any kind.

As I write, fashions for 'immersive' theatre and 'one-to-one' theatre are in the ascendant; the former tends to make use of spatial and architectural interventions, and to ask spectators to involve themselves physically in tracking down or pursuing the performance; the latter seeks a more direct relationship with the individual spectator. Both of these putative new forms often, but not always, ask the spectator to speak or act in dialogue with the performers or the performance environment, or to make choices that structure their experience: they invite the spectator to participate in ways that are differently active to that which is typical of the theatre event. Both terms serve to legitimate participatory practice, offering something more edgy and exciting than mere audience participation, perhaps.

Both trends are undoubtedly influenced by participatory practices in live art and fine art performance, where spectator/art work relationships have been a matter of experiment and innovation since the inception of this tradition early in the twentieth century, though from the basis of – and often as a specific challenge to – a set of conventions and aesthetic principles that belong to the tradition of fine art rather than that of the theatre. The borders between theatre and 'performance' in this tradition are now very porous, and though this book is centrally concerned with theatre, and titled accordingly, I will use some important and interesting 'performance' examples alongside those drawn from what belongs more self-consciously to 'theatre'; there is a growing body of theoretical work in relation to fine art performance that is vital to my analysis, as I will discuss later in this introduction. But the distinction between theatre and performance remains meaningful, even if it depends on institutional practice as much as actual performance practice: what happens in a theatre building, is marketed as theatre or created by a theatre company, rather than presented or promoted by a gallery and created by an 'artist', is recognised and treated differently, though the performance activity itself might be the same in all other regards.[1] This is not the place for a full discussion of this strange phenomenon, but it is an assumption that is the basis for writing a book about theatre, rather than the now common theatre/performance; and though I will cite several examples that might be designated as such, I am not concerned exclusively with the borderline territory of performance theatre. So the new trends, the immersive and the one-to-one, motivate an examination of audience participation at this point in time, but they take their place among a much broader range of theatre practices and traditions. Audience participation has always been important in applied and social theatre, where the aim to engage audience members in social activism and personal development has often been achieved through direct involvement in drama at the point of performance of a play. The techniques of participation that endure and thrive this tradition, as well as those in popular theatres, from the British pantomime to the musical, are only occasionally acknowledged or borrowed in the new trend for participation, but they are just as deserving of analysis and interpretation.

Throughout the book the argument will be illustrated by a promiscuous set of examples from practice across this range. Many of them will be drawn from personal practice as an audience participant or as a practitioner. Others are drawn from the literature described later in this introduction, or other people's accounts of their experience of audience participation. Occasionally I have resorted to hypothetical illustrations. Nothing here is articulated with the rigour of a case study, though some of the data was gathered and recorded in this way for other projects, it serves instead as an aid to the articulation of a set of concepts that the reader may find helpful in their own practice or analysis. Each chapter will conclude with a detailed discussion of a performance, or a set of connected performances, that illustrates how the argument of the chapter can be applied. These key examples are, to give an impression of the frame of reference of the argument at this stage: Armadillo Theatre's touring workshop performances for schools (1993–95); Jonathan Kay's fooling performances at Glastonbury Festival and his touring show, *Know One's Fool*, (2000–03); De La Guarda's *Villa Villa* (2000), an internationally toured dance performance from Argentina; and two plays by Tim Crouch, *The Author* and *I, Malvolio* (2010–12).

Of course all audiences are participatory. Without participation performance would be nothing but action happening in the presence of other people. Audiences laugh, clap, cry, fidget, and occasionally heckle; they pay for tickets, they turn up at the theatre, they stay to the end of the performance or they walk out. They are affected emotionally, cognitively and physically by the action they witness. Performers are inspired by their audiences and are dismayed by them, feel and feed off connections with audiences, or perhaps try to ignore them. Audiences and actors, writers, directors and producers work together to bind theatre and society together, so that one influences the other, inhabits and is co-extensive with the other, exists in the other as metaphor and metonymy. The balance in this relationship can be precarious, however: performers usually retain authority over the action, while the spectators usually retain the right to stay out of the action, and to watch and hear it. To change these relationships in some way asks both parties to surrender something: both give up some of the control they might expect to have over their part of the event. Should we, then, consider all theatre for its interactive nature, and analyse it as fundamentally consisting of interactions that happen in many different directions, not just between performers and from performers to audiences? Clearly yes, and many writers, such as Daphna Ben Chaim (*Distance in the Theatre*, 1981), Neil Blackadder (*Performing Opposition*, 2003) and Erika Fischer-Lichte (*The Transformative Power of Performance* 2008) take this approach. But I propose that there is a difference between the typical interactions expected and licensed in audience behaviour, and audience participation; it is not merely that some kinds of theatre are more interactive than others, but that there is a meaningful distinction to be made, from which there are useful things to be learnt.

My definition of audience participation is simple: the participation of an audience, or an audience member, in the action of a performance. The discussion that follows throughout this book uses examples of audience participation that can be understood in these terms. This kind of audience participation appears in many kinds of performance: far too many and too broad a range of practices to be considered as a movement, a school or a tradition of its own. But thinking about these things together, for what they have in common, is worthwhile because participation of this kind is exceptional, even though common. It is an exception to the familiar social occasion of theatrical performance, in the sense that we understand what an audience is in this context and understand how we should behave as part of one, so that activity that goes beyond this role *feels* different and *is* different to the activity that we expect to see and take part in. It feels different to the person who does it and to those who witness it. In this important experiential sense it is different to the action performed by those who take roles as performers, even if the actions they perform are in any other sense the same; and it is different to the activity performed in the role of spectator, even if this activity (in the form of laughter and applause, for example) might be louder, longer, and a more faithful expression of the what the spectator feels at any given moment. In this definition activity where people arrive at the event as participants – at a workshop or a rehearsal, for example – is not audience participation. Nor is the experience of audience members who respond to a performance without becoming part of its action – in their deeply or shallowly felt emotional and intellectual engagement with the work. Nor is the ritual activity that belongs to the role of audience: applause, laughter, and the vital choice to attend a theatre event in the first place. All of these things can appropriately be called 'participation' in theatre, but they are not what I want to consider as audience participation. This simple definition entails some problems, of course. What is an audience? Why should conventional audience response, which can make such difference to the course of an evening at the theatre, not be included? What is action? What is a performance?

These questions run through the book, and are addressed in many different ways. The origin and experience of action, particularly in the sense of agency in relation to events, is articulated with terms from social psychology, sociology, phenomenology and cognitive philosophy. Action in the theatre always has at least two dimensions: as everyday social action and as action within the extra-everyday space (often but not always conceived as a fictional space) of the performance. These two dimensions combine and conflict with each other in especially interesting ways in audience participatory performance, which I will show to be important to the way this action functions as aesthetic material. The audience, too, will be conceptualised in different ways through the book. For my purposes an audience is both a socially constructed practice, and a notional position in relation to external and internal phenomena: we become audiences and understand what we do as audience members because of traditions that we inherit and adapt, but we also go through our lives taking the position of spectator to the world around us, our own actions in it as well as those of other people.

The third important term in my definition is performance, a term that also has more than one relevant meaning. Performance has a register that comes before the theatrical or the artistic, in which we manage our presentation of ourselves, and in which we find the materials that allow us to become ourselves: audience participation exists in this register, as well as in the territory of theatrical and artistic performance. Audience members are performing themselves, and performing 'audience' as they watch performances. But in the definition above 'performance' stands for the theatrical and artistic register into which participants step, taking with them their performative social selves.

However, having asserted this definition, I must acknowledge the degree to which it is provisional and strategic: it serves to demarcate a field that will be meaningful to most readers, and vital to the framing of my argument. Although the defence of the terms of the argument, as outlined in the previous paragraphs, will become a useful and informative thread to that argument, it will not entirely remove a difficulty with the definition that entails from its basis on contingent (historical, institutional, conventional) practices: that these practices change, and most importantly, that the phenomena that I am observing are often instrumental in this process of change. So what constitutes action in my definition will change, sometimes quite quickly, as conventions of audience behaviour change. Rather than fundamentally undermining this definition, this invites attention to this changing context, which is often – not coincidentally – where the interesting dimensions of audience participatory performance occur. It also invites a shift in approach to this definition and the need for such a definition: if what constitutes participation is necessarily constantly in flux, why attempt to demarcate these exceptional practices at all? Why not pay attention to all social action as participation, on its continuum with dramatic and performance action? This is certainly a tactic that I will take occasionally, as my argument progresses, as it is necessary to explore this borderline just as theatre practitioners explore it. But it is not my purpose to write a new theory of the audience in theatre, so I will continue with my definition in place, as it puts some useful – if at times uncertain and porous – borders around a field.

In the opening paragraphs of *Space and Performance* (2000), Gay McAuley shows how the twentieth century's definitions of theatre (she gives examples from Bertolt Brecht, Eric Bentley, Jerzy Grotowski and Peter Brook) all acknowledge the vital communication between the audience and the performer. McAuley finds that theatre is built around the spatial relationship between these positions:

> The specificity of theatre is not to be found in its relationship to the dramatic, as film and television have shown through their appropriation and massive exploitation of the latter, but in that it consists essentially of the interaction between performers and spectators in a given space. Theatre is a social event, occurring in the auditorium as well as on the stage, and the primary signifiers are physical and even spatial in nature. (McAuley 2000: 5)

The defining spatial characteristic in this passage is the division of one group from the other, so that they can be brought together in a social order based on this separation. A social occasion becomes a theatre performance partly through the separation of performers from audiences. The manner of this separation, achieved architecturally and socially, is historically and culturally specific, as is the behaviour considered appropriate to the role of audience members. The current relative passivity of the audience in the European theatre tradition has not always been the convention, as Susan Kattwinkel (2003: ix) observes:

> The passive audience really only came into being in the nineteenth century, as theatre began its division into artistic and entertainment forms. Practitioners and theorists such as Wagner, with his 'mystic chasm', and he and Henry Irving with their darkened auditoriums, took some of the many small steps in the nineteenth century that physically separated the audience from the performance and discouraged spectatorial acts of ownership or displeasure or even vociferous approval.

Prior to this the sense of the activity that was appropriate to an audience was much broader, as it still is in many non-European cultures and other performance traditions (such as stand-up comedy or popular music). Pre-nineteenth century European and North American audiences would socialise openly in the auditorium, buy and sell, and venture opinions about the play itself, to the extent of exercising a right to 'cry down' or 'damn' a play (as in Blackadder's excellent account of the last throws of this power of veto at the turn of the twentieth century). What an audience is and does is historically and culturally contingent, often in complex ways. In this context my definition of audience participation is also historically and culturally contingent, not in the sense that it is intended to pin down what audience participation is at the historical and cultural moment at which I write, but in the sense that as understandings change of what an audience is and does, so the sense of what is or isn't audience participation under this definition also changes.

Famous examples of audience participation are often notable events in the progress of experimental performance: The Living Theatre's *Paradise Now*; the Performance Group's *Dionysus in '69*; Yoko Ono's *Cut Piece*; Marina Abramovic's *Rhythm O*; Annie Sprinkle's *Public Cervix Announcement*; De La Guarda's *Villa Villa*; Punchdrunk's *Faust*; and Tim Crouch's *The Author*. Anyone familiar with these pieces or their reputations will note also that some of them are notorious as markers of the excess of experimentation. There are also audience participation practices that are less transgressive and which inhabit quite different traditions with quite different ambitions: the British pantomime, for example, and the Theatre in Education movement. These modes of practice also stand out as exceptions to the general rules of theatre practice because they feature audience participation so heavily. Audience participation marks a border in our understanding of what theatre is and can be, and like many border zones, it is interesting as such. But in commentary on moments (even of iconic moments) of audience participation, there is often a significant gap, a lack of concern for how it was achieved, and for what moments of participation might have meant in themselves because people other than the performing company acted in them. The fact that people have participated and what they have contributed to a performance might be commented on, but how it is that they have been led to do so is most often not considered worthy of comment. In an account of Ono's *Cut Piece*: '[t]he audience was invited to cut the clothing from Ono, who sat or kneeled on the stage. Ono's placing herself as the object for unwrapping or potential destruction was rare' (Iles in Ono 1997: 14). The imagery of exposure and violence is referred to, as is the artist's place at the centre of the work, but the even more rare placement of an audience member as the subject that does the unwrapping – or as the potential agent of destruction – is not discussed here or in the rest of the article, nor is the procedure that led them to it. Without this involvement of the spectator as a performer of the crucial action of the piece, it would have been a quite different work, and yet the technique that allows this to happen goes unrecorded, as does its effect on the participant. But a consideration is necessary, because Ono clearly intended something to happen that actively involved her audience, and this intention is not the same thing as the process through which it comes to fruition. Ono has made herself and her body into a part of the media of her art, but she has also made the audience members and their bodies into media. Further questions arise about the performances of these participants: Ono has involved them in an act of symbolic violence, and it seems safe to assume that their participation is voluntary, but beyond that how far can we say that they are in control of what they do? It is quite correct that this account prioritises the agency of Ono, because she has ultimately inflicted this violence on herself, in an event that appears to have left participants with two kind of conflict to choose from: either rejecting Ono's invitation to cut, or cutting as they have been asked to. Just who has cut or not cut may be less important, in this instance, than Ono's choice to initiate the action, but we can be confident that it was important to those present whether they participated in this way or did not.

There are procedures through which participation is invited, and there are processes through which the performances invited become meaningful in a way that is different to other performances. These processes make the audience member into material that is used to compose the performance: an artistic medium. This book brings the processes and media of audience participation into focus and provides a theory for uncovering the procedures through which practitioners create the participatory processes they aim for. Most simply put, the argument is that these processes and procedures, particularly in the control they both share and withhold and in the point of view that they engender in the participant, are aesthetically important.

The range of practices brought into play by this definition and by the nature of my enquiry is very broad, but there is some narrowing of the field through a focus on the *invitation* to participate, rather than the whole phenomenon. There is more to be said about how participation is maintained by practitioners, and experienced by those who accept an invitation, but my analysis will mostly be limited to the activity that makes an invitation understood by an audience and the process through which they accept (or decline) that invitation. This includes the first few moments of participation, as the change of role takes effect, and inevitably will stray further into the implications of what kind of participation has been invited and what kind of activity can ensue. By focussing on the moment when the definition of the theatrical situation changes I aim to unpack the most important aspects of this transformation.

## Why 'aesthetics'?

In an important sense anything that provides a new component of the general theory of art is a work of aesthetics; but this is an 'aesthetics of the invitation' in a more deliberate sense than that. It is part of my assertion that the actions and experiences of audience participants is worth paying attention to: I aim to show that these actions and experiences are aesthetic material and have characteristics that need to be thought through in an appropriate way. It is an assertion of a concern with the dynamics, functions and value that the moment or episode of audience participation has as part of an event or work of art. The key questions become, in this light, concerned with what about audience participation has to be considered as aesthetic material, and what is particular about the aesthetic material of audience participation. The answers to these questions, as I have just suggested, lie with the way the audience member herself or himself becomes the artist's medium, and so the work's aesthetic material.

Aesthetics as a discipline has always been concerned with these values, characteristics and functions, but the word 'aesthetic' has proliferated in meanings in a way that is not always helpful in organising our thinking about these matters. As Leonard Koren says in his short but very useful book *Which Aesthetics Do You Mean?: Ten Definitions* (2010: 3):

> although "aesthetic" and "aesthetics" appear to agreeably elevate the tone of whatever discourse they're used in, they rarely function as mere decorous vacuity. Yet because these terms confusingly refer to so many disparate but often connected things, the exact meaning of the speaker or writer, unless qualified, is sometimes unclear.

Of Koren's ten definitions, several will be at stake in my discussion. Most of all it is the nature of my argument as a development of a small corner of the philosophy of art that qualifies it under this term. But my argument also has a part to play in continuing discussions about the place and nature of beauty, and other dimensions of artistic quality, and of the development of artistic styles and tastes. Koren also notes that the aesthetic sometimes stands for a particular cognitive mode, and the intimate relationship between audience participatory performance and the subjectivity of the participant makes this very relevant.

Aesthetics, as the philosophy of art, has always been concerned with what art is and what it is good for. One of the consequences of the enormous broadening of the available categories of art practice, and the phenomenon of the appropriation of the everyday to make art (in collage, in surrealism, in live art and so on) through which an object or an action becomes art simply because the artist says so (and other people are sympathetic enough to this claim to treat it as such), is that since the early part of the twentieth century aesthetics has had to proliferate too. It is no longer possible to have one theory of the aesthetic – if indeed universal theories of art were ever adequate – it is necessary to recognise a different 'aesthetic' for each different practice of making and receiving work. This is related to, but not entirely the same as, the sense of an aesthetic as a style of art making and its associated consumption. It is relevant to the argument of this book where the performance practices that include audience participation each evolve their own distinctive aesthetic, which include participation in their media alongside more familiar elements such as spoken language, choreographed movement and scenography. An individual aesthetic will contain an implicit definition of what art is, within its practice: what is, and by implication what is not, to be viewed or experienced in an art-appropriate way in the context of this practice. And indeed it will contain an understanding of what it means to treat things in an art-like way.

The argument of this book is that there are certain things that will appear repeatedly in the aesthetics (in this sense of multiple, distinctive associations of production, recognition and reception) of audience participatory performance practice, such that they are worth considering as foundational concepts for the analysis of this kind of work, or of the aesthetic that is in play in any example of it. The work becomes meaningful through its aesthetic, and this aesthetic – as a collection of propositions about what an artwork is and how to respond to it – if examined in detail can tell us much more about the meanings and potential meanings of the work than an analysis that takes effects as the first line of investigation: in order to understand an aesthetic we must understand its media. The 'what it is' of an artwork is built on a common understanding of artists and audiences of what the media of the work are, what is to be given attention and what kind of attention to pay to it. What I do not aim to do here, however, is to isolate and describe the specific aesthetic of any of the contemporary trends for audience participatory performance. This research is being done elsewhere, by other people, in relation to immersive performance and the one-to-one, and with particular depth and rigour regarding 'relational' performance and participatory live art, as I will discuss below. I am confident that what is thought through here will be useful to the identification of the aesthetic conventions that adhere to particular movements, trends and modes of practice, and inevitably my discussion will sketch some of these conventions as I illustrate my argument with examples; but my aim is to isolate and examine what it is that is likely to become aesthetic material when audiences are asked to take action in a performance, and what kinds of outcomes are to be expected when these things are treated 'aesthetically'.

Some trends in aesthetic theory have tried to find the root of a special 'aesthetic sense', to explain what it is about responding to art works that is so peculiarly affecting; this idea is generally rejected in the progressive aesthetics that I am sympathetic to. Some theories – Clive Bell's (2007) idea of an 'aesthetic emotion', for example, and in another of Koren's definitions, of aesthetics as 'a cognitive mode' – recognise the origin of the term and the discipline in 'aisthesis' as sensation and perception in general; which is echoed by Wolfgang Welsch's suggestion that in an aesthetics beyond aesthetics: 'aisthesis should provide the framework of the discipline while art, although important, will be only one of its subjects' (quoted in Halsall, Jansen and O'Connor 2009: 191). Art has a powerful affective dimension, continuous with the affective response we might have to other things and events – to nature, the environment, and to other people and what they do. Similarly, I am interested in aesthetic affects, in the sense that thoughts and feelings are engendered in response to audience participation. As I shall discuss throughout the book, but particularly in Chapters 3 and 4, being in a position to take action, taking action, and having a first-person relationship with that action will inflect the understanding of and the feelings generated by performance.

The idea of the aesthetic as a generalised mode of thought and being has been the subject of vigorous critique, and is treated with considerable scepticism, particularly following the work of Pierre Bourdieu; Terry Eagleton and more recently Jacques Rancière have added their considerable theoretical weight behind this critique. Bourdieu's sociology has shown how the social practices that we collect under the concepts of art and the aesthetic belong to our class and cultural structure, and ultimately serve to preserve privilege. Rancière, (2004, 2009b), though opposed to Bourdieu's particular conclusions about social structure, also opposes a sense of the aesthetic as transcendent, and portrays the aesthetic as one of a series of 'regimes' under which that which we now call art has been governed. Eagleton's *The Ideology of the Aesthetic* (1990) surveys the thought that has accompanied this regime, from Baumgarten and Kant as the originators of the enlightenment aesthetics with its project to separate the understanding of art from politics, ethics, logic and other kinds of thought, and to conceive a separate space and a separate state of being for art. Eagleton's view is broadly in line with Bourdieu, that by and large the concept of the aesthetic has been a bourgeois ideology, serving to justify – in varying and often contradictory ways – social relations in the service of capital. In *The Radical Aesthetic* (2000) Isobel Armstrong has challenged this view, proposing that the propositions of European aesthetics over this time have often been explicitly progressive, and sometimes able to put into effect the work of using art in the causes of liberty and equality; there is work to do, however:

> The project that arises from questions about democratic access to art is actually that of changing the category itself, or re-describing it, so

that what we know looks different, and what we exclude from traditional categories of art also looks different. This task is not accomplished. (Armstrong 2000: 16)

A contemporary aesthetics is implicated in this project, as is any progressive art practice. As a practitioner and teacher of 'applied' theatre myself the work of re-describing the category of art and its potential for social change is a daily task; making robust claims for emerging practice like the ambitious and thoughtful use of audience participation is also part of that task; and the following propositions about what else the idea of an aesthetics can mean are proposed with this context in mind. Identifying the media of audience participation serves this task, but further to this is identifying the way in which we relate to these media and make them meaningful.

The idea of the 'aesthetically pleasing' is often used in the making of theatre as well as in everyday conversation about encounters with things that can be subject to a simple judgement: furnishings and architecture, music and clothes, the arrangement of food on a plate, lighting, costume and sound, movement in a space. This idea is somehow included in the category of art but excepted from its more rigorous demands. Pleasure in this sense is something that has some of the characteristics of the beautiful in Kantian aesthetics, it is palpably personal, but also worth arguing in a general sense, and it can prompt the recognition of a property apparently held by the object in question. Obviously this kind of aesthetic pleasure has to be understood as part of the regime of the practice of art that we live within, so that what we feel in response to it, what we are able to say about it (and say through it) is anything but independent of who we are and where we come from. But this notion of aesthetic pleasure does point to something ineffable in art experience, the felt response that can persuade us to make claims for universality, or at least to urge others to appreciate what we appreciate. If this is something like the beauty that has fascinated and eluded aestheticians for hundreds of years, and which is now treated with great scepticism as a tool of dominant (particularly sexist) bourgeois ideologies, then it survives in everyday speech. There has been a return to the idea of beauty and the felt response to art experience, for example in Janet Woolf's *The Aesthetics of Uncertainty* (2008), which proposes a feminist approach to beauty, in Joe Winston's *Beauty and Education* (2010), which asks for a consideration of the power of beauty in pedagogy, and James Thompson's *Performance Affects* (2009), which similarly shows how emotional response to participatory drama can be as important as its capacity to facilitate measurable 'impact'. Where classical aesthetics will privilege the beautiful or the sublime, progressive and participatory aesthetics (both styles and theories) are as interested in other pleasures and other effects: the uncanny, the unexpected and the transgressive, perhaps. Most importantly they include the potential for political and ethical values and outcomes to form part of the definition of aesthetics and the work of art.

Most of the significant writing about audience participation has placed a political agenda front and centre, prior to aesthetic considerations of these various kinds. This is not the case with other kinds of performance, for which we are able to identify their formal characteristics and their media in a way that is at least in one sense prior to the discussion of politics. In music we are aware that tone, rhythm and volume are the media of the musician; in dance the moving body and its relationship to the space around it and to other bodies are the comparable fundamental building blocks of the art form; in theatre these spatio-temporal elements usually combine with the voice and words. As Bourdieu has demonstrated convincingly, none of these things can be considered as independent of their social context, or immune to a political critique. All of these artistic forms, even the manipulation of sound, space and time in music and dance, are implicated in the politics of social differentiation and its expressions of power and subordination. But in articulating these forms we allow ourselves a space for discussing fundamental elements that defers the political and ethical until a later point. What I want to do for audience participation is to suggest that there are questions of media that are fundamental to it that can be discussed in these terms, and to defer the political analysis of them very briefly. As John Dewey says in *Art as Experience*: 'Everything depends upon the way in which material is used when it operates as medium' (1980: 66). This may be the biggest contribution that will be made by this book in terms of 'aesthetics' – identifying what it is that practitioners of audience participation work with.

## The practice and theory of audience participation

Where does audience participation happen? As a teacher of applied theatre and a maker of Theatre in Education (TIE), I declare an interest: as someone who has taken audience participation for granted throughout my career, and who is determined to think and write about its application in community and educational contexts at the same time as in more conventional theatrical contexts. TIE, Theatre of the Oppressed,

Museum Theatre, Reminiscence Theatre, Theatre for Development and all the other multiplying fields that find themselves under the discursive and pedagogical umbrella of applied theatre, whenever they put on performances for audiences, are as likely as not to ask those audiences to participate. These fields deal in participation of other kinds: longer term involvement in the research, conception, devising and reception of performances, as well as participation in workshops that never reach an audience at all, are these days often considered to be the most challenging and appropriate activities to make lasting impressions on people's lives. Audience participation is no longer at the cutting edge of applied theatre practice, but nevertheless, these fields and others like them are part of the 'where' of audience participation.

Children's theatre, including British pantomime and other traditional and popular forms, often make use of audience participation, or have audience activities as familiar parts of their codes of behaviour. Commercial musicals also have their interactive components: sometimes explicitly framed invitations to sing along, (as with *The Rocky Horror Show* or *Return to the Forbidden Planet*) though also in the apparently audience-led mass singing often heard in the 'jukebox' musicals of the last decade (*Mamma Mia*, *We Will Rock You*, even Graeae's *Reasons to be Cheerful*). Though audience participation has often been a marginal and experimental impulse, it also has its place in the most commercial performance and is enjoyed by some of the largest audiences.

I have already noted a series of recognisably experimental works, some of which should be thought of as 'live art' or 'performance'; many of the most interesting approaches to participation happen in these areas or on their very porous boundaries with experimental theatre. Among the conceptual points of origin for performance in the fine art tradition is the presence of the viewer of the work in the temporal event of its creation and reception, and the relationship of the artist to that event and to the viewer. This is work that is predicated on formal experimentation, so the proliferation of positions for the viewer/participant is to be expected. Explicit connections between fine art performance and theatre are sometimes evident, as in Schechner and the Performance Group's collaboration with Alan Kaprow for their early 'environmental' theatre, while Robert Wilson and Hans Peter Kuhn's *HG* (1995, a production which is an acknowledged influence on Punchdrunk's Felix Barrett) saw acclaimed theatre practitioners adopting the style of the art installation.

Audience participation in applied theatre can be traced to early TIE and Augusto Boal's early use of 'simultaneous dramaturgy' in the 1960s;

live art performance has made use of it at least as far back as Kaprow's 'happenings'; its use in traditional and commercial performance can be traced further back than that, to the nineteenth century music hall and beyond; there is an unbroken continuity between traditional performance in some African traditions and contemporary playwriting – Femi Osofisan, for example, makes this explicit in the form and content of plays like *Once Upon Four Robbers* (1978, published in Gilbert 2001). But though it is not new, it seems to be particularly current, especially evidently in fringe theatre in London over the past decade. To say why this is so suggests a different, historical and cultural enquiry to this one, but for the moment note that over this period a brief – and not exhaustive – list of successful audience participatory theatre playing in London would include: De La Guarda's *Villa Villa* (1999/2000) and *Fuerzabruta* (2006); Shunt's *Dance Bear Dance* (2003) or *Amato Saltone* (2006); Punchdrunk's *Faust* (2005) and *The Masque of the Red Death* (2007); Tim Crouch's *The Audience* (2009–10); and Para Active and Zecora Ura's *Hotel Medea* (2009–12). Though all of these are recognisably fringe events, each (with the exception of *The Audience*, at the Royal Court, though this too has been revived several times and toured extensively) had a very wide appeal. They played to large audiences over long and often extended runs, and often charged ticket prices equal to shows in the West End. The kinds of participation on offer in these pieces vary immensely, and are often accompanied by alternative audience–performer formations and relationships. The appetite among a substantial number of theatre-goers to be or become a different kind of audience, and to accept the invitation to participate, is evident.

There is a growing tendency for theatre artists and producers to label work as immersive: Punchdrunk, for example, claim to be pioneers of 'a game-changing form of immersive theatre' (2010). This particular term is interesting in its implications and assumptions about audience experience, and about the nature and potential of theatre and performance. Perhaps the term will become the point of convergence for a trend towards experimental audience strategies, but its usefulness in this study is to point up an attitude to the experiential nature of participation. Not all audience participation would be claimed under the rubric of the immersive (vague though that is, at this stage), but the suggestion of being inside that comes with the idea of the immersive has resonances with the experience of being able to take action within the work, and with the changed point of view that is gained through this experience that I suggest are the special characteristics of audience participation. To be inside the work, not just inside its physical and temporal space but inside it as an aesthetic, affective, phenomenological entity gives a different aspect to the idea of a point of view, and of action, so that the idea of immersive theatre will be a particularly useful reference point for parts of my argument.

Despite its significant presence in diverse fields of theatre and performance, and this growing popularity among theatre makers and audiences, comparatively little has been written about the processes of audience participation, even when the phenomenon has been documented. Two books, which bear the title *Audience Participation*, serve as examples of two different ways in which the field has been addressed in print up to now. The earlier of the two, Brian Way's 1980 volume (*Audience Participation: Theatre for Young People*), is a practitioner's guide to a specialist practice: the children's theatre of which he was a pioneer. In contrast to this is Susan Kattwinkel's collection of essays (2003), each of which is concerned with different performances, rather than forming a single continuous theorisation. Both are useful books, but do not present the broad-based theorisation that is possible. What they do offer is a variety of accounts of audience participation events and audience participation techniques: Way's book of practice with young children and teenagers, in theatre buildings and in school halls; Kattwinkel's of a range from avant-garde dance, eighteenth-century theatre, pantomime, to community-based drama. Writing that provides this kind of material is fairly common: work that records audience participation as a part of its description or analysis of performances without making it a main focus. It appears in work that surveys counter-cultural theatre in the sixties and seventies, by Kostelanetz (1994), Kershaw (1992), Craig (1980) and Ansorge (1975). In surveys of performance art and live art, such as Goldberg (1979), Kirby (1965) and Case (1990), more experiments appear sometimes including the same personalities. Mason's (1992) guide to street theatre and Coult and Kershaw's work about Welfare State International (1990), show both how these progressive audience participations grow and become part of practice that consolidates and diversifies in the years that follow. More recent use of spectator involvement in fine art performance has been theorised as dialogical, by Kester (2004), and relational, by Bourriaud (2002), and the claims of both these writers have been contested by Bishop (2004, 2006, 2012). Applied theatre's literature contains many accounts of audience participation, for example, Haedicke and Nellhaus (2001) on community-based theatre, and Salhi (1998), Byam (1999) and Byram (1985) on Theatre for Development. Where writing on applied theatre draws heavily on Boal's practice, his participatory techniques inevitably receive a lot of attention, in Cohen-Cruz and Schutzman (1994), Babbage (2004), Dwyer (2004) or Mda (1993) for example; and Cohen-Cruz's recent *Engaging Performance* (2010) places Boalian practice within a continuum of participatory practices. O'Toole (1976) and Jackson (1997, 2007), offer analytical views of audience participation practice in Theatre in Education.

Boal's own writing is easily the most influential by a practitioner theorising his own practice, both in terms of the work done in applied theatre and in the way it is thought about, though both his theory and practice attract a degree of criticism. For the reader in English, *Theatre of the Oppressed* (1979) provides his alternative theatre historiography, critique of the non-participatory nature of conventional theatre and proposal for a participatory theatre practice, though one has to look to his other books, such as *Games for Actors and Non-Actors* (1992) or *Legislative Theatre* (1998) to find more detailed account of the techniques. Schechner, in *Environmental Theatre* (1994) gives some detailed consideration to the practicalities and the ethical difficulties of asking for participation in progressive theatre. Less well known is Gary Izzo, whose *Interactive Theatre* (1998) is concerned with commercial applications of similar techniques and sets out a new terminology of its own. Johnstone's (1981, 2000) writing about improvisation contains many passing references to handling audience suggestions, and effective ways of making use of participants, but only against the background of improvisation by 'performers'. Where there is sustained writing about audience participation the perspective is usually that of a maker of theatre rather than of an observer, the emphasis, at least for Boal, Izzo and Johnstone is on understanding work as it is done, explaining it rather than examining it. For Boal certainly, and partly for Schechner and Izzo, audience participation is presented as a solution to questions asked about conventional theatre, rather than as something to be questioned in its own right. Schechner does go further, offering unresolved questions about what can be achieved with audience participation; some of these unanswered questions are addressed in this book.

Claire Bishop has established an influential body of work on the subject of participation and interaction in fine art performance. In it she challenges romanticism about the emancipatory potential of participation, and the contradictory thinking that underpins some of this critique, drawing significantly on Jacques Rancière and taking issue with Pierre Bourriaud's *Relational Aesthetics*:

> To argue [...] that social participation is particularly suited to the task of social inclusion not only assumes that participants are already

in a position of impotence, it actually reinforces this arrangement. (Bishop in Halsall, Jansen and O'Connor 2009: 254).

Far from active engagement in itself being enough to open an intersubjective space that will alter the social relations at play around the space of the interactive work, it is in danger of reproducing the assumptions of that dominant social space, if it does not put itself to work in opposing them specifically. An art that does not focus on the harmoniously social, but on the capacity for 'relational antagonism' (Bishop 2004: 79) within the aesthetic frame of an interactive work has the potential to scrutinise 'all easy claims for a transitive relationship between art and society' (Bishop 2004: 79), and to properly critique society itself. This antagonism can be expressed both within the work and in its relationships with its social and political contexts: interactive work must be allowed to clash with those that it invites to participate, as well as to create convivial spaces for them to come together. She notes that in the work of Jeremy Deller and Phil Collins:

> intersubjective relations are not an end in themselves but serve to unfold a more complex knot of concerns about pleasure, disruption, engagement, and the conventions of social interaction. Instead of extracting art from the 'useless' domain of the aesthetic and fusing it with social praxis, the most interesting art of today exists between two vanishing points. (2009: 255)

To occupy this space between two poles it needs to engage with both – the aesthetic and the social; it follows from this that in order to be able to understand and assess this work we need to have a full understanding of what is aesthetic in this context.

In re-orienting the agenda of the political and ethical claims of participatory art, and asserting the importance of considering the aesthetic characteristics of the work as well as its work in the social sphere, Bishop helps to set the scene for this study of audience participatory performance. What I pursue in this book is not an extension of this debate: for a start the work with which she is concerned is clearly part of a different institutional environment, and the terms in which she addresses it are drawn from that tradition; equally, this practice is not always participatory in the sense that I am interested in. Its characteristic, as 'social' art, is that it makes explicit extensions of the art work into the social contexts that surround it, and makes these extensions and their impact into aesthetic material. Sometimes this is through audience (or spectator, given the different viewing practices of the field) participation, but often the participation of the 'public' is invited and contracted in very different ways. Think, for example, of Santiago Sierra's 2000 work *Workers Who Cannot Be Paid, Remunerated to Remain Inside Cardboard Boxes*, presented in Berlin, Havana and Guatemala City, where 'the imagery of boxed people both metaphorised and literalised local refugee and labour politics' (Jackson 2011: 61). Clearly this imagery is assembled around the bodies and subjectivities of these 'boxed people', but they are not the audience, their own relationship to the work is relevant – as well as troubling and problematic – but the key orientation of spectator to art work has not been fundamentally altered in this work. My citation here is to Shannon Jackson's *Social Works* (2011), which is a substantial contribution to the debate initiated by Bishop. Jackson takes steps to undermine the binaries that are instituted in this debate:

> (1) social celebration versus social antagonism; (2) legibility versus illegibility; (3) radical functionality versus radical unfunctionality; and (4) artistic heteronomy versus artistic autonomy. (Jackson 2011: 48)

And while some of these terms have more resonance in the discourse of fine art than theatre art – polarities of functionality and autonomy certainly – Jackson's nuanced discussion of how politically and socially engaged work can operate across these poles rather than at their ends gives a significant lead in showing how effects and aesthetics can entwine with rather than undermine each other. The terms under which Bishop and Jackson propose we address the value of participatory art will not form a significant part of my discussion, but they are important to its context. Instead I will use two of the contrasting theorists that feature in Bishop's discussions in order to set the terms of a different agenda.

## Emancipating spectators

As with the advocates of the 'social turn' in live art performance, some of the champions of audience participation in theatre simplify and overstate their case:

> Spectator is a bad word. The spectator is less than a man and it is necessary to humanise him, to restore to him his capacity for action in all its fullness. He too must be a subject, an actor on an equal plane with those generally accepted as actors, who must also be spectators. (Boal 1979: 154–155)

This is an extravagant claim. While it is entirely possible to show that the practice of Theatre of the Oppressed, with its audience participatory and extended participation techniques, can be instrumental in stimulating a capacity for (social, political) action in individuals and communities, and promoting an idea of a 'humanised' subjectivity (and some of the works cited above do this, in relation to particular examples of the techniques in context), it is not necessary to exaggerate the failings of conventional spectatorship in order to make this point. More modest claims are made for other kinds of audience participation, which similarly define participatory performance as an improvement of the relationship between performer and spectator:

> Since 2000, we have pioneered a game changing form of immersive theatre in which roaming audiences experience epic storytelling inside sensory theatrical worlds.
> Blending classic texts, physical performance, award-winning design installation and unexpected sites, our infectious format rejects the passive obedience usually expected of audiences. (Punchdrunk 2010)

The liberation on offer here is comparatively limited, but still the conventional audience is denigrated in favour of one that is free-roaming and adventurous. This kind of over-statement can serve as an easy target for those who would prefer a more distanced relationship between spectators and performers. Jacques Rancière's *The Emancipated Spectator* (2009a: 1–23)[2] is a text that might already represent a cornerstone of a sceptical approach to experiments with actor–audience relationships, and it is welcome as such. In brief, Rancière's argument is to address what has he says has falsely been identified as the 'paradox of spectatorship', and to critique the most famous responses to it. He looks for the grounds for influential theories of the spectator, specifically those of Brecht and Artaud, and finds them in Plato's *Republic*. The paradox is this: 'There is no theatre without a spectator, [...] but being a spectator is a bad thing' (2009a: 2). It is said to be a bad thing because seeing is inferior to knowing, looking is inferior to acting, and in Plato's opinion watching theatre actively stimulates vice and disease. The problematic response to this, for Rancière, is to manipulate spectatorship in either direction increasing or decreasing aesthetic distance, and ultimately tending towards a theatre without spectators. Though Rancière does not make the point explicitly, this can be read as a polemic against the most extravagant claims for audience participatory theatre, especially when we remember Boal's injunction that 'spectator is a bad word'.

His argument is based on an analogy between theatre and pedagogy, in which he casts theatre makers, 'the dramaturges', as traditional 'masters' who know what they have to teach, and collapse distance in order to bring their pupils into possession of that knowledge. This urge to collapse distance is based on a fixation with the inequality of intelligence: on knowing how one's knowledge is greater than another's, and how to give that knowledge to them. In contrast to this, it is the thesis of his *The Ignorant Schoolmaster* that:

> The human animal learns everything in the same way as it initially learnt its mother tongue, as it learnt to venture into the forest of things and signs that surround it, so as to take its place among human beings: by observing and comparing one thing with another, a sign with a fact, a sign with another sign. (Rancière 2009a: 10).

On this basis his suggestion is that we dismiss methodologies designed to bring audiences into our superior understanding, and allow them the autonomy to encounter performances as part of the 'forest of things and signs' and thus we respect the intelligence of our audience, and allow their emancipation, which consists precisely of 'the process of verification of the equality of intelligence'.

Among the strengths of the essay are that he makes us wary of manifestos, and ask us to question the dismissal of the spectator – though he may exaggerate Brecht and Artaud, sometimes his caricature of the radical dramaturge reads as if he is quoting Boal; Rancière shows how reductive such arguments can be. He also reminds us that the contemporary potential to cross-borders and blur roles and forms can lead to nothing more than another form of 'consumerist hyper-activism', which 'uses the blurring of boundaries and the confusion of roles to enhance the effect of performance without questioning its principles' (2009a: 21): theatre as shopping, with more choice but to no purpose. But there are a number of things we might take issue with. This is a brief sketch of Rancière's argument, but in that argument Rancière himself makes use of a cartoon of the practice of most theatre makers, in which they have a mission to pass on superior knowledge, and are in thrall to a mistaken, Platonic, antipathy to spectatorship. The essay seems less aware of contemporary practice, than of the manifestoes that inspired it at sometime in the past. It simply isn't the case that most practitioners these days (and arguments could also be made on behalf of Brecht and Artaud in this respect) have a thesis that they wish to transmit, so the analogy with the pedagogical master that is at the centre of the argument is weak.[3] If there is an anti-theatrical prejudice in the contemporary avant-garde, it is more likely to be inherited from Michael Fried's influence on fine art performance. The conclusive suggestion of the essay is that we should 'revoke the privilege of vitality and communitarian power accorded the theatrical stage, so as to restore it to an equal footing with the telling of a story, the reading of a book, or the gaze focused on an image' (2009a: 22); this reads like a manifesto too.

Rancière says that distance is the proper situation: that it allows us equality in relation to the maker of the work, through the mediation of the work itself. Others suggest that intimacy, to the extent of the loss of autonomy, might represent both a materially productive and ethical approach. For Fischer-Lichte, in *The Transformative Power of Performance* (2008), there is no distance between the spectator and the work, because the spectator is part of the work. For her, in all performance, but in a self-conscious and strategic way in performance since the 60s, there is an 'autopoietic feedback loop' (2008: 39). Autopoietic because it is self-generating, an emergent system that arises from itself, with only the input of raw materials rather than an exterior guiding hand; and a feedback loop because the activity of the spectators, however subtle, becomes part of the event, generating the variations in the activity of the performers and other spectators that generate more variations, and so on, and produce the liveness of the theatre event. This is part of her ontology of performance, and if performance makers have made a virtue of it, it would be foolish of theorists to leave it out of the account: 'If "production" and "reception" occur at the same time and place, this renders the parameters developed for a distinct aesthetics of production, work and reception ineffectual' (Fischer-Lichte 2008: 18).

Rancière's 'emancipated spectator', however, knows no feedback loop. He or she meets a performance as a set of 'things', 'signs', that are autonomous, and in the face of which he or she remains autonomous. For James Thompson in *Performance Affects* the intimacy of participation in performance creates its ethical force. Meeting the other in a situation where the forces of affect are working upon us both enhances that encounter, and shows us: 'the limits of our autonomy, and thus our limitless responsibility to others, that I believe should be at the heart of an ethical practice of applied theatre and the starting point for its politics' (Thompson 2009: 153).

This is especially powerful in applied theatre, where the sources of affective response can be so personal and therefore more powerful, but it applies in other performances too. These are two recent proposals for a sense of what theatre is, and what is ethical about it, that come from very different sources: Fischer-Lichte is writing about the European avant-garde, Thompson about participatory applied theatre. But both offer a definition of theatrical performance that does away with autonomy in the moment of reception, without ever saying that spectatorship is in any sense a bad thing.

The thesis in *The Emancipated Spectator* can be pursued a little further. Rancière's political subject depends on being heard as such: on having a relation similar to that of the emancipated learner available to them.[4] But crucially, the process by which they should come into this relation is not one that can be imposed from above. The fullest political subjectivity is achieved through a self-initiated democratic outburst. What is in common between this view and that in *The Emancipated Spectator* is that the gap that exists between teacher and learner, between performer and audience, has the potential to allow dissensus, rather than to enforce consensus.

Another contrasting theory of emancipation through performance is found in *Relational Aesthetics*, where Bourriaud draws on the theory of Felix Guattari to suggest that participatory engagement with artworks promotes the fluidity of subjectivity, in positive ways. He describes relational art thus: 'A set of artistic practices which take as their theoretical and practical point of departure the whole of human relations and their social context, rather than an independent and private space' (Bourriaud 1998: 113), which is a very broad definition, but the kind of work he describes in the book is more tightly bound than this. It is conceptual art predicated on interactions with the social world outside the art gallery and the system of art production. The principle of his theoretical development of this is that the best way to understand contemporary art, and especially relational art, is as an operation on and through subjectivity. For a definition of subjectivity, he turns to Felix Guattari: '"All the conditions making it possible for individual and/ or collective agencies to be in a position to emerge as sui-referential existential territory, adjacent to or in a relation of delimitation with otherness that is itself subjective". Otherwise put, subjectivity can only be defined by the presence of a second subjectivity' (Bourriaud 2002: 90–91). He insists that we must de-naturalise subjectivity, recognising that as it comes into being through encounters with otherness, it is assembled and re-assembled through these encounters. Art's job in this process is to resist the neurosis produced by capitalism, ideology, supplier–client relations and all those forms of otherness that press us into rigid, narrow, and frozen assemblies of subjectivisation. Ultimately, 'the only acceptable end purpose of human activities is the production of a subjectivity that is forever self-enriching its relationship with the world' (Bourriaud 2002: 113). In another striking image, he says that art has the capacity for thermodynamic effects: melting the frozen relations produced by homogenising culture.

Bourriaud's proposal collapses the work itself into the relation between subjectivities, but does not collapse the subjectivity of the spectator into the work, so it escapes Rancière's specific objection in *The Emancipated Spectator*. But they would not agree on the political nature of art, or on the nature of political art. Rancière is very sceptical about a political art that seeks to raise consciousness, as ultimately Bourriaud would like to, as it is akin to not just the old-fashioned schoolteacher but also the general form of political discourse that presumes to make a place for the participant – as opposed to one where the individual has taken that place for themselves. But he is not averse to art which makes propositions or to the possibility of genuine politics emerging from or around artworks. The programme of the relational artwork does not impress him, as it seeks to operate on the subjectivity of the spectator: bringing him/her to the boil. Rancière would rather see this boiling point reached independently.

So there is no synthesis of Bourriaud and Rancière, but there is something more useful at this point in the task of beginning an aesthetics of participation. The synthesis is not in finding a combination or middle ground between these two, but in recognising how both possibilities address something fundamental about subjectivity, and that they suggest why moments like this work powerfully in participatory theatre.

## Subjectivity as material and medium

> By 'subject' I mean someone who recognises herself as having an 'I', as having her own peculiar perspective; a subject is an agent who is able to be self-reflective, and to assume responsibility for herself and for some of her actions. (Cavell 2006: 1)

Subjectivity in itself can be said to be largely a matter of the point of view of the subject, and their capacity for action, and of the recognition of this position by the subject herself and (missing from Marcia Cavell's definition) its recognition by others. For both Rancière and Bourriaud these things are at stake in the spectator's encounter with an art work, and especially at stake because they are dealing with a proposal for an encounter which is up-close, responsive or invasive: that is, participatory. For Rancière the point of view of the spectator must remain at some distance to the work, and their agency is to be defended to the degree that we would not expect them to take action within the work at all. For Bourriaud's understanding of relational art the point of view is within the work, and has become part of the work, and he seems to have a very flexible sense of agency: if a spectator is participating in an artistic encounter while the work is having a powerful 'melting' effect on their everyday subjectivity, their autonomy must be in question.

To look at it another way, these two component parts could be thought of as the recognition of the participant as a subject within the field of activity of the performance with the potential to enter into dialogue with it, and the addressing of the performance to forms of subjectivity or subject positions that have a special point of view in relation to the performance by virtue of their participation in it. Audience participatory performance has among its building blocks – its media – the agency of the participant, and their point of view within the work.

These two theorists, like Boal, raise the possibility of an emancipatory spectatorship; they see the matter of the recognition of the spectator as subject as a political effect as well as an aesthetic one. It would be possible to reach a similar conclusion about the central position of these dimensions of subjectivity through an analysis based on less politicised theory, through psychoanalysis or analytical philosophy for example, but I find my way there through two politicised approaches and place this discussion here for a reason: to set aside, for the majority of this book, the polemics about emancipation and the political possibilities of audience participatory performance. My strategy is not to avoid politics, but to strategically defer it, and to invite it back into the discussion when my terms are ready for it. The theory that I will exploit in the analysis I present is often social theory concerned with power relationships and how they are enacted in the microcosmic interactions of everyday life. So this deferring of the political does not take it out of the discussion entirely: each of the chapters that follow will move fairly swiftly from some assertions about the various media of audience participation as suggested above, to how they come into play in the interactive, social, and often contested space of episodes of audience participation. Each chapter will begin with questions that are initiated by the logics available when making audience-participatory work. As these questions relate to interactions between people, people as located social subjects, the best approaches to answering them will be found in the – often political – theories through which we can understand social subjects, just as those subjects themselves are embedded in a social life that is thoroughly penetrated by the politics that govern us. But the questions themselves relate to the logics of practice that arise in the work, and the politics implied by the answers offered here are left to some brief remarks in the conclusion, and to the reader to elaborate for her or himself. As Halsall, Jansen and O'Conner say in the introduction to *Rediscovering Aesthetics* (2009: 7):

> the 'aesthetic turn' as a curatorial strategy is [...] contentious because it is feared to prioritise aesthetic (i.e., sensuous, playful, or pleasurable) effects over critical social and political dimensions of contemporary art practice.

I, too, am wary of allowing this priority to hold sway beyond what is needed in order to recognise how audience participation becomes sensuous, playful or pleasurable – or whatever other qualities will arise under this particular sense of the aesthetic. But I am certain that a political and ethical critique will be sorely limited if it does not have the conceptual equipment to show how an art work or event engages us on these terms.

## The structure of the book

Examining agency means being interested in how people are led to perform, and in how far they can be said to be made to perform, and to give performances that have been conceived by theatre practitioners. By extension this will suggest how people are able to give performances that they invent themselves: the agency of the participant as the inverse, the flipside, of the control of the theatre practitioner. These questions will form the bulk of the analysis of Chapters 1, 2 and 3. The matter of the participant's point of view will inform this analysis, but will be taken up in its own right in Chapter 4.

Chapter 1 'Process and Procedure' sets out an initial theoretical framework for the analysis of audience participatory theatre. Following Anthony Jackson's example (in his work on participatory practice in TIE) I explore some ideas from Erving Goffman's *Frame Analysis*, supplementing his terms with ideas from Pierre Bourdieu and Hans-Georg Gadamer, to give this theory a broader capacity to address differences in response through a hermeneutics of social signification. The chapter concludes with a detailed discussion of a Theatre in Education workshop performance by Armadillo Theatre, an event that both facilitates and manipulates participant agency. In the second chapter, 'Risk and Rational Action', this initial theoretical framework is used to account for the powerful influence of perceived and real risk in performance. Contrasting practices of disguise, exaggeration or informed consent are discussed as elements of the dramaturgy of participation, with much in common with techniques of facilitation. Jonathan Kay's fooling performances are explored, to test and elaborate the theory in relation to practice that seeks to enact a challenge to audience members' inhibitions.

Disrupting this model of participation as rational action, the third chapter 'Irrational Interactions' considers embodied influences on participation, and how they shape both decisions to participate and the character of participation itself. The terminologies and mode of questioning deployed here are quite different, drawing on cognitive science and the phenomenological philosophy associated with it, as well as ideas from anthropology and evolutionary psychology. These ideas are put to work in an analysis of De La Guarda's *Villa Villa*, a performance that addressed itself directly and deliberately to the bodies of spectator participants. Chapter 4 'Accepting the Invitation' shifts the focus again, onto the experiential aspect of the moment of response, and its effect on what follows. Ideas about the phenomenology of acting and spectating are deployed to unpick the peculiar situation of doing both at the same time, as well as to re-orient Fischer-Lichte's proposition about the autopoietic feedback loop of performance, before turning to Tim Crouch's *The Author* and *I, Malvolio* for an opportunity to consider strategies that encourage reflexivity in the audience experience, using discrete and focussed participatory procedures.

The focus of the book on the moment of invitation means that similar elements of practice and the problems associated with them return many times, to be picked apart in different ways. Though the frame of reference, in terms of the range of theatre practice, is very broad, its focus in these terms is narrow – in effect taking a thin slice across audience participation practice as a whole. Returning again and again to the invitation and its response, and looking at them from different angles and with different theoretical lenses thus gives some hope of saying meaningful things about such disparate practices.

# 1
# Process and Procedure

In this chapter I will introduce three questions that relate the issue of the participant's agency to the practicalities of devising, facilitating and taking part in an audience participatory performance. These three questions present areas of uncertainty in the understanding of interactive artworks when we consider them alongside more conventional works. They are also concerned with the nature of the artwork, especially in relation to the contribution of the audience participant. The questions are:

- Who 'authors' audience participation and how?
- Who is in control when participation is happening?
- Where does the 'art' happen – in the event itself, or in the preparation for the event?

To explore these questions I will propose and articulate some terms, most importantly 'procedural authorship', 'invitation' and 'horizon of participation'. Each is either borrowed from or develops from earlier work in aesthetics, sociology or phenomenology; they provide the basis of the discussion for the rest of the book.

Like most performances, those that include audience participation usually involve a lot of preparation. Like most performances they cannot be considered to be fully realised until there is an audience present to watch, listen and appreciate, and to interact. But the quantity and quality of the interaction that is needed to realise audience participation is different to that which is needed to complete a more conventional performance. Though any performance maker and regular performance watcher knows how much performances can change from one occasion to the next, we are in the habit of considering each performance of the same production to be an iteration of the same work. Does this make sense when audience participation is a significant element of the performance? The answer may be yes, but if so it is yes in a quite different way.

The contribution of the participant is the important difference. It is important to a conception of a work as interactive, and it is important, though to varying degrees, to practitioners who ask for interaction. An interactive work is an event made through the collaboration of artists and participating audience members, and the way this comes to happen is something we will need to ask questions about. If, as I have suggested in the introduction, interactive work is characterised by the recognition of the audience participant as a subject through their actions in the performance, the way those actions come to happen is fundamental. We cannot understand interactive performance without considering the provenance of these actions and interactions: how invitations to participate are made, and how people are able to respond to these invitations.

Once again, most performance involves a great deal of preparation, but does not come into being properly, as a work of art, until it is performed for an audience; performance is an event. But the interactive work is prepared so that it has gaps to be filled with the actions of participating audience members (as well as, of course, gaps for the coded participations of applause, laughter and other 'normal' audience responses) and gaps that require the thought and felt response of the audience to make sense out of its various material.[1] So a significant part of the work of an interactive work consists of creating the structure within which these particular gaps appear, and the work of the interactive performer consists of repeating this structure and allowing the participants to fill the gaps in different ways in each fresh iteration of the work. So does the audience participatory event consist of the structure or the action that happens in the gaps that it creates? The answer must be that it is both; to understand this dual nature of the work we need good terms for it.

In drama education the emphasis is on drama as a process as much as a product, and it is from this idea that much Theatre in Education (TIE) has evolved,[2] building a body of process-oriented practices with audience participation at its heart. This chapter takes a theorisation of TIE practice as a starting point: the terms appropriate for this kind of process-based practice can, with some modification, provide a basis for others not normally associated with it. A process involves uncertainty, spontaneity, responsiveness and the chance for participants to express themselves and make choices; these characteristics are also common in audience participatory performance outside educational settings. But every drama educator knows the value of preparation, and carefully constructs the activities from which such processes arise. This preparation and the presentation of prepared activities, in educational settings and elsewhere, are the procedures that create process.

I have borrowed the word procedure from Jan Murray's *Hamlet on the Holodeck* in which she discusses the way that participation is manipulated by computer game designers to create a system with which players to interact, and designing the procedures that allow and respond to their activities. She insists this is a creative activity comparable with that of poets, authors and playwrights: it is very similar to the work of the creators of interactive drama, and Murray's definition is one that will transfer easily:

> Procedural authorship means writing the rules by which the texts appear as well as writing the text themselves. It means writing the rules for the interactor's involvement, that is, the conditions under which things will happen in response to the participant's actions. It means establishing the properties of the objects and potential objects in the virtual world and the formulas for how they will relate to one another. The procedural author creates not just a set of scenes but a world of narrative possibilities. (Murray 1999: 152)

Murray's procedural author is involved in telling stories, as narrative is important to these digital entertainments as it leads us to immerse ourselves in a game, but narrative is no more essential to this concept of authorship than it is to authorship of other kinds. What is important is the suggestion of both the authority of the practitioner who makes such a framework, and the distinctive character of the procedures they use. It also implies that authorship here is quite different from authorship elsewhere. The creators of interactive performances are procedural authors, though narrative is not always as important to their work as it is to most game designers. In this chapter I will discuss how this concept is helpful, as well as some of its limitations.

Does this mean that the procedural author is only in control up to the moment where the procedure creates a gap, at which point an audience participant steps in and takes control of the event? Clearly not. The exchanges that can happen between performer and participant are extremely complex, so that control – and authorship – is shared, and passed back and forth between them. The most nuanced analysis of audience-participatory performance will address this sharing of the control of the performed action, and will show how the initiative, the power to make choices, and the freedom to express – in other words the agency within the event – is shared by participants and those who facilitate their action. The terminology and approach proposed in this chapter is intended to allow this kind of nuanced analysis.

## Antony Jackson and frame analysis

To begin to develop a theory in response to these questions, it is helpful to look at an existing set of terms that relate to a specific mode of practice, to see how they can be generalised and developed to apply in other areas. Anthony Jackson (1997: 48–60), in a discussion of interactive strategies in TIE, introduces an interpretation of Erving Goffman's *Frame Analysis* (1986). He describes a series of frames used to facilitate different kinds of participation, first a 'Pre-Theatrical Frame' in which children are prepared for the theatrical experience, and an 'Outer Theatrical Frame' in which a theatrical space is established. In these two frames the audience does not yet imaginatively take on another a new role, but they recognise the distinction between theatrical space and normal space, and the expectations placed on their behaviour (that they will watch) and that of the performers (that they will perform). He goes on to name a number of 'Inner Frames' that can operate within this outer theatrical frame, and between which TIE programmes move. In the 'Narrative Frame' a story is told or introduced, in the 'Presentational Frame' the actors present the story. Though the audience watching in these frames remain just watchers and listeners, they may be 'contextualised', given a fictional role related to the situation they are watching, perhaps one that gives them something to watch out for. The 'Investigative Frame' allows the audience to join the action, usually with a specific task, and where the progress of the story is often suspended. The 'Involvement Frame' is where the audience and performers occupy the same space, physically and imaginatively, and the audience have become participants with a significant influence over the course of the action. Jackson's analysis of M6 Theatre's *Grounded*[3] shows something of how these frames might be found in typical TIE of the time:

> The play opens with a brief scene between mother and daughter at the clinic, awaiting the results of Joanne's pregnancy test. Unambiguously, we watch through a presentational frame. Then, before the scene is resolved, the mother turns to the audience and, in direct address, she recounts the events of that day and all that has led up to the current crisis, thus establishing a narrative frame, in

present time. [...] The workshop begins as soon as the play ends. Still within the outer theatre frame (the students are not yet returning to the classroom), the dominant frame is now the investigative – established by the facilitator (in this case one of the actors who played a less pivotal character and can thus be more 'neutral'). It is clearly signalled to the students now that they have a distinct role to play – not merely to clarify but to engage with and test the action and the characters (who stay in role throughout). (Jackson 1997: 56–59)

The benefit of Jackson's approach is that he suggests a way of describing procedural authorship: as the manipulation of frames of interaction. As I will go on to demonstrate, Goffman's *Frame Analysis* offers a structure for thinking about the procedure of participatory work and the processes that arise from it, and for how performers and participants interact with each other as the event evolves. Jackson has named some categories of frames, but not described them in great detail, nor elaborated a set of terms for this more detailed description, but the theory he draws on offers such a set of terms. Jackson's frames, as he describes them, are appropriate to the work that is common in TIE, but they will not serve to describe all kinds of audience participation. In particular, there will be a greater variety of 'inner frames' available in addition to the ones he describes, and also a greater number of variations on the ones he describes.

In De La Guarda's *Villa Villa*,[4] for example, there were several kinds of involvement frame in the middle section of the show, the 'Fiesta China'. Here the performers improvised dances with the audience, flirting with them, kissing them, carrying them off to other parts of the building. In this section the content of the performance depends upon the actions of the spectators who interact with the performers – and it is certainly an inner frame. But it differs markedly from another episode a few moments later in the show where one spectator is chosen to be hoisted into the air above the audience, where most of the action up to this point has taken place. This is also an inner frame, but it is quite different: the participant is much more the focus of everyone's attention, but is much less in control of what happens, so this is not consistent with what Jackson calls integral participation. His essay points the way but does not tell us how to differentiate between different modes like these. He does not develop a way of describing in detail how facilitators begin and end participation, nor how they guide interaction when it is under way, but such an elaboration can begin with the terminology he borrows from Goffman's *Frame Analysis*. This chapter develops these ideas and renders them adaptable to a wider variety of circumstances and practices, setting out a scheme for the discussion of audience participation that focuses on how it is 'marked off' from the usual interactions of theatre.

## Goffman's *Frame Analysis*

*Frame Analysis* develops a vocabulary to describe how we organise our perceptions of the multitude of different situations we observe and find ourselves in. The most basic distinction made is between two different types of 'primary frameworks': the natural and the social. In the natural order we understand events to be determined beyond social control, and not guided by human agency; and in the social order we perceive the choices and efforts of other social beings like ourselves. Thus, at the most basic level, we look at our experiences in different ways, bringing to them different assumptions about their meaning: we place them into frames that enable our understanding. As well as structuring our perceptions, frames allow us to manage the different episodes of life, and our behaviour in social life in particular. We clearly use different kinds of behaviour in different situations, and in social life the movements between the different kinds of behaviour are subtle and complex; the problem is how to describe and account for these changes in behaviour. Goffman's idea is that we do this through 'organisational premises' (1986: 247) that make the situation real to us as well as manageable: we have ways of understanding what kind of activity is going on, and what kind of activity would be appropriate and beneficial for ourselves. When Goffman uses frame to describe our functional understanding of interactions in everyday life he indicates a network of shared assumptions about what an interaction means for its participants, and what is appropriate behaviour at these interactions. A key phrase for Goffman is 'the definition of the situation'(1986: 1), the agreement between the people involved in an interaction about what it is they are engaged in, and what can or should happen.

Gavin Bolton gives an interpretation of *Frame Analysis* in an educational context, focusing on how it is necessary to 'build belief' in the social context and our role in it (1992: 2). He gives the example of a class, which begins like any other class with the teacher (Bolton himself) following his own pattern of teacherly behaviour to assert himself as the focus and leader of the group, and the students signal their understanding and acceptance of this by following their own student-like routine. Once this is achieved they can all go about the business of learning and teaching, and become less concerned with demonstrating their roles. In Bolton's example the class was interrupted when one of the students was taken ill, and another social order had to be hurriedly put in place while this situation was dealt with; in order to begin the class again he and the students had once again to go through a period of demonstrating the ascendancy of the 'classroom' situation. Bolton sees everyday life as an oscillation between demonstrating the kind of social relationship that is appropriate and submitting to that relationship and the process that ensues from it. Though Bolton uses this term 'building belief', neither he nor Goffman intend that we disbelieve one definition of the situation in order to move on to another, nor that we need to hold conflicting beliefs in abeyance in order to move from one frame to another, merely that it is necessary to agree on the current definition:

> Together the participants contribute to a single over-all definition of the situation which involves not so much a real agreement as to what exists but rather a real agreement as to whose claims concerning what issues will be temporarily honoured. (Goffman 1969: 21)

Clearly there is an issue of trust involved in this building of belief, a need to establish that a 'proper' or 'correct' frame is being employed, and in the idea of 'whose claims' are honoured; issues around trust will inform the discussion of risk in participation in the following chapter. Goffman indicates, in this phrasing, that frame is always to some extent a matter of power, that those who are able to control the definition of a situation are able to control what is talked about and how it is talked about, what is done or not done, what is decided, what action taken. How control of this kind happens is the concern of the second half of this chapter.

In drama work in the classroom, the rehearsal or in a workshop, we can observe this oscillation between the setting up and settling into the drama, and the work when it is properly under way and the actors are committed to it. Relationships are set up where participants know what role they are to play, and what others are to play, how they are to play them, and when they are to stop, but once they are involved in this 'playing' it is no longer necessary to think about these parameters. Drama work is clearly a frame that can contain behaviours of different kinds – 'acting' or 'not acting' for example[5] – and where people move easily from one kind of behaviour to another with some ease. The situation in the theatre – as opposed to the classroom, the rehearsal room or the workshop – is different, at least at first glance. As Goffman observes, 'the central understanding' of the theatre is 'that the audience has neither the right nor the obligation to participate directly in the dramatic action occurring on the stage' (1986: 125). When some members of the gathering at a theatre performance appear to change frames, to move into another definition of the situation where they follow, for example, scripted behaviour, others appear to remain outside the frame, aloof from it and not part of the interaction except in the most cursory way, in their laughter or applause. When Goffman applies frame theory to the theatre he sees the divisions of roles that cut across both sides of the divide between stage and auditorium, the actor is present both as 'stage-actor' and as 'stage-character', both as professional person and as a role within the constraints of the presented world; the spectator is present both as a 'theatregoer' and as an 'onlooker', both as a patron of the theatre spending time and money, and as a recipient and passive participant in the events of the play.

These roles, those that exist within the play and those that extend beyond it, are constructed by and through frame processes, and as such they are conceivable in different forms. If we can accept that we see the actor in different roles during the evening's show, as when he takes a bow he leaves behind the character in order to be celebrated in the role of professional, we can also accept this flexibility for the theatregoers too: they too can take on more roles than that of onlooker. As Goffman says, it is not a matter of interactions between the stage and the audience that we should attend to, but the frame that has been engaged to facilitate an evening's entertainment, and whether or how this frame allows such roles to be taken by different people (Goffman 1986: 127).

Goffman provides a more detailed terminology for the way that these frames of activity are constructed, both in everyday life and in extra-daily activities like drama, theatre and performance. The frames of behaviour that can contain fictional, 'non-serious' behaviour such as theatrical acting, storytelling, or practical jokes, are called in *Frame Analysis* 'Keyed Frames'. He uses a musical metaphor to imply that they may resemble serious forms of behaviour, but they are being played 'in a different key', in a frame that has made it clear that this activity is not to be taken seriously: at least not so far that promises made have to be kept, views expressed have to be maintained, or that action undertaken by a participant in the interaction is to be taken as part of their presentation of their 'real selves'. Theatre's material and ritual trappings are designed to assert this definition of a situation where the behaviour of a privileged section of the participants is seen as keyed. Though we all take part in other kinds of keyed behaviour, in games and sports, in play, in jokes, most people do not enjoy the privilege of playing in one of the keys of drama with any frequency.

Though keyed frames are 'non-serious', just like all other frames they must be connected to patterns of behaviour and context that surround them. Keying is an approach to the autonomy of art-related behaviour, how it is able to resemble, but also detach itself from, everyday activity. For Goffman putting interaction into an art-like key enables this detachment, while also enabling its anchoring in the frames that surround it. A very useful set of terms is presented in Chapter 7 of *Frame Analysis*, 'The Anchoring of Activity' (Goffman 1986: 247–300): 'episoding conventions', 'appearance formulas', 'resource continuity', 'unconnectedness' and 'the human being'.

The 'episoding conventions' (251–269) of a frame are the signals or conventions through which an activity is 'marked off' from other activities, from the 'ongoing flow of surrounding events' (251), this might be the opening of a curtain in a theatre or the opening remarks of a conversation. These conventions help us to learn from others what kind of activity is going on, and to signal what role we are going to take in this activity and when we are doing so. They also allow us to move – not always seamlessly, but fluently – from one mode of behaviour to another, assuming that the conventions used have made it clear and acceptable to all that a change in frame has happened. The 'signalling' and 'settling into' a frame that Bolton describes is what constitutes the use and the acceptance of an episoding convention by those involved in the interaction.

'Appearance formulas' (269–287) are made up, first, of person-role formulas: relationships between the presentation given in the frame and the other presentations given outside it by the same person, in the general continuity of other frames. An appearance given by a player in a frame is never entirely divisible from the person who gives it, so 'casting' a person in a 'role' as part of a frame makes the other roles they play available, adding meaning to the frame of activity. Second, in drama and theatre, Goffman reconstructs this as the 'person-character' formula: citing restrictions on the kinds of people who are allowed to perform and what they are allowed to play as an obvious example of a formula – the close physical resemblance between character and performer demanded by western naturalism, or the Onnagata tradition in Kabuki, where the female 'romantic lead' is played by a very experienced older man.

Alongside appearance formulas as the permissible differences between the person and their role, there is 'resource continuity' (287–292), the ways in which individuals bring aspects of themselves to different roles and maintain a connection across various activities: among other things this might constitute what we could call an individual's style, but it is also the use within the framed activity of the cultural and personal skills they possess. 'Unconnectedness' (292–293) is the irrelevance of much of the context of the frame to the meaning or the pursuit of the activity within it. Some of what surrounds us during most kinds of interaction is incidental, though the higher the degree of formality in a situation, the more likely it is that the context is being used to 'stage' the interaction in some way.

Finally in this chapter, Goffman makes a defence of the notion of 'the human being', not because he wants to persuade us to believe in an essential soul or subject, but because such an idea is fundamentally important to us in the way that we anchor our behaviour – because we generally do, in a practical sense, behave as if there is a single indivisible and consistent self at the centre of our actions and experience. Goffman himself is often cynical about this, one of several aspects of his work that brings him close to the ideas of those who have less optimism than he about the ability of the individual to act on the world rather than to be acted upon by it. Battershill says that in Goffman's work we see an early theorisation of '[t]he post-modern self [as] an interactive terminal, its unitaryness an illusory effect of communicative process' (Riggins 1990: 167). The self as an effect – illusory or otherwise – of communication with others, and among different aspects of our mind and body, is a development of the principle that the meaning of experience is derived from interaction, that comes to the fore in the pragmatist philosophy of which Goffman is often considered an adherent. The problematics of ideas of self, subjectivity and intersubjectivity, and their relevance to participatory performance, are explored in more detail in Chapters 3 and 4.

It is through these concepts of anchoring that Goffman describes how people use common ground to establish frames for participation: marking the move from one frame to another, selecting those resources that are to be used or ignored, maintaining a personal and collective narrative that ties them together. The procedural authorship of audience participatory performance anchors itself to the common experience of its participants, grounds itself in the frames that they use in the rest of their lives. The idea of episoding conventions can be used to describe how people are invited to take part in an interaction, and the other anchoring concepts to describe what the relationship is between this interaction and their 'everyday selves', and other aspects of the context of the event, looking at how these factors together produce a range of possible activities that can take place within the frame. In this way we can construct an idea of the frame produced by the procedure that is separate from examples of the procedure in action: not what the performance is or will be, but an indication of the possible performances it will give rise to.

## The frame analysis of audience participation

Episoding conventions in audience participatory theatre can work in a number of ways. Goffman's term and his description imply that they are conventional, that they work through shared experience and shared assumptions, and in the majority of framed activity this has to be so: the purpose of the idea of frame is to explain how we go from one kind of activity to another without constantly instructing each other or asking questions about what is going on. The kind of social negotiation that shapes a frame in everyday life is generally tacit it is achieved by a shared, implicit process of recalling previous occasions of action in similar frames. Where a person enters a frame for the first time they might be instructed explicitly about what is appropriate behaviour, and what are the limits; or perhaps they might have been instructed in preparation, in how to behave in a frame:

> When the individual does move into a new position in society and obtains a new part to perform, he is not likely to be told in full detail how to conduct himself, nor will the facts of his new situation press sufficiently on him from the start to determine his conduct without his further giving thought to it. Ordinarily he will be given only a few cues, hints, and stage directions, and it will be assumed that he already has in his repertoire a large number of bits and pieces of performance that will be required in the new setting. [...] He may even be able to play out the part of a hypnotic subject or commit a 'compulsive crime' on the basis of models for these activities that he is already familiar with (Goffman 1969: 79).[6]

The individual might 'sit back' and observe the actions of others, and judge what similar frames they can associate with the new one, and as Goffman's two examples here suggest, we can often convincingly play roles that are apparently far from our previous experience. As there are likely to be neophytes at most participatory theatre they must be catered for. This can happen through the use of established social or cultural conventions of audience participation through traditions of volunteering or responding in a group, or the appropriation of such traditions into forms where they do not normally appear. But not all frames can be established through the appeal to known conventions, sometimes the nature of a frame needs to be introduced explicitly, to make clear when interactivity is invited and what kind of activity is wanted, and often this is done by stopping the progress of a performance and clearly describing what is to happen next.

To distinguish between these degrees of conventionality, it is a helpful heuristic device to supplement Goffman's vocabulary detailing some of the kinds of episoding convention that can be found in audience participatory theatre. The episoding conventions used by procedural authors to introduce a participatory frame can be described as different kinds of 'invitations': *overt*, *implicit*, *covert* and *accidental* invitations, as well as making an allowance for uninvited participation. An *overt* invitation is one where the performers make clear to the audience what they want them to do, for example, in the kind of explanations given by The Joker in Forum Theatre, usually necessary because the technique, widespread though it is, is not likely to be familiar to everyone in any given audience. An overt invitation need not always be as explicit as this, it could consist of a performer, in or out of character, addressing spectators directly in a way that makes it clear that they are being asked to respond in some way, something as subtle as a change in tone of voice, or a gesture, and a particular sequence of words, as in the initiation of an 'oh no he doesn't!' 'oh yes he does!' routine in a British pantomime. Or an overt invitation might have been given in advance, before the moment of participation arises, as for example, in Felix Ruckert's *Hautnah*, where the programme read:

> Look around, relax and get ready for an evening full of encounters, to be performed for a unique spectator. You will find the name of each performer under each frame, as well as a badge/key holder. You may take a badge as soon as you have made a choice. A missing badge means that the performer is already busy (Abrams in Kattwinkel 2003: 3).

Thus prepared, the audience members became participants in the action of choosing a performer – a process which made them visible to the other participants, and involved some negotiation, competition, and the prospect of disappointment – before becoming spectators again, anticipating the arrival of the dancer and further invitations to interact.

Alternatively, there are examples of audience participation where the invitation is *implicit*, where a convention does exist for participation and nothing has to be described to the audience. Enough of any audience at a British 'panto' will be familiar with its traditions that if they see one character (a pirate in Robinson Crusoe for example, a ghost in versions of almost any pantomime story) begin to creep up on another (Ben Gunn, Buttons) they will shout, apparently spontaneously 'he's behind you'. These are learned, culturally specific traditions, in the case of pantomime often baffling to spectators from outside the United Kingdom, but familiar to most natives from an early age.

A simpler implicit invitation is employed every time a well known sing-along song is begun, and an audience which is familiar with it joins in. Implicit invitations can be ambiguous, creating moments where spectators do not know whether invitation is intended or not: in Shunt's *Dance Bear Dance*,[7] there were two different kinds of implicit invitation, the first when one half of the space was transformed into a casino, and the actors became croupiers. There was no formal announcement that we should now take places at the tables, but it did not take long before people began to take their seats, were given some chips, and began playing. Later the show reached a hiatus, the actors all left the room, and a telephone rang; the action did not continue until someone answered the phone to receive instructions. Again everyone knew exactly what to do with a ringing telephone, but this time it took longer for someone to step forward, first perhaps while they interpreted the ring as an invitation addressed to them rather than being framed as only an 'onstage' ring, and probably also because it would make them the centre of attention – making the action that is invited more risky. Ambiguous invitations like this are interesting cases that reveal risky situations and changing power relationships.

It is possible to invite interaction in ways that are covert, neither implicit nor overt, but lead an audience or a spectator into participating without letting them know that this is happening, though definitions of audience participation can become tricky here, as many examples of this kind will involve hiding from the participants the fact that they are involved in a piece of theatre at all. Boal's 'Invisible Theatre', for example, is ultimately a politically motivated confidence trick that covertly leads people into an interaction that they believe is 'real' and for them is framed not as 'performance' but as everyday life (and, strictly speaking, falls outside my definition of audience participation, as the 'audience' do not understand themselves as such). Any covert invitation relies on the same deception: that the action anticipated will not become a part of the theatrical performance, that a frame change will not occur, or that it will not be the change that it turns out to be. In Box Clever's *Something Beautiful*, (a piece of TIE toured to schools in England in the late 1990s), I would often initiate an interaction by offering to shake the hand of an apparently random boy in the audience, seeming to invite a simple interaction, with the words 'Hello mate, what's your name?' When I followed this with 'nice to meet you, could you just give me a hand?', and, keeping hold of the boy's hand, pulled him onto the stage; I was rarely refused. The 'volunteer' in this was not randomly chosen, instead he was always one of the more confident boys in the audience, pre-selected as the audience came into the performance space, so that his performance of reluctance – sighs and shrugs – was enjoyed by their peers, but being on stage and joining us in a brief scene did not seem too difficult.[8]

To follow the logic of categorising episoding conventions it is necessary to include two peripheral categories of unwanted episoding: the accidental and the uninvited. It is possible to produce signals that are so like the episoding conventions of known interactive theatre that spectators will read them as such and respond when a response is not wanted. It is also possible, and probably more frequent, that spectators interject deliberately when no invitation of any kind has been given or misunderstood; heckling in stand-up comedy is a conventionally understood episode where the heckler deliberately changes the frame into an interactive one, challenging the comedian to prove that he or she can thrive in this new frame and end the episode authoritatively to return to their routine.[9] Of course the general tolerance of heckling in stand-up suggests that it is a conventionalised practice, that there is a standing implicit invitation to heckle a performer. There is disagreement among performers about the place of heckling, and the nature of its invitation is open to interpretation. Bim Mason describes the usual approach of street performers to the interruptions of hecklers:

> To a good performer most interruptions are not a problem, on the contrary they are a gift. Because they present a situation that could not have been rehearsed, the audience is fascinated to see what will happen and how well it is handled [...] However some hecklers can be destructive, especially if they are children or drunk, repeating their once funny witticism ad nauseam. The best policy in this case is to ignore them. (1992: 101)

He insists that ordinarily the street theatre performer must acknowledge interruptions, that the frames of street theatre must be participatory, remaining alive to the unpredictable nature of their setting. Children, dogs and drunks can all be allowed into the frame for a while and then sent back, having demonstrated the performer's versatility. The interventions of the police, which are usually intended to end the performance frame and re-introduce the utilitarian frame of a commercial thoroughfare, Mason suggests, are best dealt with by the performers leaving the space altogether, joining the audience and re-framing the uniformed officers as the focus of a performance they had not anticipated (Mason 1992: 103). The gist of most recommendations for dealing with unwanted interaction seems to be a confident re-assertion of the frame, as if the performer's own conviction that this is how business is to be perceived and conducted will be enough: 'Answering a heckler is all a matter of not showing fear, of showing that you are still in control of the situation' (Double 1997: 134). Early in Shunt's *Dance Bear Dance* there were peculiar moments when the audience was seated around a large table with the performers, who frequently addressed them directly by the names – of countries, as delegates to the United Nations – on the badges given to them as they enter the room. If this drew a reply from the audience member, the dialogue was not continued. It was not clear whether this was an accidental or an uninvited participation, or a deliberate invitation to participate, but intended so that the participation could be ignored. If anything the unease that this might have created for some members of the audience suited the strange atmosphere of the show.

The invitation itself is not the change of frame. It has to be understood by the spectators so that they perceive themselves as potential participants. From the point where they understand that a new frame has been offered, they will read a performance differently, though they still may not – either as individuals or as an entire audience – engage in any active participation. After an initial invitation is given, facilitation through further invitations might continue, to encourage the spectators to accept it and engage in interaction in the new frame. In the workshop section of Greenwich Young People's Theatre's *Stop!*,[10] a scene was repeated in which a character waited at home for an abusive partner to return, and the audience had been invited to offer suggestions for how she should act. An extra piece of narration was added to the scene, which was not in the play in its first exposition: 'Look, he's on his way home, he's got his key in the door, she's got to think fast!' At this point the invitation had been made, and the change in perception of the frame had been assumed by the facilitators, but it was unclear whether they had accepted the re-framing, and whether they would engage in new kinds of interaction. The effect of this narration was to make the intervention of the spectators seem more urgent, and to draw attention to the new frame in which they had the responsibility for making the character 'think fast'. In this instance the performance continues, with an overt invitation to participate in place, and encouraged by this facilitative narration. This technique, which puts pressure on the audience members to interject, is explicit and overt, but it is also manipulative. It makes use of an emotive, urgent demand put upon them by the facilitator, and it is not entirely clear what will happen when a spectator makes the choice to interject; the audience's empathy for the characters is exploited to give them greater investment in the situation, and more motivation to explore it through participation.

As will become increasingly clear as my argument progresses, there are overlaps between the different kinds of invitation that I have given, where perhaps they can be read as either overt or covert, depending on the response of the individual, where an implicit invitation leads to an unexpected interaction, or where other ambiguities, accidents or strategies come into play. As I noted at the beginning of this section, these are heuristic tools to unpack a procedure of participation, but they will require more subtle and specific analysis for the character of an invitation to become clear. The following section, however, concentrates on what kind of activity is invited, and how participants are able to respond.

## Roles and resources

As the different kinds of invitations that function as episoding conventions in audience participation are very important, I treat them separately to the other 'anchoring' ideas, and subdivide them into types. The other kinds of anchoring can be considered together as 'continuities'; they are different ways of observing how an action in a frame is connected with its context. The sense of context here is very broad, so that even the idea of the person connecting the actions performed by a certain body is part of the context, as is the performing body itself, and the role played by the person/body in the frame. Appearance formulas, as I have said, concern role and person and person and character, two different transformations of the participant in the frame. They can help to establish if the frame calls for a person to take up a role – a position in the framed activity that might come with obligations or expectations – or take up some kind of character – a make-believe of being someone that they are not. But as well as this we should consider how the role or character has to be anchored in other roles the person plays, for example, are they reproducing a role they play at other times, as when a teacher plays a teacher in a TIE exercise, or a student a student?

Appearance formulas, if the work within a frame is at all fictional, place the performer in a matrix of time-place-character, as Kirby (1965: 44) proposes, where the fictions of the theatre insist that these three variables are presented as other than those of the performer, whereas all kinds of other combinations are available, up to and including a performance of now-here-me. Goffman describes how theatre relies on 'transcription practices' (Goffman 1986: ch. 5), which adapt 'real' life so that it fits the frame's necessities of communication, suspense, unity, and so on. Taking a character – a role that is matrixed in a fictional world – will also mean taking up some of these practices, 'transcribing' the behaviour being shown into a usable form for the stage, a process that will involve using the properties of the person in different ways in different styles of theatre; the person-character formula employed is one of these 'transcription practices' in the way it makes aspects of the person's appearance relevant to the performance they give.

Neelands, writing about drama work in the classroom, also describes a nuanced idea of the differences between 'person' and 'role' and 'character', making a larger number of subtle distinctions showing that a simple difference between playing a character and not playing a character is not necessarily helpful, when considering the variety of different role-plays and activities that students might undertake:

1. Public self in the social setting of the classroom.
2. Public self but operates as a role in the social setting of the drama.
3. Operates as a role, but now projects a social or cultural attitude to events, which is different from normative or habitual self.
4. Operates as above but role taken is representative of a social or cultural group with its own history and characteristic response.
5. Uses technique to 'become' a character that is physically and psychologically unique.
6. Projects self as actually being the character – the performer's 'self' is masked by her physical manifestation of a 'flesh and blood' character. (Neelands 1998: 16)

These detail the different relationships a student in classroom drama can have with the performance they give, but can easily be applied to other examples of performance in very different contexts. When a spectator picks up a pair of scissors to cut off part of Yoko Ono's clothing (Ono 1997: 14, 126), he or she retains a 'public self', but operating in the social setting of the gallery, the behaviour is 'keyed' by the gallery frame as non-serious, but has not taken a key that allows us to make-believe that anyone but this individual did the cutting. A spect-actor intervening in a Forum Theatre show often does pretend to be someone else, to 'become' a unique other person, though the amount of technique used might be minimal. In looking at audience participation these distinctions can be useful, and we can look more closely at the list through the filter of Goffman's anchoring terms. The first two of Neelands' levels are clearly person-role formulas – the participant in Ono's *Cut Piece* is involved in a person-role formula – and the last two are clearly person-character formulas – the spect-actor in Forum Theatre, for example, is involved in a person-character formula. But the two levels in between do not fit these categories so easily: they seem to be made up of some aspects of a fictional setting and some aspects of the person's place outside the fiction, it would be possible to say that they take on only some of the variables in the matrix – the time and place variables, but only limited parts of the character variable. I might describe them as person-role-situation formulae, but it is more worth-while to note these different kinds of appearance formula here, and to leave the idea open, so that specific formulas can be ascribed to roles following specific invitations.

The invitation thus establishes the relationship between the partici-pant and the performer, and it will do this by drawing on other shared resources, roles that are understood by all. It will simultaneously create the network of associations that give meaning to the role, its conti-nuities with the other parts played by that person. Another thing that will be established at this point, which is not developed in depth in Goffman's theory, is the goal that is associated with the role. In much of Goffman's work the goal that is uppermost in the minds of the people he conceives is the maintenance of a successful 'front', a performance that benefits the team to which the person belongs (Goffman 1969: ch. 4; 1970). Self-presentation to serve a team may be the dominant goal of a frame or role in audience participation, but there will often be a more specific aim given to participants in order to focus their perform-ances, or to generate experiences of some kind. The resources that they have been given, or that are indicated as part of their role, constitute the techniques and tools that they will use to reach that goal. John O'Toole (1976: 24) gives an example of a TIE piece in which a group of children had been introduced to performers playing members of a tribal community in a situation where water was very scarce, and left alone to safeguard a supply of water, before meeting a different char-acter: a thirsty traveller. Their resources in this case were no more than their social selves, their ability to interact with others, and the bowl of water itself. The explicit goal of conserving the water, in conflict with the needs of the new character, amounted to a dilemma that created a meaningful experience from the drama.

A person's ability to construct a role or a character, to adapt to a formula of any kind, and to work towards a goal depends upon their use of 'resource continuity', the continuity with the cultural and personal resources that are available to them. The cultural resources might include language, genres, and stories that will be shared by the spectators and the performers at an event, allowing participants to take the roles offered to them or the conventions of how to behave during audience participation. When a performer in improvised comedy (professional performer or volunteer from the audience) acts a scene 'in the style of...' they make use of shared resources in an obvious way, but so does a guest at a visitor attraction, who interacts with actors representing characters or types from familiar literature, films or history. Personal resources might include skills – the ability to play a musical instrument for instance, that can then be played on stage – or knowledge – experience of the disciplinary procedure in a school that can be used when interacting in a TIE performance. Kaprow (1993: 50) makes clear the importance of the intelligibility of the invitation, and of the shared language necessary for interaction: 'This may seem truistic, but participation presupposes shared assumptions, interests, meanings, contexts and uses. It cannot take place otherwise': but there is always the possibility that resources will be shared by some and not by others. When, in *Dance Bear Dance*, the performance space is transformed into a casino, those who know the games available will be able to participate more fully than those who do not.

A play that is presented, or partly presented, in the outer theatrical frame is always a shared resource specific to the event, there for all to draw on as they produce their own performances. In a procedure that works through stages of interactivity from the presentational to the investigative to the involvement frame (using Jackson's terminology), the experience of a simple interaction gives participants not only confidence but also some shared resources of experience and language to use in the later frames. There will also be a shared resource in the participation itself, when for example, there are repetitions of the same scenario in a Forum Theatre show, the previous (perhaps failed) attempts will be in the minds of all participants as a resource in the next attempt at the problem. But just as a performance will be received differently by each spectator, it will be useful to each participant in different ways, as each individual's experience will make available different interpretations of its content, and will shape how they choose among these interpretations, suggesting that relatively homogenous audiences will provide more consistent or predictable reactions to participatory performance, as they will have similar resources available to them.[11] Punchdrunk's various re-workings of canonical texts – Shakespeare, Edgar Allen Poe and Goethe among them – allow the participant to explore environments and scenes that are not shown in the original plays, and to interact with some of the characters. The use that can be made of these opportunities will be very different for a participant who knows the play, and for one who does not. This difference in cultural resources is not trivial, of course, and will be considered more carefully later in this chapter.

This kind of dilemma – judging what resources are available to spectator-participants – has some similarity to the judgements that have to be made when making conventional theatre, the need, usually, to consider whether the content of a performance will be understood as it is intended. But a failure to understand can be more damaging to a participatory procedure: if no-one understands the participation that is being invited, or no-one has resources in behaviour, language, or skills with which to participate, then the interaction will fail. Kaprow's observation that participation has to be tailored to its audience is reinforced by the way that participation in popular performance is built up around routines that have become known to all, rather than around innovation:

> Audience participation shows have evolved as popular art genres along with political rallies, demonstrations, holiday celebrations, and social dancing. Parts of the common culture, they are known and accepted, the moves individuals must make are familiar, and their goals or uses are assumed to be clear. [...] The complex question of familiarity never arises in vernacular communal performances, [...] Everyone knows what's going on and what to do. (Kaprow 1993: 185)

Goffman's idea of 'unconnectedness' concerns me because so much of the context of theatre (contemporary Western theatre at least) is designed to emphasise a kind of connectedness. The use of the stage itself and especially a proscenium arch instructs us so explicitly that what is in this space is to be attended to that it is difficult to 'disattend'[12] anything that enters onto it. It is vital, if interactive theatre involves the playing of characters, that some elements of the person as context for the role have to be disattended, simply because it is usually impossible to cast or costume or rehearse audience participants in order to allow all aspects of their performance to be consistent, convincing or relevant. In audience participation, clothes for example usually have to be seen to be unconnected to a character, as do physical and vocal attributes of the person. Unconnectedness in this sense appears to be merely the opposite or the lack of the two kinds of anchoring that have come before, and to a degree this is so. But Goffman notes it separately as a way in which activity may include, even make use of in some peripheral way, elements that are not in a significant way part of the frame.

## Working inside the frame

As well as understanding how a frame is initiated, and how it is anchored in relationship with the other frames of social life that it emerges from, it is also necessary to take account of how the frame is managed while it is under way. In other words, how the procedure is maintained and developed by the facilitators and facilitating performers: what further signals elaborate or reinforce activity once it has begun. As well as the continuing work of procedural authorship, there will be influences on action from other participants who have joined the action from the audience, influences from those who remain in the audience, and other factors such as the performance environment and even inanimate objects.

Procedural authors can use in-frame activity in a huge variety of ways, some of which are worth noting here to give an idea of their scope. Performers in a facilitating role, of course, do more than just deliver the invitation, they can give further instruction, advice and encouragement to participants after they have become involved. A facilitator often has a position that is in the frame, but also observing it, not from outside, but with an outsider's eye, thinking ahead, aware of the consequences of actions in the frame, and ready to anticipate the adjustments to the procedure to keep the frame functioning. The Joker in Forum Theatre is an example of this facilitator, who manages the procedure 'live', so to speak, sometimes giving out rules as the 'game' is running, or modifying the rules according to the needs or whim of the audience. Such a facilitating role need not be held by one person (it need not always be present at all) performers might step in and out of it, as an episode of interactivity opens and closes, or they may remain in a character role throughout, facilitating through role-play within the fictional context. The actors in Izzo's interactive theatre (see Izzo 1997, 1998) work entirely without coming 'out of character' and without any non-character facilitators to introduce the frame. They guide their 'guests' by improvising with them, giving them roles to play in scenarios by implication: covert invitations.

Props can be introduced to a frame in order to provide a focus for action and to motivate action: the bowl of water given to the children in the TIE show cited above is such a case, the children in this play had to decide which was most important, the thirst of a friendly stranger, or the trust placed in them by their elders, a dilemma facilitated by the idea of their guarding some water, but made concrete in the presence of the water itself. The microphone is a powerful symbolic as well as functional object to viewers and performers in broadcast media. Its functional role is to allow the transmission and recording of sounds and voices, but it is also used to signal who is speaking, and when they should speak. It can be made invisible, but often it is not, with large hand-held microphones used where it would be possible to use smaller ones. The hand held microphone is a symbol of the control held by a television presenter over the conversational order, allowing them to give or withhold the licence to speak by placing it in front of the face of a interviewee (it is like the theatre stage, which also has functional, acoustic and visual properties, but whose symbolic properties are equally important). Other props can be used to show that a participant has become a performer, as well as to show the role that they are to play – a hat for example, or another small piece of costume; or an object can be used to signal turn taking.

The clapping and cheering that is encouraged in some interactive shows is a way of using the audience as a motivator for action within a frame, they can show their encouragement to those brave enough to take part, or they can try to influence the actions of the participants, to make them take one course or another. Other rewards or incentives can be offered, conceivably of a quite tangible kind – Keith Johnstone insists on giving gifts of free tickets to people who participate in 'Gorilla Theatre' (2000: 20).

The activity of the participants who become active in the frame is not entirely in the control of the procedural author, but it is to some degree. The resources provided or suggested to them, with the goals and techniques given in their role means they are at least partly predictable, and the mixing of these roles and stimuli is one of the key techniques of designing a procedure, of allowing the participants themselves to provide the stimulus for a frame to maintain itself. Forum Theatre is a framework for very successful processes because it allows for an expanding number of roles for 'spect-actors' to take, each fitting into a simple set of goals and techniques. The first spect-actors have to break the oppression set out in the forum play, later spect-actors have the option of stepping in to show how the oppression might be reinforced, and later again others can step in to further help to break it. The Joker and the facilitating actors might have very little to do by these later stages, as the roles set out in the procedure provide plenty of structure for the participants to work without them.

## Control and social structure

The theory of frames, as I have used it so far, allows the agent to deploy resources as rationally and strategically as they see fit, and to their own advantage. It does not address how this deployment is itself a skill and a resource, as determined by experience and social background as the resources that are there to be deployed. It suggests, therefore, a theory of procedure and process of audience participation in which the procedural author merely has to judge the resources available to participants and create a procedure that addresses them, in order for an open space to appear. It does not take account of the myriad inhibitions, reservations and obligations that will come into play in a micro-sociological exchange like an episode of audience participation, and which will make the deployment of these resources a much more complex matter. This is not satisfactory, but by augmenting Goffman's theory at this point with ideas from Pierre Bourdieu, it is possible to introduce a component – the habitus – that allows us to think of the disposition towards the use of resources as another factor that the procedural author has to strategise for, to work around and with, as both an obstacle and a resource. The following two chapters explore how perceptions of risk and unconscious embodied responses will inform participatory choices, while this section – and the remainder of this chapter – adapts what has come before to account for differences of class and culture among prospective participants.

Goffman's idea of resources has affinities with the notion of capital that Bourdieu employs to show how different symbolic attributes can be viewed as goods at a social market. There are many varieties of capital in his writing. Richard Jenkins distils them into three:

> social capital (various kinds of valued relations with significant others), cultural capital (primarily legitimate knowledge of one kind or another) and symbolic capital (prestige and social honour) (Jenkins, 1992: 85).

All of these can have a part to play in a participatory event: social capital coming into play when a participant has useful, or inhibiting, connections with other participants, either audience members or performers; and symbolic capital when status relationships affect participants' perceptions of each other and ultimately the way they interact with each other. Most importantly, cultural capital will consist of the skills and knowledges that participants can bring into the interaction with them. Though all three are kinds of resources that can be important to a social interaction of this kind, it is the idea of cultural capital that reflects the resources that have been discussed in detail so far.

Bourdieu's *field*, too, has some resonances with Goffman's *frame* – though he is much more at pains to define the interconnections between capital and field. It is the specific field of social interaction that will dictate the relative value of the different elements of capital that can be brought into use at any time. Academic qualifications, as symbolic capital, are more valuable in fields of work or education than they are in fields of recreational interaction, among friends, family or strangers; the social capital of friendships of family connections will be of greater value in creating more and stronger such connections, and will be valuable in some fields of work and education, but probably only a limited range of such fields as are connected, through class or sub-culture, to these family and friendship networks. Goffman's frame is a more microcosmic view of this, engaged with the smaller scale of immediate interactions, and concerned with perceptions in the moment rather than permanent or persistent institutions and practices.

Bourdieu achieves this by insisting that capital cannot be used without recourse to the 'structuring mechanism', which indicates what its value is, and how it is to be deployed in an appropriate field. This structuring mechanism is the habitus:

> the strategy generating principle enabling agents to cope with unforeseen and ever-changing situations [...] a system of lasting and transposable dispositions which, integrating past experiences, functions at every moment as a matrix of perceptions, appreciations and actions and makes possible the achievement of infinitely diversified tasks. (Bourdieu and Wacquant 1992: 18).

These dispositions give the individual a way of interpreting and making use of the ideas, objects and situations employed in a field. In Bourdieu's analysis habitus is intimately connected with class identity, and while Goffman is generally less interested in a theory of social classes, his idea of resource continuity is also a framework for how the individual interprets a situation according to experience, background and learned disposition. Habitus, for Bourdieu, is the reason why the same things are understood and used differently by people from different backgrounds – why capital has different value in different settings, and the reason why people from similar backgrounds tend to respond similarly to situations they understand on the basis of this shared experience. Bourdieu's landmark text, *Distinction: A Social Critique of the Judgement of Taste* (1984), is a study of culture, class and education in France in the 1970s, revealing and theorising the persistence of social immobility in the face of initiatives to remedy it. This matter of the defining character of social background, and the way it shapes not only the resources available to us, but also the way we are disposed to make use of them, is of some importance when we consider invitations, especially by procedural authors who do not know their audience personally, as is often the case in audience participation. Supplementing Goffman's conceptual structure with Bourdieu's allows us to see how class, gender, age and other cultural distinctions will determine how frames of participation are used.

There is disagreement amongst commentators on Bourdieu: some say that his theory clearly denies the choice-making of the individual, their agency, and that habitus is a variation of the theory of a powerful hegemony that penetrates the individual's psyche and overrules choices that are not pre-determined by social structure. Others protest that Bourdieu himself has misunderstood the capacity of his theory to account for agency, that the habitus is a 'strategy generating mechanism' rather than the entirety of the strategy itself. These theorists are inclined to see how resistance to social structure is not only possible, but also necessary if we are to understand phenomena within that structure: for example, the changing nature of the structure, and our ability to commentate upon it. To de Certeau, for example, Bourdieu treats habitus as an 'immobile stone figure', and 'throws a blanket over tactics' (de Certeau 1988: 58–59), where he himself uses the idea of tactics to show people as able to resist domination through improvisations in the spaces left by structure. Structure, for de Certeau, works at the level of strategy, where it has command of the terrain and that which is 'proper' to it; beneath this we operate tactically, without autonomy from the strategic level, but with trickery, tenacity and challenge. He is interested in a theory that has room for the agency of individuals and groups within social structure.

In an essay on the dichotomy between structure and agency, Hays finds that although this dichotomy is almost ubiquitous in social theory, it is often disabling rather than useful. In place of this opposition, she looks for a balance in which:

Agency explains the creation, recreation and transformation of social structures; agency is made possible by the enabling features of social structures at the same time as it is limited within the bounds of structural constraint (Hays 1994: 62).

This is a reciprocating relationship. She doesn't eliminate the tension between a lasting and self-perpetuating structure, and an impulse for change or independence: 'structurally reproductive agency' is contrasted to 'structurally transformative agency' (Hays 1994: 63–64). Habitus, according to this interpretation, allows us to place the operation of the relationship with dominant discourses (or fields) back with the individual, by insisting that the ways that a person or a group can engage with them is determined differently according to their background and experience. We will each be disposed differently towards events such as participatory performance, and will respond differently, so that the determinations of our learned responses are particular to each of us, and thus even more unknowable for the procedural author. We will also each bring different capital to these interactions, different materials with which to resist, subvert or enjoy the control of the procedure, to work tactically, in de Certeau's terms.

The frames of audience participation are always citational, always make use of the material of the rest of everyday life, and our actions within them are always mediated by our learned dispositions towards behaviour (habitus) and our usable social attributes (capital). In giving an invitation to participate, the procedural author articulates a relationship between the participant, these contexts of pre-theatrical and outer frame of performance, and the performances that might be given in the frame of participation.

For the most part practitioners are happy to cite whatever vocabularies they can access with their participants, the shared resources that make it easy for people to speak and act in public. At best this might produce the Freirian ideal of validating people's understanding of the world, allowing them to speak for themselves using the words and actions they use every day. At worst it runs the risk of reproducing discourses that perpetuate oppression or discrimination, or fails to articulate any viewpoints except those of the dominant culture. A potential benefit to a politically motivated practitioner can be an interrogation of the ideas available in the dominant discourse, emphasising the contingency of these vocabularies over any presumed universality because of the need for negotiation between participants to secure understanding. But using genre resources (as Izzo does so enthusiastically in his work) gives a short cut to a kind of universalised vocabulary, a conceptualisation separated from the world and its contingencies, and so with a fraught relationship with free expression. The characters, and the roles they play, in a Western or a historical romance, for example, have some room for manoeuvre, but it takes some ingenuity to escape from the demands of the stereotype when inventing action on the hoof. Even the non-matrixed performances described by Kirby (1965: 44), make use of shared resources, the discourses of the body are particularly emphasised when the performer is not fictionalised, and references to the person are more closely associated with that person: the continuity is with resources used in everyday contexts as well as in artistic or political contexts. Thus even the subject matter adopted in a procedure will be limiting in itself, it will create the boundaries of the action.

The terms that can be taken forward from these theorists will allow a more nuanced understanding of the determinations at play in a frame of audience participation, or the way that action is shaped. Procedural authors will work according to their own habitus, just as their participants will; their agency could become structurally reproductive or structurally transformative; and they will make tactical moves under the strategic influence of the dominant disciplines of theatre culture. But the microcosmic social structures of participatory theatre will also mimic the influence of social structure in the way that a procedure, and the processes that result from it, shape and dictate the action of participants. Inevitably, the way participants can deploy their capital will be guided by habitus, but they will also be able to use tactical approaches, within what at this level is the strategic field set out by the procedural author. However, it is the procedural author who has control over the action at the level of strategy, in de Certeau's sense, while the participant has the possibility of a tactical response within this dominated field.

## Horizons of participation

To unpack further what emerges from the interaction of procedural authors and audience participants, and to offer another perspective on the framing of activity, it is worth turning to an account of the reception of art work in its usual, more passive form. Reception theory celebrates the agency of the reader of literary texts, and the interaction between text, author and reader. But even in appropriations of this theory for the different conditions of the theatre audience – by Susan Bennett for example – the proposal is for agencies and interactivities of a different order to those that are possible in participatory theatre. Bennett makes some inroads in developing these theories for use in performance analysis, taking into account the different conditions at work for 'readers' of performance: the broader range of sign systems in play, the effect of the presence of other spectators, the chances and contingencies that can change a performance from one day to another, and, most importantly, the direct effect audiences can have on the performance. Though her analysis does not extend to full audience participation, it provides a grounding for any discussion of the perceptions, and by implication the behaviour of theatre audiences. Bennett makes good use of the notion of 'horizons of expectation' for how audiences come to the theatre with preconceptions that guide how they view a performance. This is based on Hans-Robert Jauss's introduction of the term to the field of literature, accounting for how readers approach a text.

> A literary work, even when it appears to be new, does not present itself as something absolutely new in an informational vacuum, but predisposes its audience to a very specific kind of reception by announcements, overt and covert signals, familiar characteristics, or implicit allusions. (Jauss 1982: 23)

These predispositions amount to the horizon beyond which a reader cannot see, and beyond which the audience of a performance cannot see. For Hans-Georg Gadamer – Jauss's key source for this idea – the recognition that all perception involves preconceptions is of fundamental importance, and is required for a full appreciation of the nature of understanding. Gadamer and Jauss are not simply saying that the encounter with a text is limited by preconception, but that the understanding of a text is facilitated by the pre-judgements that tradition and experience make available to us. The text, of course, must contain the cues which alert us to what in tradition we must make use of:

> The psychic process in the reception of a text is, in the primary horizon of aesthetic experience, by no means only an arbitrary series of merely subjective impressions, but rather the carrying out of specific instructions in a process of directed perception, which can be comprehended according to its constitutive motivations and triggering signals, and which also can be described by a textual linguistics. (Jauss in Holub 1984: 61)

There is a circularity to this – the text can only be understood through the 'triggering signals' but these signals are themselves part of the text; nevertheless the notion that the perception of a text is guided by the codes that the text itself declares is robust. Though Gadamer's discussion in *Truth and Method* is founded on hermeneutics – the interpretation of texts – he is interested in understanding in a much wider sense, so that the everyday situation and the social action that derive from it are implied too:

> Every finite present has its limitations. We define the concept of 'situation' by saying that it represents a standpoint that limits the possibility of vision. Hence an essential part of the concept of situation is the concept of 'horizon'. The horizon is the range of vision that includes everything that can be seen from a particular vantage point. Applying this to the thinking mind, we speak of narrowness of horizon, of the possible expansion of horizon, of the opening up of new horizons, etc. (Gadamer 2004: 301)

Audiences at the theatre are also guided in their perception of the performance, by an even greater organisation of contextual material than that which can be controlled by the authors of books. But more interestingly for my purposes, the 'psychic process' occurs within a social process, which is also established through signals embedded in the event and its conventions: and as has been discussed at some length, theatregoing is such a social process, where audience *behaviour* is guided as well as audience perception. Gadamer extends this 'range of vision' to all matters of experience and understanding, and though he does not make the link to a notion of horizons of action, the Goffman-like proposition can be made that action is determined by perception, and by expectations of what is appropriate within a perceived situation. I propose a 'horizon of participation', in which audience members perceive the range of behaviours through which they are invited to participate in a performance. Gadamer's use of the metaphor implies finite limits, but like Jauss, he is also at pains to point out that the horizon also implies a perception beyond the immediate, the transcending of narrow limits of perception, and that horizons continually extend and adapt; the notion of a horizon as a limit does not indicate a fatally restricted viewpoint, but should suggest the opposite: 'A horizon is not a rigid frontier, but something that moves with one and invites one to advance further' (Gadamer 2004: 238).

Authors, too, have horizons, in how they anticipate the reception of their work, and in the potential they perceive in the traditions at hand. They arrive at the conjoined practices of writing and reading – or theatre making and theatre going – with these practices in place, and when they attempt to exploit, adapt or revolutionise practice they must confront their own interiorised expectations of practice, as well as challenging those of readers and audiences. Reading a text or receiving a performance is not a matter of adopting the author's horizon, but the 'fusion' (Gadamer 2004: 305) of the reader's horizon with that of the text, which occurs as an event of understanding:

> [t]he horizon of understanding cannot be limited either by what the writer had originally in mind, or by the horizon of the person to whom the text was originally addressed (396).

For Jauss there are works that extend horizons. The literary text itself, when first encountered, is seen within horizons of form or genre, a 'paradigmatic isotopy', but then presents its own movement within this paradigm to establish an 'immanent syntagmatic horizon' – each work moves within the apparent rules of its type to create the structure for its own reception as an individual utterance. As forms and genres are challenged:

> A corresponding process of the continuous establishing and altering of horizons also determines the relationship of the individual text to the succession of texts that forms the genre. The new text evokes for the reader (listener) the horizon of expectation and rules familiar from earlier texts, which are then varied, corrected, altered, or even just reproduced (Jauss 1982: 23)

How far these horizons can be extended, however, and into what behavioural territory, is another matter, and here the question of control becomes more acute: not only do traditions and practices in performance influence very closely how audiences participate, they also circumscribe the opportunities in which participants get to make choices of their own about what their participation consists of. Umberto Eco (1979) is notable among semioticians for considering the active choices of the reader, for example, in his idea of 'open' and 'closed' texts: an open text is one where there are fewer textual imperatives, and more opportunity for interpretation, and a closed text being more conventional in telling the reader what it is. We can, similarly, expect there to be participatory events that are more or less open in the sense that they create spaces in which participants have a wider range of choices about how to respond to an invitation. Similarly Iser gives us the idea of the textual 'blanks' or 'gaps' where the reader or spectator has to infer meaning from what the text or play does not show or say:

> Blanks allow the reader to bring a story to life, to assign meaning, and by making his decision he implicitly acknowledges the

inexhaustibility of the text: at the same time it is this very inexhaustibility that forces him to make his decision (Bennett 1997: 44)

The production of texts, including performance texts, is also a matter of
creating gaps for readers and spectators to fill, though often this might
be an entirely unconscious element of the creative process. A procedural
author creates gaps of a different kind.

The horizon of participation, like the horizon of expectation, is a
limit and a range of potentials within that limit, both gaps to be filled
and choices to be made. Unlike the horizon of expectation these gaps
and choices are about action rather than interpretation. When invited
to participate we construct, in this way, an initial assessment of the
potential activity appropriate to the invitation – in Goffman's terms we
understand a frame, in Gadamer's we perceive a horizon – which has not
told us what to do, but offered us a set of limits and a perception of the
potential values of action within those limits. The horizon metaphor
describes limits and the possibilities within those limits. The horizon is
a limit in the sense that it stands for the point at which we recognise
(correctly or incorrectly, in the sense that other people, including a procedural author, may understand or intend something different), invited
and appropriate action ends, and inappropriate responses begin. Within
perceived limits there are multiple possibilities, which if we extend the
metaphor of the horizon a little, we can conceive as a landscape or terrain to be explored or navigated.

Horizons, in this sense, are not set by the procedural author, but
arrived at through the interaction of all the contributing elements of
the process as a perception of the audience participant. Just as physical
horizons change as we move through a landscape, the horizon of participation changes as we interact and perform, moving with us and inviting us to advance further. Alternatively, we might read the metaphor in
conjunction with Bourdieu's idea of 'field', as a situation in which it is
necessary to take a place, to plant oneself, and thus to alter the meaning
of the landscape around this place. Either way, seeing the invitation to
participate as revealing a horizon through which to choose a path or to
take a position, becomes a subtle and flexible tool for understanding the
processes of participation.

The procedural author can work to change the horizon, both as a
limit, as they might indicate that the invitation is open to more than
had previously been understood, and in the sense of landscape, as they
guide the participant towards certain paths or terrain. The range will be
comparatively broad or narrow in different procedures, where some are

designed to produce very specific actions – singing along, or shouting a set response – others are intended to give opportunities for creative expression to participants.

To continue the example of the pantomime given earlier, the invitation is to shout 'behind you'. To shout something else would be quite possible but it would be inappropriate, it would break the frame, exceed the horizon, and it would be churlish behaviour at a children's event. A procedure that successfully invites participants will see them explore the horizon, play within it to produce performances that are both theirs, and the procedural authors, as Abrams, again, notes in Ruckert's Hautnah:

> Tactility was the central element in this piece: two props – a knife and a peacock feather were present in the space, she caressed herself with them, caressed me with them, offered them to me to do the same. I echoed but changed the movements, responding rather than imitating. She led, I followed – here the solo became a duet. (Kattwinkel 2003: 3)

Goffman's terminology for the construction and interconnection of frames, and my additions to its relation to the invitation of participatory frames, will transfer easily to the interactive process of perceiving a horizon. Invitations will either be explicit about the acts wanted, or will imply (conventionally, covertly or accidentally) a known frame, or an audience member will begin to use another convention, (or there will be a combination of explicit and conventional instruction and generic implications). The continuities will produce limitations and indications of what is expected through appearance formulas, resources, and disconnections, and facilitators will work in-frame to provide the context for the actions, again limiting the range while suggesting which parts of it to explore.

The horizon that participants perceive maps out the possibility of their agency in the event, thus using these concepts to describe and understand this horizon and how it is created will help to answer the question of the relative agency of the participants and the initiators of the event. It will also serve to show the control that the procedural author has over the participants, as the horizon is established primarily by the invitation to participate, and by the relation between the event and its context, and the further activities of the facilitators in the frame, all of which are to some degree expressions of procedural authorship. Much of the 'in-frame' activity just described can be thought of as shaping this terrain, closing parts of it and making other parts seem open – obvious or attractive to participants. Sometimes facilitation might become 'difficult-ating', when a horizon has established itself and people are participating wholeheartedly, new problems can be introduced, and thus work can be advanced by developing the terrain that is being worked in rather than moving to a different frame. The horizon therefore, rather than a fixed set of possibilities, is a changing landscape that develops as participants take action and as practitioners intervene.

Although the horizon is arrived at for each participant through their interaction with the invitation given, rather than a direct imposition, it is through controlling these aspects of a procedure that theatre practitioners – procedural authors – can to a degree keep control of the actions of their participants, and hence the performances that arise from their procedures. Complete control of these actions is not possible, but there are a number of ways in which performances will be suggested and limited, so that what happens remains within a horizon and its terrain has been largely foreseen by the procedural author. First, they construct this horizon in ways that are available to theatre makers and authors of more conventional kinds – defining the immediate pre-theatrical frame and the outer theatrical frames – and provide many of the resources that the participants will use in their performances. In the selection of the setting, and in the writing of the performance, continuities are implied between the performances to be given in the participatory frames and the performances given by the participants or known by participants, in other parts of their lives.

Second, the procedural author can use the invitation to participate and in-frame activity to describe the horizon explicitly. At the point of invitation they have the opportunity to define the range in ways that can make it more open or closed, most decisively when giving goals for the participants to achieve. The actions of facilitators and facilitating actors following the invitation will continue to shape the horizon and its terrain, closing off some possibilities and opening others, and these actions are manifestations of procedural authorship. All of the actions of the facilitators will have an effect upon the horizon, though they may not be entirely in control of their own behaviour in having these effects, and might suggest performances in ways that they have not foreseen. As these varied actions will shape the opportunities in different ways in relation to different kinds of action, and in relation to different participants, the horizon can be thought of as having a constantly shifting landscape. This landscape, however, has always been shaped by procedural authorship, whatever efforts have been made to keep this influence to a minimum.

Some ambiguity may be detected in the way I have described horizons in this section. Just as Jauss writes of horizons as belonging to texts or traditions, as well as to readers, I have suggested that horizons of participation belong to individual participants, but are shaped by procedural authorship, and implied in performance traditions. Though a strict sense of a horizon that manifests when an individual encounters a situation and comes to an understanding of its possibilities and limitations on the basis of the pre-dispositions given to them by experience is worth keeping in mind, horizons that are culturally shared or assumed by practitioners and audiences are useful as long as we remember that the manner of their actual manifestation depends upon real people in real situations. Horizon is a metaphor, first of all, and it is flexible and has many useful correlates.

## The aesthetic meaning of agency

This chapter has introduced an analytical framework for the analysis of audience participation, based on questions of authorship, control and the nature of the art work. The creation of audience participation has been shown to be a collaborative process in which a horizon of participation is arrived at through the interaction of expectations about theatre and performance events, the invitation strategy of the procedural author, and the availability of social resources to be used in performance by individual participants. The work has to be seen as both the procedure, which is designed to create this process, and the distinct iterations of the process and performances it gives rise to. Authorship has been shown to be a dynamic property of this process/procedure evolution, where the horizon of participation manifests limits and opportunities shaped by the invitation of the procedural author, but which is arrived at individually by each participant, and within which the participant has agency to make choices about their action. Giving this interplay of agencies an important place in the active generation of performance material and into the experience of the participant, I propose, makes it into not just a practical problem to solve, but an aesthetic property of the work.

Antony Giddens suggests that the absence of intention can be considered the absence of real agency:

> It has frequently been supposed that human agency can be defined only in terms of intentions. That is to say, for an item of behaviour

to count as action, whoever perpetrates it must intend to do so, or else the behaviour in questions is just a reactive response'. (Giddens 1996: 95)

This intention, however, is not necessarily a rational process: the intentions do not have to be careful, beneficial or right in order to display agency. Agency, though, can apply as a meaningful term to only part of our behaviour:

> I am the author of many things I do not intend to do, and may not want to bring about, but none the less do. Conversely, there may be circumstances in which I intend to achieve something, and do achieve it, although not directly through my agency' (Giddens 1996: 93).

In this view, to achieve something through a reactive response is not agency, to achieve something by accident is not agency, and to merely intend and achieve nothing is not agency. For an end to have been achieved through our agency there must be a connection between our actions and the results we intend: our actions must have power. So if a decision to participate, or how to participate, in a performance, is made on the basis of incomplete information where that information is withheld by another party, the agency is undermined: it is not based on an informed decision. The weakness of this perspective on agency is that no-one ever has a full understanding of circumstances surrounding an action, so all actions are taken with incomplete information. If the implication that an informed agency is therefore impossible is to be avoided, the threat of mis-information must be a relative one: a reasonable degree of information is necessary, but some element of ignorance is inevitable. An agent who has this capacity to act or not, on the basis of reasonably complete information, whether fully rationalising the situation or not, can be held responsible for their actions. They have the benefit of being able to take credit or blame; this makes their actions meaningful, as Daniel Dennett says: 'blame is the price we pay for credit, and we pay it gladly under most circumstances' (2004: 292). Responsibility is a freedom worth having.

The apparent opposite of creating positions of (reasonably) informed agency for participants is to create positions in which their actions are manipulated, because they cannot be said to have sufficient information to intend the consequences of their actions. The result might be to create experiences, but not experiences of choice, and to provoke performances by audience participants that are not meaningfully created by them. But the discussion in this chapter has shown how complex the matter of choice in social interaction is, how moments where we make choices are informed and structured by experiences and learned dispositions; and the following chapters explore other aspects of choice making, action and experience. Agency in the context of these ideas is a matter of feeling as well as a matter of a reliable connection between conscious action and its results. The experience of making choices – whether they lead directly to desired outcomes or not – or of having choice taken away, makes up one part of the aesthetics of participation.

An example of participation of this kind occurred in the closing section of Gob Squad's *Kitchen*,[13] when several audience members were given headphones, and asked to take the place of performers. The performers then took places in the audience, with microphones, and gave instructions for action and dialogue to their replacements through the headphones. As ever these volunteers had the option to refuse the invitation to participate, or to adopt behaviours outside the frame offered, but when they accepted the invitation, the horizon available was very limited indeed: they became puppets for the performers who instructed them. The quality of this sequence – to me as an audience member who did not perform – was informed by the style and content of the preceding material, made up of pastiches of several Andy Warhol films and their rhetoric of transforming everyday life into art. The framing of these puppets as part of this attempt to reconstruct a utopian experiment was inflected by the participants' evident anxiety and uncertainty, their growing confidence in the parts they were playing and the inflections they began to give to what they were evidently being instructed to do. So even in this very tightly controlled horizon choices were available, albeit tiny ones, which were magnified for those watching by the process through which they were put on show. In this sense the experience of becoming a performer was revealed for the rest of the audience; perhaps it was meaningful in this sense for the participants themselves.

Agency changes the quality of all action taken: an action that belongs to me feels different; and conversely (and perhaps perversely), when we take action that does not belong to us in this sense it also feels different on that account. But the extent to which action can belong to an audience participant has not been solved in this chapter. In further chapters this dimension of the recognition of the subjectivity of the audience member through participation will be explored in more detail, and challenged in different ways. The model of the subject as it has been theorised in this chapter is more-or-less secure and monadic: it needs to be considered that, as well as the social influences on our behaviour accounted for by Bourdieu's habitus, field and capital, there are physical and psychological influences too, particularly when we are in the company of others. The depth of the influence of these factors draws attention to the embodiment and intersubjectivity of human experience, understanding and action. Intersubjectivity – the way in which the presence of other people in our world both gives us a point of view, and draws action from us – will have to be examined explicitly, for the way it creates our ability to respond in audience participation, and for how it becomes part of the substance of these performances. The embodiment of culture as expressed in the dispositions of Bourdieu's habitus intersects with pre-culturally embodied physical processes in both conscious and unconscious responses to stimulus, again dictating or inflecting how we act in any given situation. These factors add significant dimensions to aesthetic theory, particularly around the ontology of the artwork and the engagement of the spectator with it, dimensions which will be especially pertinent to the aesthetics of audience participation.

## Armadillo Theatre

A detailed analysis of a procedure of participation that deploys a complex of choice and manipulation will help to demonstrate further how the concepts of this chapter can be used. The description that follows outlines a procedure and its invitations in some detail, to start with, before discussing the processes that arose from it. It is drawn from my own experience as a co-creator of the workshop, and performer and facilitator on many occasions over a number of years. No formal documentation of the participants' experiences was made at the time – any speculation about this aspect of the work is just that, speculation, but based on many observations of behaviour, response and informal feedback. The form is fairly typical of Theatre in Education of its time, a conflation of a Forum Theatre style, but unhitched from the strictures of Theatre of the Oppressed, and other interactive techniques. It is not offered here as a model of good practice – my critique of its potential failings will become apparent, as well as its strengths.

Armadillo Theatre's workshop around bullying in school was produced in conjunction with a research project at the University of Sheffield in 1991–92. It continued to tour for several years independently of this project in forms that developed from the original described and has been assessed by Smith and Sharp in *School Bullying: Insights and Perspectives* (1994). The version detailed here is from some time later, and was used with larger groups of children, up to three classes at a time, and with a fairly broad age range, from nine up to thirteen. The aim of the workshop was to promote awareness of bullying as a problem that involves and affects everyone in the school, which should be dealt with openly, and to encourage children to think of bullying as something that they can all help to change rather than just a problem for those immediately affected. In this version Forum Theatre takes a central role in the process along with the performance of a play, 'hot-seating' of characters, discussion led by a facilitator/joker, and short passages of 'teaching in role'. There are four actors, two of whom stay in character most of the time, two of whom take turns to facilitate the exercises.

The programme begins with a very brief introduction delivered by one of the actors to the students, who are gathered as an audience in the school hall, usually in a large circle of chairs, several deep. One of the four actors introduces the company and asks the students to watch a short play, and to watch carefully. The play has four scenes and four characters: we first see Ian and Mark kicking a ball to each other in a games lesson, talking. Their friend Nicky arrives, taking a short cut because she is late for school, and Ian talks to her, pointedly excluding Mark. In the second scene she returns a homework book to Mark, Ian snatches it and refuses to return it, dropping it on the floor and making Mark beg for it. He does not return the book, but says that he will give it back at youth club that evening instead. There is a brief scene in which Mark tells his teacher, Mr Jenkins, that he has forgotten his homework, and refuses to admit that anything is wrong. The final scene is at the youth club, where Ian tosses the book to Mark, then asks him to lend money for the pool table. When refused, Ian grabs Mark by the collar, and the play ends. The whole thing lasts a little more than ten minutes, uses no set, and only a book and a football as props; all the characters are played by adults dressed in their own clothes. As an outer theatrical frame it draws on generalities of school life rather than on the realities of any school in particular: the conversation revolves around football, watching videos and avoiding homework. The characters are not caricatures or stereotypes, but they have only the characteristics to make them seem ordinary, and also to fall into clear categories of 'bully', 'victim' and 'innocent onlooker'. The banality of these thematic resources is designed to allow participants to pick up the threads of conversation easily, and to identify and play with the interests of the characters. The theatrical conventions – the lack of set and costume, and the adults playing children – are the shared resource of a theatre technique that is easy to pick up, and present person-character formulas that are very flexible.

At the climactic moment of danger, when Ian has taken hold of Mark, the performer playing Nicky comes out of character and explains that the children now have an opportunity to talk to the two boys, and divides them into two groups, sending one to one end of the hall, where Ian is waiting, and to the other where Mark is. They are left to talk to each actor, who remains in character, for around ten minutes before swapping. When questioned, the actors respond freely according to how they see the characters (a number of different actors played each character, sometimes alternating the roles morning and afternoon, and each had scope to interpret it within the parameters described here), but with some very specific constraints: neither offers anything in the boy's background that would explain the behaviour, even if they are directly asked about it: Ian likes fighting and getting what he wants; Mark knows he's not good at fighting and wants to be friends with everyone, he even considers Ian to be his friend. Mark appears unhappy and can be persuaded to see that Ian, and even Nicky, are not behaving as friends should. During the hot-seating Ian can be persuaded that his actions make Mark unhappy, but will not agree to change, or even recognise that there is any compelling reason why he should.

After telling the students that they have a chance to ask the boys anything they want, the facilitators do nothing to ensure that a dialogue gets going, and the teachers who are present are asked not to intervene, even if it appears nothing will happen. As in-frame facilitators the actors make some effort to keep the discussion relevant, answering all questions as long as they maintain 'belief' in the situation. Some answers given are shorter than others, and Mark ensures that at some point he describes his feelings about Ian's bullying. Little is done to control the students' performance as questioners; they are not allowed to wander away, or to give up on the task entirely and the actors take some measures to make sure the overall performance of question and answer produces some useful information. As an invitation it is fairly explicit, but also fairly open; it draws on the students' expectation that they will be asked by responsible adults to undertake tasks – on this disposition in the habitus of the school-child – but begins to neglect some of the clear structuring that such activities normally take.

After this the facilitator asks the two groups to return to their seats, and explains that the play will now be shown again, and that this time the audience should watch out for moments were Mark could do something different, and to shout 'stop' at these moments. This is a limited Forum Theatre introduction, no more instructions are given at this point, but when the play runs, and the first 'stop' is offered – usually quite early on, where Ian ignores Mark, or interrupts him in conversation with Nicky – she asks the student to describe what Mark should do, then asks him or her to show everyone. Often this first volunteer is nervous about doing so, and so she offers the service of the actor who has played Mark, who listens carefully to instructions from the child, and acts the forum scene for them. But the tactic at this point is for the actor to get it wrong, to make sure the intervention fails, with the intention of inspiring the child or one of his or her friends to offer to do it right. When they do, Ian makes sure that it works, and that the child looks good doing it. After this there is usually no shortage of volunteers. This strategy manipulates the suggested interventions – ultimately manipulating the idea that has been offered by the child – in the interests of overcoming any initial nervousness about participation. The invitations, again, are explicit at each stage, and create an increasingly broad horizon of participation, though they do not explain all the details of what will happen when the invitation is taken up.

It is only after this that the facilitator explains that the actors will also try to show how a suggestion might fail, and the forum begins to alternate between suggestions offered, and shown working, and then repeated with the actors improvising to make them fail. The usual Forum Theatre rule of not allowing any suggestions that are 'magic' (or asking the spectators to shout out when they spot such interventions) is not included, so 'unrealistic' ideas, such as for example 'get a gun and shoot Ian' are shown, in slow motion, action movie style, (and usually then repeated showing Mark – for example – being arrested and sent to jail), and are included alongside the sensible ones. Shared generic resources from popular entertainment are deliberately included, such as gunfights and martial arts battles, and explored on their own terms. A short discussion is encouraged after each intervention, principally consisting of The Joker asking whether Mark is better off, and why, but also allowing some discussion of whether an intervention is realistic, or morally right or wrong.

Without drawing conclusions from the forum and the discussions of it, the facilitators move the process on to another episode of hot-seating – this time of Nicky. The questioning soon turns to why she doesn't stop Ian from behaving as he does, to which she replies that she doesn't know how to go about it, and she'd feel better if she had some help. When the help is volunteered by the children she makes them agree that the next time they see him picking on Mark, they will intervene with her. Sometimes they offer to beat him up for her, but she insists that they do not do this, because he is still her friend.

'Nicky' manages the conversation so that it seems she is following the implications of the students' questions, but in fact is ensuring it leads to this conclusion. As soon as this agreement has been made Ian and Mark re-appear; the actors simply make themselves seen somewhere behind Nicky, striking up a simple routine of Ian pushing Mark around. Nicky approaches and tells Ian, uncomfortably and ineffectually, that he should stop. This is an implicit invitation – the frame has changed from the clear-cut question-and-answer hot-seating to one of situated conversation between characters, but without the children being returned to their audience role. They have been led to offer their help if Nicky speaks to Ian, so at this stage the children either join in with her verbally, threaten Ian or attack him physically. In any case, but more quickly if the latter, Mr Jenkins, the teacher reappears and reprimands them all for picking on Ian. He then questions them carefully about what had happened, but tells them that they should be speaking to him about it rather than taking matters into their own hands. This closing sequence is ambiguous, it leads the group into an action that is then disapproved of by an authority figure; it is certainly coercive in the way it leads them in this way, but it also serves to leave the programme as a whole with an open ended message, which has to be developed and explored by a teacher in follow-up work for the programme to become coherent.

## Analysing Armadillo's procedure

The invitations to participation are given so that they are coercive in a way that Theatre of the Oppressed processes are not – or should not be if they seek to be true to the values set out in Boal's books. There is a gradual revelation of the nature of the interactive frame, so that participants early in the event are not entirely aware of what they are to do when they shout stop, or even when they make their first intervention in describing what they want Mark to do. The use of the actor in the frame to make this limited kind of participation unattractive is also manipulative in making it necessary to take the role in person in order to make the intervention work. It is these in-frame activities that are the real closing strategy in this process, the work of actors who have thought about and prepared for the interventions that will be offered, and are ready to make them look good and to look bad. Ideas that might challenge 'proper behaviour' are given a hearing, but the negative development has the advantage of coming second and last, and might remain more memorable. The Joker has control over which suggestions are to be played out, and while there is a policy to play all kinds of suggestions, perhaps more so than might be expected in a school setting, this episoding convention – the decision of whether the invitation to suggest and discuss becomes an invitation to take the character and play the scene – remains in the control of a person in authority, an adult among children. The most manipulative of the episoding processes comes at the end of the programme, where a clear invitation is not given, but the action moves from a frame of hot-seating with one character to a frame of free improvisation with another character, while a third waits in anticipation of the interaction that is certain to follow.

Some of the important openings in this process are properties of the style: the freedom to shout 'stop' at any moment when the play is running, the invitation that is open to all – at least as far as the stopping and discussing is concerned – and the freedom, once on the stage, to play with the content of the scene. The openness of the hot-seating conversations helps to develop the atmosphere of freedom, and encourages the students to take responsibility for the progress of the action before the Forum Theatre begins. There is also an important freedom in the availability of the 'victim' role to whoever wants to play it: there are no particular person-character formulae, although the implication is generally that the teachers who are present will not participate in this way. In the forum section the range of action is constricted initially by the resources introduced through the plot and characters, and through the goals set out in the invitation: it is fairly broad, and to an extent broader than in many Forum Theatre performances because of the exclusion of the 'it's magic!' rule.[14] The nature of the relationship between the performers and the participants, however, shapes the range of action in a different way: they are adults working with children, having rehearsed for some time to produce a procedure, and inevitably able to influence each intervention substantially once it is under way. The controlling strategies are more obvious here, to the practitioners, and to observers, but it is not until they have done their work that they will be obvious to participants.

In the final section of this procedure Armadillo Theatre has taken such a strategic control over the horizon of participation that they leave very little tactical space for the students to make use of. The pre-prepared sequence can absorb any response and use it as material to re-enforce something like a moral for the piece, an officially sanctioned message about the role that school authorities should take in this kind of situation. Credit is given to the resources that the students bring to the Forum Theatre section, to what is meaningful to them, but it is undermined by the resources brought to bear by the company, in a more serious manner, in the section that follows. There are two kinds of resources at work: the students draw on their own resources to show their understanding of the problem, and argue with each other and the company about it; the company draw on their understanding of school life and of the problem, which is close to an 'official' understanding of bullying. The capital of the official understanding is, however, more highly valued, is placed last, and is not followed at this point by an examination of it in discussion.

The participants in this work have spaces in which to exercise their cultural capital, to speak in their own language, in a manner that conforms to their 'habitus', but only in parts of the event does this equate to an agency that avoids manipulation through either the withholding of information or the creation of restricted ranges of action. The final sequence has an outcome which they cannot intend – leading them into a performance as bullies being disciplined by a teacher – because they are unaware that their actions will be re-framed as an interaction with a teacher. The procedure that leads to this doesn't give them informed consent about how they perform, or about what will be done with their performance. But it does give them access to experiences of choosing to reject victimising behaviour, as well as choosing aggressive behaviour of their own. They are likely, in these moments, to feel a variety of emotions – excitement, shame, confusion, perhaps; the success of the process as pedagogy depends upon the follow-up work of the teachers who see it with their students, who must interrogate these feelings and the actions that give rise to them. Post-hoc reflection on an aesthetic experience is always an important – perhaps the most important – element of how it becomes meaningful to us, in this case choices, the actions that arise from those choices, and the feelings that arise from this action, are the material that needs to be reflected on.

The young people in Armadillo Theatre's workshop, who stumble, uninformed, into a role play in which they exemplify a lesson in cycles of victimisation are essentially humiliated, precisely because they have been seen to make a choice – and have presented themselves as making a choice – but in a situation in which the only likely choice (the horizon of participation) is then re-cast as a wrong choice. This results from the use of an implicit invitation that has no clear explanation, and an address to the specific plot resources already introduced, and to the dispositions towards behaviours that can be expected from these participants. This results in a narrowly delineated horizon of participation, and hence to the performance desired by the procedural authors.

For James Thompson, applied theatre is 'a practice that engages in the politics of prepositions. The theatres "of", "by", "with" or "for" question each other because none is given primacy in the term' (2003: 15). Audience participation is always a theatre *with* the participants. It can generally lay claim to being a theatre *for* its participants, but the territory of a theatre *of* or a theatre *by* is more difficult to confidently assert. When authorship is shared, in a balance that will be specific to the moment of interaction, these labels might apply, but if the participant has been reduced to the status of the object of performance, perhaps they cannot. In this example what has been made with these participants, at worst as puppets of the procedure, is still an experience for them, and potentially a meaningful one.

This lengthy discussion of a procedure of participation, without in this instance any exploration of specific iterations of it, is placed here to show how the terminologies of the chapter can be applied. It might also unpack the ethics and ground-level politics of a procedure, but although my references to humiliation and manipulation have an ethical flavour, my concern is not (at this point) with the ethics of the work. A further analysis might consider whether what I have called humiliation, and the clear manipulation of the participants, might be ethically valid when viewed in a wider context – most importantly taking into account the continued work of class teachers in following up the programme with the young people after the event. My point, however, is that the crafting of these experiences is a kind of authorship, through the shaping and bringing into heightened attention the experience of choice and action.

A further development of my proposition that the experience of making choices is an aesthetic property of the art work depends on hearing what these moments felt like as they happened, and as they are remembered. In the chapters that follow the experience of process – as opposed to the structure of procedure – is examined through my own experience as a participant, through interviews with other participants, and through observation of participation in work where I didn't become a participant, as I explore other influences on whether and how to accept an invitation, and what accepting an invitation means to an audience participant.

# 2
# Risk and Rational Action

## Risk in performance

An action staged in a theatre is a relatively contrived illusion and an admitted one; unlike ordinary life, nothing real or actual can happen to the performed characters – although at another level of course something real and actual can happen to the reputation of performers qua professional whose everyday job is to put on theatrical performances. (Goffman 1969: 246)

Real and actual things can happen to characters in interactive plays, insofar as participants can in some cases change the characters' destinies. But the characters we watch most closely in audience participatory performance are often the people who perform, rather than the characters they portray. Audience participants are not professionals, so they do not put their reputations in jeopardy in the way that Goffman describes here, but they have reputations nevertheless, which can really and actually come to harm in a performance. In everyday life the risk of embarrassment has a disciplinary effect on people. We are under injunctions to control ourselves, to present performances of ourselves that fit the personae we present to the world. So when participatory theatre invites performances from audience members, it presents special opportunities for embarrassment, for mis-performance and reputational damage, such that the maintenance of control and the assertion of agency that protects this decorum is important to the potential audience participant, especially at the moment of invitation.

It is, therefore, also of vital importance to the practitioner of audience participatory performance, the procedural author. Participation is risky for these practitioners too: the presence of non-professional volunteers on the stage is a risk. A participant may do almost anything or they may do nothing; they may do what is invited and do it badly. Practitioners who are used to the conventional roles in the theatre will not find it easy to make the sacrifice that has to be made by the procedural author. To have an unrehearsed performer on stage might go against the instincts of the writer who wants his or her words to be said and to be said well. It might go against the instincts of the director who cannot direct the actions of the participant. It might go against the instincts of actors because they do now have to direct, and because they can be made to look foolish. A principle of Western theatre, at least in its orthodox traditions, is that the show should be as controlled and complete as possible before being presented to an audience; in interactive theatre this must be sacrificed as some of the performers cannot be fully rehearsed. The payoff for this risk is that a performance is produced that is even more ephemeral and unique than most live performance, and that is demonstrably a product of the people who are present at the event. However, my focus for this chapter is on the inhibiting force of risk and the perception of risk for potential participants, and on three key questions:

- What do participants risk in performance?
- How does procedural authorship manage risk and the perception of risk?
- What does the element of risk mean for the aesthetics of participation?

A detailed consideration of how risk manifests when participation is invited affords an alternative viewpoint on the role and activity of procedural authors: considering them now as facilitators of the potential performances of participants, rather than as the co-creators of these performances. The audience participant is seen differently in this light too. In the previous chapter I discussed the continuity of their brief life as a performer with the rest of life outside the performance, but now turn to the difficulty presented by the potential contrast and conflict of these two modes of being. In a sense this is a re-focussing of the theme of the previous chapter: the agency of the procedural author is brought to the fore as they take responsibility for the safety, and the perception of safety, of the participant; while the participant's agency is re-cast from the perspective of their need for self-protection and rational minimisation of harm.

This dimension of the relationship between these two roles is never the whole story, but its importance to the practice of creating audience participation, (from both creative positions), and therefore to the performance produced, will become evident. An initial characterisation of this aspect of the work of the procedural author can be drawn from the comparable work of the workshop leader in participatory theatre work of other kinds, where the importance of this issue is taken for granted. As Hahlo and Reynolds acknowledge at the beginning of their guide to building an effective workshop:

> Those taking part, especially if it is a new experience for them, have to be encouraged to get to a point where they can begin to take small but significant personal risks, and prick the bubble of inhibiting self consciousness. The workshop leader [...] won't physically or even metaphorically have to drag spectators into active participation; but she or he will inevitably gently need to persuade and cajole sometimes reluctant spectators into positions where they can become active participants in making a dramatic event of their own. (Hahlo and Reynolds 2000: xxiv)

Spectators, in this passage, become active participants, and even in the private format of a drama workshop take on a more public role. Good facilitators have strategies for overcoming the inhibitions that haunt this change of role: gradually building up involvement over several sessions; disguising participation by asking only for verbal contributions from more inhibited participants; raising the tempo and physicality of the activities through games and moving swiftly into physical role-play; or 'trust games' might feature, and an atmosphere of trust consciously developed. Through these and other strategies people are led to do things that they would not have expected, to surprise themselves. Performances that are the culmination of an extended workshop process, happening privately or semi-publicly, also work with the dynamics of risk, for example in Westlake's account of a Seattle Public Theatre project with homeless young people:

> To establish a safe environment the facilitators closed the workshop to everyone but the participants, SPT staff, me, and the occasional journalist. Also anyone who was late or who missed a day was not allowed to come back. This reduced the group to a few committed youth. [...] The facilitators led a series of ice-breaking exercises geared towards knowing the body. The work helped the participants get used to moving around. It also helped them to develop trust and become comfortable with one another. (Haedicke and Nelhaus 2001: 70)

Safety is engineered at three levels here: in the environment, in the membership of the group, and in the activity itself. It is in these events that we can see the workings of risk-management openly exhibited, though other strategies may be hidden or may be implicit in the procedure in a way that even the facilitators themselves are unaware of. The first read through of a play, for example, might be presented as the natural starting point in a rehearsal process, but it also masks a moment of high anxiety and allows actors a managed forum in which to begin working together, it is a facilitative strategy for the group. In these contexts participants are persuaded that what they put at risk by taking part is worthwhile given the potential benefits. This kind of investment – to continue the metaphor of resources and markets used in the previous chapter – is encouraged partly by explicitly addressing and reducing the actual risk, but also by managing anxieties that might exaggerate the feeling of risk. This chapter explores how this risk management is the basis of the facilitation of audience participation too.

## Real and perceived risk

This reluctance to perform in public is not based on an irrational fear, it is based in an understanding of a real risk. To expose unconsidered thoughts or emotions in a semi-public space is risky, just as it is to display incompetence, inappropriate enthusiasm, neediness, distress or loss of poise. The risk in all these cases is that we undermine the careful (though not often entirely conscious) performance of a consistent and functional persona: a public self. Jonothan Neelands gives us a list of issues at play when leading drama with young people:

> The sequencing and staging of the learning process of the lesson – the realising of the objectives – has to be mediated through the imperative of making the student's lived experience of drama comfortable enough for them to want to join in. Whatever the planned objectives might be, students' inhibitions, physical embarrassment, fear of censure, transient moods and relationships to others in the group need to be taken into account. (1992: 44)

Adults also get embarrassed and fear censure, and have relationships that need protecting; we also need to overcome these things in order to enter a worthwhile engagement with any participatory material, whether in a workshop or audience participation. We go to great lengths to 'save face' in everyday life, especially in avoiding unfamiliar or un-habitual public activity, to protect our public personae and other people's perceptions of them; we even go to some lengths to protect other people's 'face':

> When an individual employs these strategies and tactics to protect his own projections, we may refer to them as 'defensive practices'; when a participant employs them to save the definition of a situation projected by another, we speak of 'protective practices', of 'tact'. (Goffman 1969: 26)

People are likely to employ defensive practices in avoiding public performance, and, to a degree, have a right to expect that theatre practitioners will demonstrate some tact in the way they engage with their participants, that they should take some steps to protect their dignity. In his essay 'Where the Action Is' (in *Interaction Ritual*, 1972),[1] Goffman raises the idea of 'gambling the self', of knowingly taking risks with public esteem. Public performance is one of the settings in which it is possible to gamble 'self', where (as we have seen) the resources employed in performances are continuous from one frame to the next, and though their value might vary in different frames, a resource expended in one frame – overstretched, shown to be insubstantial, contradicted – might then be undermined for use in the other frames that follow.

The genuine risks involved in performing in public come in a variety of forms, of which this risk of embarrassment is only the most persistent. There are also potentially risks in taking part in an activity that is not enjoyable, or which might even be distressing, actual physical risks involved in the activity, and risks that a performance will bring dangerous consequences after the show is complete – unusual, but a real possibility for participants in Theatre of the Oppressed in a site of conflict, for example. These actual risks may not, however, be as important to the procedures of audience participation as the perception of risk in the minds of the participants. If the initiation of participation is a rational response by the audience member to an invitation, as it has been portrayed so far – and which entails some problems, which will be taken up in the following chapter – then the choice depends on this potential participant's assessment of risk rather than on the risk itself. And where the resources in play are as varied and individual, and the potential outcomes so personal and specific, at the same time as the anticipation of adverse outcome determined by such diverse experience and disposition – perceptions of risk will be highly unpredictable, much less predictable than the relative difficulty of performance tasks, and the risks of failure or physical harm that they involve.

## Actual risk in audience participation

Following this logic and this language, then, each procedure of audience participation will produce, in the landscape of possibilities available to its participants, a challenge to their abilities and to their desire to remain safe from loss of face. The topography of each horizon of participation presents different risks generally, and different risks to each participant, and whether an invitation is accepted and how it is navigated will depend fundamentally on the perception of these risks. Before exploring the ways that procedural authorship consists of manipulating risk and perception of risk, a few manifestations of risk in participation are worth outlining; but, as will become obvious, any discussion of specific instances of audience participation inevitably leads to accounting for the facilitating strategy of the performers – this element of their procedural authorship.

The obvious thing that will affect the real risk involved in a public performance will be the nature of the performance task itself. Some activities clearly risk humiliation; some are evidently physically dangerous; some more likely to provoke an adverse reaction from people in the audience. Jonathan Kay, in his *Know One's Fool* performances (which are described in more detail at the end of this chapter), sometimes challenges his spectators to demonstrate that they are not inhibited by social convention, and to kiss the person sitting next to them; those who follow the invitation make a small transgression against normal sexual mores. When a fire juggler asks for a volunteer – to throw a club, or hold a hoop – the risk that someone will get burned, whether performer or participant, inevitably increases.

The difficulty of the task to be performed will also make a difference to the actual risk of physical injury – if there is any such risk – or injury to public esteem because of failure. Virtuosity is a key part of many public performances, we applaud musicians, dancers, jugglers and magicians because they can do things that we cannot, as well as for the beauty of their actions, and the same is true to a degree for actors. And while there will be different attitudes to failure at different kinds of tasks it can generally be said that a difficult task lays the performer open to a bigger risk of embarrassment through failure. Even the most apparently minimal performance can expose the performer to judgement, the audience at an improvisation or Theatresports (Engleberts 2004) show vie with each other to provide the most spontaneous and original suggestion, and these suggestions will be judged by the other specta- tors as acts in themselves, even though the performers may find them uninteresting and choose to use others. In Jane Munro's *Invitation*,[2] an interactive dance performance, participants are wordlessly invited to learn the steps of a restoration partner dance, and to begin to perform them for other audience members. The atmosphere and effect of this piece derives from the way individuals accept or reject the invitation, while watched and watching each other, as well as from the subtle strat- egies of body language used by performers to lead them to take the risk of performing a dance in front of others.

The relationship of the act to its audience can increase the actual risk of embarrassment, especially in the amount of exposure that the performance brings to the performer. An act that takes place in front of a large audience, and fails in some way, is magnified; if the audience is small the potential for embarrassment is not so great. For example *You, Me, Bum Bum Train*'s pieces take individuals through sequences of encounters where improvisatory responses are required of them:

> Wheelchairs transport ticketholders, at staggered intervals and one by one, through a labyrinth of rooms, each providing a different, explicitly rendered environment. And you, dear audience mem- ber, become the undisputed focus of that environment: you're an American football coach, urged to exhort his team to victory; a patient in an M.R.I. machine (that winds up transporting you, lying down, into a Japanese restaurant); a bungling apprentice to a cat bur- glar, prowling through a sleeping woman's bedroom; an evangelist in a chapel; a government minister (with supposed financial interests in BP) at a news conference; and an idolized musician, encouraged to leap into the extended arms of a throng of fans. (Brantley 2010)

These acts are in a sense private, though given in a public place. They are seen by the performers that invite them – at some points crowds of many performers at once – they are not on show to the rest of the participants.

Pantomime provides another example, the children who offer 'behind you' warnings to the characters don't usually leave their seats, while there is often a game in which a group of children are taken onto the stage; this group of children leave the designated space of audience and enter the space of the performer, visibly becoming part of the show, while those who remain behind may shout as loud as they like, they will always remain physically part of the audience. Similarly a performance that is given by one person with many watching has more potential for embarrassment than one given by many people at the same time, or even many one after another, as in the latter cases one's mistakes or discomfort will be less visible. In the Forum Theatre described in Boal's texts – as opposed to other pragmatic adaptations – spect-actors come into the performance space to present their arguments one at a time. Although they may interact with a number of other spect-actors and actors once involved in the action, they generally take the step from audience space to stage space individually and detach themselves from the crowd that makes up the audience. Variations on the technique may allow spect-actors to offer their ideas from the safety of their seat, giving instructions to others to act on their behalf. Alternatively in pantomime the audience shout 'Oh no he doesn't' or 'He's behind you' as a crowd, not individually, and will therefore not put themselves on show, and will not take as much risk.

Ontroerend Goed's *Internal*[3] is notorious for manipulating several levels of intimacy and public exposure, making the embarrassment of participants into a feature of the work. In Tom Phillips' review in Venue magazine he describes how his participation consisted of a private, one-to-one encounter with a performer where he shared some information about himself, shared an imaginary journey and an imaginary kiss. The second 'act' of the piece involved various pairs of performers and participants being interrogated about their interactions:

> Compared with what happened to the others, my conversation with Maria seemed entirely normal and sane. Then the two of us became the focus of attention. I was asked (by another actor) if I thought that we'd "clicked". I said "Yes". Why wouldn't I? Maria and I had got on. We'd had a chat, shared a laugh, made a toast to friendship. "Prove it!" said the other actor, quite aggressively. I looked blank. How on earth do you do that? Before I could think, Maria had opened her arms and she was kissing me. Warmly. On the lips. Suddenly, I was emotional jelly: euphoric as a 17-year-old who's just copped off with the best-looking girl in school. Then Maria very matter-of-factly announced to everyone that I'd been with my partner for 25 years. Ouch. (Phillips 2010)

The private encounter appears to be low-risk, but proves otherwise when a further public performance is conjured out of it. Phillips' review elaborates how this public embarrassment, nevertheless, subsequently led to complex and meaningful reflections about loyalty, sexual politics, and his own ability to be tricked using everyday ploys involving body language and flattery. There is a deliberate strategy of embarrassment, and the risk of damage to participants' relationships is also real, the covert nature of the invitation has brought criticism, but some audience participants at least have found the work to be worth the investment.

## Horizons of risk

Real risk, however, being only the potential for harm in a situation rather than known or intrinsic harm as such, is not what prevents people from participating. It is perception of the risks by the individual that leads to conscious and unconscious choices about how and whether to participate, and there are some obvious and some less obvious factors that shape these perceptions.

While prior experience of the actions invited will make successful performance actually more likely, familiarity – which can be read as the anchoring of the frame in shared resources of performance traditions – also has a great influence on the perception of the difficulty of an act. Asking an audience to clap or sing along to a familiar song repeats a routine they are familiar with, and is quite different to asking them to sing a new tune, or clap a strange rhythm. A member of a community that is used to using Forum Theatre as part of a decision-making process is going to think less of standing up to contribute than someone seeing it for the first time. The individual's perception of themselves as a performer or potential performer will be very important, as will perceptions of the other people at the event, and of the meaning and atmosphere of the performance.

Being in a crowd that participate together can make people feel safe, for a number of reasons. First, simple safety in numbers prevents an individual from either being seen to be choosing to give a performance individually, or even just from being seen while they are participating. Second, we are more likely to associate ourselves positively with an action that we see a number of other people undertaking. Third, the understanding on which we build our assessment of risk is ongoing, and will be influenced by the evidence of the actions and implied risk assessments of others: in effect the shared aspect of the element of the horizon of participation that relates to risk (of which more below) is exaggerated when participants are in a group of some size when invited.

Perceptions of risk in performance will be culturally determined. As Felix Ruckert observes about audiences in different countries, 'Americans take fewer risks, they are open but less actively [...] in

Germany the people are very controlled [...] the Italians are very play-ful' (Kattwinkel 2003: 8); and as Boal recalls of working with prisoners:

> Amongst other things the macho men were embarrassed about doing physical exercises and hostile to the idea of man-to-man bodily con-tact; in one particular exercise they were standing in a circle with their eyes closed, and when I said I was going to pass behind them and tap them on the shoulder to designate 'the leader' their protests were vociferous. 'Don't creep up behind me, mate – stop right there!' they chorused, almost to a man. (Boal 1998: 42)

Specific contexts will bring powerful shared horizons of participation: work with prisoners, for example, must take into account that vol-unteering will imply risks that are magnified beyond what might be expected in other situations or institutions. The incident remembered by Boal illustrates how prevalent attitudes embedded in the context – in this case homophobia – require a performative conformity. Public embarrassment, or a performance of complicity with the official regime of the prison, or the appearance of weakness, will all have implications that are not easily understood by those who do not share this world and its way of life. Schools will often have similar dynamics. The 'economy' of self-presentation in any social milieu, but especially in a closed insti-tution, will shape the horizons of those who inhabit it.

As every teacher knows children's perceptions and expectations regard-ing public performance change enormously at different ages, though they are never entirely easy to predict. Younger children understand social risk in very different ways, sometimes appearing fearless, sometimes very shy, teenagers are notoriously reluctant to perform, except for those who are inveterate show-offs. The issues of procedural authorship are the same with children and young people as with everyone else, though sensitivity to the needs of different age groups, and even specific groups of young people will be invaluable in assessing their horizons of participation.

The mood of the audience member of any age is fundamentally important, and often hard to anticipate or account for. Pre-theatrical and outer theatrical frame activity can obviously have a significant effect, but the initial individual mood of audience members is generally beyond the control of practitioners and the understanding of commen-tators. People arrive at performances in very individual states of mind, and might have radically different attitudes to their capacity to per-form, or to the potential for engaging in interaction to do them harm, depending on all sorts of contingent circumstances of the day, states of mental or physical health, or positive/negative anticipation of the performance event. State of mind, emotion and its relationship to decision making, empathy and intersubjectivity are discussed in the next chapter, where the problems of the model of participation, as a rational response that maximises benefit and minimises risk, is explored. Clearly the perception of risk is a matter of emotion and affect, of a set of irrational anxieties and excitement, as much as it is of rational assessment.

All of these factors and dimensions, then, will shape the horizon of participation that has been outlined as a key part of my conceptual framework: the risks perceived by audience members are self-evidently part of the make-up of the horizon of any moment of interaction. However, viewed from this perspective it appears more like the horizon of expectation brought to an experience (Gadamer) or a text (Jauss), in the sense of a limit defined by preconceptions, and this reflects the potential of perceived risk to prevent potential participants from accepting an invitation. But we can think of the horizon from the point of view of more flexible readings of Gadamer and Jauss, in which horizons of expectation account not only for fixed limits but for the space of potential, and for the possibility of extensions and adaptations of capacities. This allows the handling of risk by procedural authors and audience participants to be conceived in a full and flexible way. In other words, pursuing the landscape metaphor implied by the idea of a horizon may suggest inviting paths or dangerous terrain, or a precipitous and dangerous route that is a worthwhile challenge.

Nevertheless, a horizon of risk, as a dimension of the horizon participation as a whole, is given structure by the negative impulses of the audience participant, and the positive exertions of the procedural author who tries to anticipate, elide, ameliorate and/or overcome these perceptions. It is also where the landscape within the horizon is given further shape and character by felt responses of a negative kind, by anxiety or trepidation.

## Risk management as procedural authorship

The simplest strategy available to the procedural author is to anticipate a general horizon of risk and make sure that all interactions are contained within it in a way that is comfortable to most of the audience. Other strategies that work on the basis of a general horizon of risk might be characterised as:

- changing the general horizon somehow;
- making the audience feel that they want or ought to explore the horizon;

- misrepresenting activities so that the horizon is not a fair representation of what they will be asked to do; or
- beginning well within the general horizon of risk and gradually becoming more difficult and more risky, broadening the horizon from the inside rather than challenging it straight away.

A procedure of gradually including one participant after another, being sure to take good care of each, should have the effect of expanding the horizons of those who are more reluctant, as Brian Way recommends, when working with children:

> Many will wait until they see what kind of thing they are going to be asked to do. When they discover that there is nothing to be afraid of, that no individual is going to be picked on and watched by the rest of the audience, and that no one is going to criticize them or hold them up to ridicule, then confidence will grow and grow and with the confidence will come fuller participation and the probability that more people will become involved. (1980: 41)

Way says that his participants will 'discover that there is nothing to be afraid of', but perhaps, really, they change their perception of what danger is presented by the activity, they change their horizons as their confidence grows. Other forms do this too: Forum Theatre initially allows audiences the security of distance and then invites, inspires or provokes them to abandon this in favour of full involvement in the 'theatrical game'. Inspiring and provoking are both different strategies for expanding horizons of participation, rather than ways of honestly proposing an interaction.

The invitation that changes an ordinary theatrical performance frame into an interactive performance frame works on the basis of these expectations and perceptions of the event. Where the outer theatrical frame makes it clear that interaction and participation are going to happen, especially where this changing of frames is something traditional or familiar, the audience will have a clearer perception of the risk or difficulty of the performances that might be asked of them. In these circumstances the episoding might be entirely conventional, tending towards an implicit invitation because many people will know what is required of them, and their perceptions might not need to be addressed by the performers or the procedure. Where a more overt invitation is given, the facilitators may explicitly address the perceptions of the audience and attempt to take advantage of the flexibility of their perceptions, using language and tone to construct the audience's understanding of what they are to be asked to do. Covert invitations can make a play on people's expectations and perceptions of an event so that they do not perceive their performance as a performance per se and so perhaps bypass their sense of the show as risky.

In the earlier examples – the fire juggler and Kay's invitation to kiss another audience member – the perception of the risk is nuanced by the performance of the invitation and after it: fire jugglers create an air of real physical danger around their shows, which is not entirely fictional, but the risk to performer and participant is much less than it is made to appear. Like Kay, Las Furas Del Baus sought, in *XXX*, to make a point about conventional inhibition, not merely to invite exhibitionism, but to follow it up with further invitations in a manner which this observer considered bullying:

> At the end of row J, 20-year-old Nina from Australia removes her bra and reveals her naked breasts. The large audience stares and claps. She volunteered, and her boyfriend Seth is standing next to her, but she's being bullied by the maestro into getting down to the flesh. She won't let him remove her trousers, but Seth – perhaps to spare her blushes – removes his own and reveals his pierced penis to the world. (Benedictus 2004)

The risk is managed not to reduce it but to guarantee its outcome, as a rhetorical strategy. Like Ontroerend Goed, this company are not wary of taking a risk themselves, of giving offence to their audience; but their manipulation is not to covertly invite participation and lead participants into something unexpected, but to overtly invite a performance that seems challenging enough, only to follow it up with another invitation. It seems they will remain unsatisfied, and performing their invitations as demands, as bullying, inflects the horizon of participation of audience members, as well as the way others will respond.

The activities of facilitators and facilitating actors will continue to affect perceptions once a frame has changed and an interaction has begun, both for those who are performing and for those who continue to watch and may be considering what to do if another invitation is given. They can give encouragement, which builds confidence, giving the impression that a performance is better than it might otherwise be thought, or conversely they can criticise,[4] so that a performance seems to have been of lesser quality. In either case the risk of entering the performance will appear different, whether because the audience fall for this manipulation and perceive the actual activity differently, or because they see through it and now consider the facilitators to be more unfriendly. The apparent difficulty of a task, as it is evidenced in the achievements of participants who actually undertake it, will be a very great influence on the perception of the difficulty and risk involved for those who might follow, and the appearance of difficulty is something that can be manipulated by the facilitating performers or other techniques of procedural authorship.

Seeing someone fail and embarrass themselves makes it seem likely that this might happen again, though of course some people will take this as a challenge rather than a disincentive. Interactive performers, as well as the obvious facilitators, can take part in the provocation and inspiration that serve to change people's horizons of participation, as in Mark Weinberg's observation of community based theatre with young people:

> During the scene a gay couple danced together, was hassled by others at the prom, and forced to leave by the chaperones, ostensibly 'for their own safety'. At the end there was applause, but also signs of distress in the audience. However, when I asked for someone to replace the protagonist no one moved. Fortunately, one of the students not in the scene stepped in as one of the protagonists. She chose the worst possible option – to say that dancing with her partner was a joke and deny his sexual identity... I did not have to prod anyone again. (in Kattwinkel 2003: 195)

The student here appears to be an audience participant, and is not a plant in the sense of performing a pre-planned action that engineers participation. But she is aware of the process that needs to happen, and intervenes with her own contribution to the procedure: an action that challenges the young people present to defend their values, and the values that they think should be presented at this event.

Individual performances can be invited from within the audience, to make distinctive contributions but from a position of security, as in a Forum Theatre event described by Frances Babbage, in which Richard and Matthew are audience participants (spect-actors), and Kirk a performer:

> It was clearly too soon to expect either of them to enter the performance space – Richard, anyway, was adamant he would not act – so Kirk, as Jennifer, simply came into the audience. Matthew was prepared to adopt the teacher's role from where he sat. (Babbage 2004: 84)

The important thing for the practitioners in this case is that some action is taken for the forum to proceed; for the participants the important thing is that they don't draw attention to themselves in the wrong way: the compromise works for both parties. Detaching oneself from the crowd can be exhilarating, because of this perception of danger; Liepe-Levinson considers this experience of risk to be one of the distinctive elements of participation in striptease shows:

> This thrill consists of voluntarily exposing oneself to some sort of perceived external danger, such as standing up in front of an audience and being scrutinised by the group. It is the possibility of being carried away or done in by the event; it is the pleasure produced by a mixture of fear, the hope for a positive outcome, and the exhilaration of having experienced 'danger'. (1998: 12)

The 'possibility of being carried away', rather than just the anticipation of this possibility, is on the agenda of the next chapter, and the uses of exaggerated risk will return later in this one, but this thrill is made possible, in Liepe-Levinson's account, by detachment from the crowd, and the risk of scrutiny that it entails.

The seriousness of a performance is also important, though it can produce risk in complex ways. A trivial performance might have less serious implications for public persona than one taken seriously, but equally it may be seen as less embarrassing to fail at something worthwhile than at something pointless – the Armadillo Theatre workshop programme described in Chapter 1 took place with groups of teachers and school support staff as well as with children, and though many of these adults insisted that they wouldn't actively join in the role-play, often the most adamant performed with conviction once they understood the exercise as a tool of serious debate. In part these teachers may have been inspired by an empathic relationship to the characters, they came to care about the situation just as audiences of young people did, but as well as this their anxiety may have abated when the complexity of the situation presented a genuine challenge. Again Babbage tells of a nervous participant who finds courage when it appears that she is not being taken seriously, Jennifer, once more is the character at the centre of a Forum Theatre model:

> Julie proposed that Jennifer try talking to her mother properly, confronting the situation rather than avoiding it and cosily watching television. She was invited to enter the scene and replace

Jennifer, which perhaps surprisingly she did immediately. But once 'onstage', even though this was only three steps from her chair, she lost confidence – 'I don't know what to do, what am I supposed to say – I can't believe I'm doing this' – but regained it when Dave got up to go; she told him smartly to sit back down, and he did. (Babbage 2004: 82)

Julie's relationship with Dave is important to this behaviour, but in Babbage's re-telling it is clear that she wants him to hear what she has to say, and does not want her performance to be undermined by his departure. A direct relationship between seriousness and risk, and its inverse, where people are able to laugh about an activity they will consider it to be of less consequence, and so to be less likely to make them lose face, seems logical; but where a serious subject is engaged in a performance, to say or do the wrong thing can make one look ignorant or stupid, but it can also produce embarrassment if a serious subject is not engaged with seriously.

The casting of participants can be arranged so that facilitators have control over who will be offered a task, and they might use this as an opportunity to try to make sure that a suitable person is invited to take part. There is huge scope for error in this of course, unless the facilitators know their audience beforehand. With Box Clever Theatre Company, touring to young audiences in schools, we would always try to talk to children as they came into the performance space, to spot those that were confident but not too rowdy, and that seemed popular with other students, and by having brief conversations as they took their seats. Choosing such a participant for the first piece of audience interaction in the play helped to make sure that they would respond positively, be able to do the simple tasks required and also that others would be willing to follow; it was, of course, a strategy to reduce risk to us, the performers, too.

This doesn't mean that facilitators will always make safe selections, with Box Clever I made the mistake of choosing a boy who was bullied by his schoolmates, and was heckled when he participated, and a girl who had just left hospital, still wearing an ID bracelet on her wrist. They had both volunteered, and initially appeared good choices for the reasons given above, but participation was risky for each of them in an additional, real way, that we could not have known about.[5]

It is also possible to cast participants appropriately by creating roles that suit them; this would be the case in a workshop drama process, but a quick thinking facilitator will apply the same idea in an audience participation, as did Adrian Jackson of Cardboard Citizens in this account by Babbage:

> The scene was set; Jackson drew in two others, casting them as mourners with the assurance that they wouldn't have to speak. Payne played the vicar, Still the boyfriend-in-waiting. Jackson inserted additional theatrical touches, giving the mourners a box to represent a coffin, directing them to make an entrance and help establish the solemn atmosphere; they ended up doing more 'acting' than they had intended, and seemingly enjoyed it. (2004: 88)

Covert invitations deal with a different set of expectations, and different behavioural horizons, because they are not explicit or honest about the fact that a theatrical interaction is to take place. Their place in a procedure that manipulates perceptions of risk is a tricky one – they can lead people into a very different set of expectations, and a different horizon of participation, or they may simply annoy or alienate participants, who, thinking they have been tricked, will restrict their horizons drastically. Again, where facilitators choose participants before asking them to participate, they may sometimes try to anticipate their attitude to participation, and try to choose someone with a broad horizon so that they will be more likely to agree to join in, and will be relaxed and enthusiastic when they do.

## Ethical issues in the management of real and perceived risk

So far my discussion has been concerned with managing risk and perception of risk to ensure that participation happens, but there are also ethical reasons for making these choices. Real risks, and to some extent the perception of risks, bring with them obligations on the theatre maker and rights for the participant. The interrelationship of these two factors brings not just questions about what should be done and how, but also some perspective on the dynamics of what it can mean. A useful comparator – though not directly applicable in a great many cases – is the principle of informed consent and the capacity for such consent. This principle, that comes into play in academic research wherever a human being is involved in a research project,[6] as well as in medical practice, is designed to protect individuals taking part in research whether that be medical, scientific, sociological or in the humanities. That this applies across the board validates, to some degree, what I have said about risks to social and mental well-being as well as physical – subjects in social science research are rarely put at risk of physical harm, but need to judge whether they risk reputational damage through sharing personal information or memories. Having begun to argue that the performances of audience participation are always to some degree performances of the social self, the relevance of this is clear.

I do not want to argue for the treatment of audience participation in strict accordance with this principle – far from it. I have seen participatory performances which, under the influence of a misreading of the obligations of research ethics in a university context,[7] have been preceded by a notice announcing that participation would be invited and that audiences were free to choose whether they took part, and which thus lost an important element of surprise and the delight that comes with it. But there is a capacity for audience participatory theatre to be distinctly unethical, to manipulate participants into situations they did not anticipate or were not informed about and which expose them to significant public embarrassment or the revelation of private material; and more commonly there is work that plays on the boundaries of this, where embarrassment might be acute and painful in some cases, but in most cases not damaging in the long term, where the harm caused might be better characterised alongside 'taking offence'. Often the discussions of the ethics of such invitations are concerned as much with the nature of the manipulation as with the actual performances invited or given.

Where children and other vulnerable people are involved in research the principle of informed consent is not applied, consent must be given by another responsible party, and the law is very clear about who such people are and who is empowered to consent on their behalf. But the law is silent on who should consent on a child's behalf in audience participatory theatre: there is an assumption, perhaps, that the adults responsible will be familiar with the conventions by which children (so often) will be asked to participate, and consent implicitly to the presumed minor risks involved. The comparison is not entirely fatuous, in a culture where child protection has become increasingly regulated, performance for children, especially outside school buildings, gets off lightly.

Is there a similar implied consent for responsible adults attending theatre performances? To a great extent there is. The theatre is an institution made up of a myriad of institutions each understood by its constituent public – there are traditions in which we understand the conventions and thus imply consent to them when we attend, and there are other sites – festivals, venues, companies –- where the challenging of conventions is to be expected, and thus a degree of consent also implied. Anyone attending an Ontroerend Goed performance is likely to expect their sensibilities to be challenged as part of the performance, and for a kind of participation to be invited which could be potentially humiliating. But their reputation did not always precede them.

Where participants are vulnerable – by legal definition or through a dangerous context, rather than as a result of accepting the invitation in itself – the logic of how to make an ethical choice about informed consent might be read as a pragmatic cost-benefit analysis, or as an absolute obligation to fully inform all participants. Think, for example, of the use of participatory performance to discuss domestic abuse, and where a 'conspiracy of silence' perpetuates the normalisation of abuse; is a manipulative invitation to participate that leads to a revelation about such abuse in a public forum ever justified? Most practitioners would probably agree that it would not be; but might be less certain if the participant manipulated into revealing the truth was the abuser and not the abused – in other words if manipulation was used to expose and embarrass the oppressor rather than their victim.

The techniques for reducing risk or giving consent do not have to consist of excluding certain kinds of material or giving full and clear explanations to every audience member. Some TIE and children's theatre shows include a stage of rehearsal where acts are prepared away from the large audience before being put in full view of their peers. If a participant is prepared and rehearsed for a task they will be more likely to complete it well, and they may also have an opportunity to anticipate and get advice on how to perform difficult or potentially embarrassing material, or to consider carefully what they want to present.

Obviously in many situations the manipulation of perceptions of risk is not a serious ethical consideration, the street performer who asks a child to help them for example, but uses all their skill to make the task for the child look difficult – throwing a club up to the juggler when on a high unicycle for example – and when they succeed they make sure that the child feels that they are getting most of the applause. The game of taking risks then becomes the mechanism through which the event becomes meaningful for the participant, where the apparent risk is so well judged that it produces a frisson of excitement appropriate to their perceptions of what is challenging behaviour to their horizon of risk. But this kind of game can be introduced in more ethically fraught situations: as in Liepe-Levinson's observation of a Chippendale's performance in New York:

> After the lead dancer completes his routine, three more bikini clad male strippers enter and wrap crepe-paper streamers around the

women's bodies so that they look as if they are tied to their chairs. The trio of strippers then alternately dance for and caress their bound amours. In contrast to the first half of the scene, the women remain motionless. The play concludes with the strippers kissing the captives and then releasing them. The symbolic and practical use of paper bondage in this scene demonstrates the importance and underlying mutual consent necessary for the playing out of such erotic encounters. To be in bondage is presumably to be controlled and therefore to be placed in real jeopardy. But here, the 'bonds' are conspicuously under the command of both the dancers and the tied-up spectators. If the male sex and courting show isn't up to par, the captive women (even though they may be subject to peer pressure and the intimidation of the theatrical scene) can still get up and walk away. (1998: 22)

This erotic thrill of this challenge is turned on its head in Barbara Smith's *Feed Me*, in which she greets her audience one at a time while naked, inside a constructed domestic space inside a gallery.

Although the space may have been safe and nurturing for Smith, it might have not have seemed so to the visitors, witnessing private acts in what was, no matter how it was disguised from the inside, a public space. Indeed their very presence transformed the space from private to public. And, as with any solo performance, they were essential to the event as performance, as was their willingness to 'take risks' by becoming active participants. (Kattwinkel 2003: 159)

This might be an example of what Claire Bishop characterises as an 'agonistic' encounter, in her treatment of socially interactive live art. Designed to be uncomfortable and quietly confrontational, the feeling of social risk provoked by the disjuncture of public and private acts, clothed and unclothed bodies was perhaps as important to the substance of the work as the legible meaning of Smith's performance. The ethics of audience participation, then, aren't as simple as removing all significant risk or ensuring explicit or implicit consent. At times effective participation – and politically challenging participation – will be that which puts participants in compromising situations.

Keith Johnstone's attitude to the ethics of invitation in improvised theatre is ambivalent, and the strategies he suggest for handling invitations interesting. This is one form of public theatre where the audience have a clear role to play, but in *Impro for Storytellers*, which describes the form that Theatresports and Gorilla Theatre should take, he warns strongly against handing over too much responsibility, mostly in order to avoid giving volunteers work to do which is too risky. When discussing inviting spectators on to the stage to take part in improvisations themselves, he is enthusiastic, and he clearly expresses an awareness and concern for the risk that these participants are taking:

> Audience volunteers interest the spectators in a fresh way, and the time spent improvising with them doesn't feel like 'part of the show'. Never abuse them (as happens in stand up comedy), and when they kill idea after idea – as they will – you must somehow manoeuvre them into being successful. Always be seen to be making them the centre of attention (they will be anyway, so you might as well take the credit for it). Give them free tickets or T-shirts, or tokens for the concessions. Treat them with love, courtesy and respect; yet I've seen volunteers who were wandering about in a scene with the players ignoring them; who were asked to be the hero of an adventure which became an excuse for the players to shine; who were not introduced; who were not given prizes; who were not thanked; who were not accompanied back to their seats. (Johnstone 2000: 20)

Johnstone's volunteers are to be handled with kid gloves, and rewarded for their bravery. This care for the volunteers in fact might not always allay the sense of risk, if anything it might heighten it. By giving prizes for coming onto the stage the performers draw attention to the risk taken, rather than taking attention away from it. The way people are brought onto the stage can make the act appear more significant:

> Be inventive. I've lain down on the stage and said that nothing will happen until we get eight volunteers to play a ten-minute Theatresports match. We listened to music until eight sheepish people emerged. The audience cheered everything they did with wild enthusiasm. (Johnstone 2000: 20)

The invitation here goes against the grain of what happens in workshop drama, albeit playfully; it puts pressure on the participants instead of taking the pressure off. And as the danger of public performance is almost entirely to do with appearance, with how one presents oneself to the social world, the risk is increased by drawing attention to it, even though the scope for individual invention, and therefore personal embarrassment, is being carefully contained by the performers. The acknowledgement of the volunteers' lack of expertise and the assistance they will need in order to 'succeed' betrays Johnstone's lack of confidence in what they will produce when left to their own devices. The strategy seems to be to make volunteers look good by exaggerating the task they undertake and avoiding giving them responsibility for the performances they give; sometimes the sense that they are to lose their agency entirely becomes quite clear: 'let volunteers open and close their mouths while the players dub their voices, or tell the players to be puppets, and have the audience volunteers manipulate them in scenes (the 'puppets' providing the dialogue).' (Johnstone 2000: 20)

There are two different kinds of audience participation, which Johnstone describes: participation on stage in ways that are controlled and almost risk free, and the use of suggestions by participants to be enacted by performers. The first he encourages, though it is to be used with restraint, the second he discourages, though it is widely used by others. The kind of interactivity recommended tends to involve inviting people onto the stage, in small groups or individually, to act in scenes that they have never read, with people they don't know, and in front of an audience. In most elements these acts will therefore be towards the riskier end of the scale: in being located on the stage, in being separated from other audience members, in being asked to do unfamiliar and unrehearsed things. The fact that they are going to be under the control of the performers means that the actual risk is reduced, the acts are designed to keep the responsibility for the resulting performance with the actors, though it might be made to appear otherwise; but the situation places them at the centre of attention, so the perception of risk might be very high. Though we must not underestimate the seriousness of trying to be funny, the game-play frame makes the consequence of success or failure into something frivolous. Johnstone is adamant that the participants are not to be left stranded on the stage, that when they get into trouble they are to be rescued, and preferably, what they do is to be clearly led by the actors, not by their own impulse. The ethics of participation he proposes are entirely to do with the safety of the participant from embarrassment, and not at all to do with giving away the control of the theatrical event.

## Protecting participants into involvement

As mentioned at the beginning of the chapter, workshop techniques pay close attention to risk management. But in the best practice the approach is designed to lead to deep involvement rather than simply to ensure participation. Often a workshop will follow a path of progressive exercises that starts with less risky activities and becomes more challenging, gradually expanding the participants' horizons of participation rather than challenging them outright to start with. Warm-ups also serve to draw people gradually into activity and similar strategies are sometimes employed in interactive theatre. The aim of the warm-up for the participants, to prepare them for heightened physical and mental activity, is genuine, but disguises other benefits to the workshop process. It is a way of marking off the workshop activity from everyday life, like a kind of rite of passage:

> The warm-up is always necessary, because the beginning of any workshop is like going through an 'air lock', moving slowly from a highly pressurized environment to one where the pressure is radically reduced. It helps people clear away some of the daily clutter that they bring with them into the workshop and which needs to be ditched if they are to establish the necessary focus on the work in hand. (Hahlo and Reynolds 2000: 5)

The pressures of everyday life are various and persistent, but by denying their power within the workshop a facilitator makes it possible to focus on the specific kinds and qualities of interaction that are at the heart of the educational or therapeutic workshop. The airlock effect given by a warm-up helps to frame these intense representations of social life safely, and to allow the distractions of real social life to be set aside for a while. I think the metaphor can be interpreted differently, that the work that happens in participatory drama and theatre is in some ways more 'high pressure'. It is magnified, distilled action, and it puts people more overtly into the position of performing for others than is true of most forms of everyday behaviour, but it serves to show how the change of frame is a very significant one. For audience participation the outer theatrical frame can serve some of the functions of a warm-up by developing emotional investment in an event, by creating a space in time and behaviour between the outside world and participation, and by modelling some of the work to be done in participation.

Writing about classroom drama with children, where problems may more often arise from over-eagerness than from reluctance, Gavin Bolton introduces a useful idea of protective strategies to take people into activity.

> The notion of protection is not necessarily concerned with protecting participants from emotion, for unless there is some kind of

> emotional engagement nothing can be learned, but rather to protect them into emotion. This requires a careful grading of structures toward an effective equilibrium so that self-esteem, personal dignity, personal defences and group security are not over-challenged. (Bolton 1984: 128)

Although with children the emphasis will as often be on engaging with emotion at the right pitch rather than encouraging engagement for the inhibited, which it more often will be with adults, that which Bolton describes as needing protection – self-esteem, personal dignity, personal defences and group security – is the same across all kinds of group drama work. The warm-up, with its role as demarcation of the special nature of workshop time and space, is an example of an important protective device. Classroom drama practitioners like Bolton might not use a warm-up in the same sense as Hahlo and Reynolds describe, but instead some introductory activities or games that have a similar function. His comment not only illuminates what the opening sequences of workshops and classes and participatory performances can do, but also indicates the second major task of the facilitator – to ensure that the participants engage with the purpose of the work in a significant way. The facilitator will bring material to the process, but also needs the participants to bring something of themselves to it. Of course, the contribution required will depend on the kind of work being done – a workshop programme with children will often need to engage them with information that is new to them, while a therapeutic process may rely on contributions of a deeply personal nature.

Although this might appear to be a process of making interaction safe and easy it is, as Bolton makes clear, a matter of protecting participants to allow them a more serious involvement – the strategy, in his terms, is to protect children into emotion rather than to protect them from emotion. This can also take the form of balancing one kind of risk with another, so that a performance is safe in one way but risky in another. In the *Rocky Horror Show* it is the appearance of the performers and audience – in both theatre and cinema versions the audience often attend cross-dressed, in make-up, or in 'fetish' clothes – that is the site of the mildly transgressive behaviour that all of the 'safe' activities – singing songs, scripted interjections into the play, throwing things – are designed to facilitate for the crowd.

The terminology of participatory drama implies a certain kind of procedure; practitioners describe themselves as 'facilitators', seeing the role as making things easier. It is obviously potentially a waste of time to design a theatre that asks for participation that is bound to fail, or that scares people away from interaction, but the alternative to these strategies is to make it seem hard. People respond to challenges, and might 'gamble' more of their public esteem if it seems there is more kudos for success, or more stimulation on the way. Faking the difficulty of an activity, so that the performer does all the work and the participant gets the applause, as in street theatre, intensifies the feeling of risk for this purpose. In some performances the nervousness of the participants may be foregrounded, to exploit the tension and fear, as Bim Mason observes:

> Another way to create tension, and therefore keep attention is by interactions with members of the public either as participants or as part of the crowd. Improvisation between performers is often exciting, but with volunteers from the audience a different sort of drama is created because the rest of the audience identifies with the volunteer. Therefore, it is important that they come out of the situation well – the audience will feel a collective sense of relief and achievement. These feelings will be the greater the harder the challenge. The danger is going too far so that they become fearful and embarrassed. (Mason 1992: 98)

Making some kind of challenge apparent to participants in workshops or classroom drama is acknowledged as good practice, as identified by Helen Nicholson for example: 'a general atmosphere of trust, where there is familiarity between participants but no element of risk, is unlikely to lead to drama which presents students with new challenges' (Nicholson 2002: 85). This 'general atmosphere of trust', bred, in the examples she is concerned with, through familiarity, is not the same as the more valuable trust that must be harnessed for a group of students to embark on new and unfamiliar tasks, in new relationships with each other. This is what Johnstone is trying to provoke very quickly when he lies on the stage and waits for a volunteer to take responsibility for the show, and in another sense what Ono is referring to in works like 'Cut Piece' where:

> the woman [...] is intruded upon physically, by subjecting herself, sitting or kneeling on stage, to the actions of the audience, who have been invited to cut off parts of her clothing with scissors [...] the performances question the limits of the boundaries of trust between people. (Ono 1997: 126)

The question of trust is presented in a powerful visual image, but also in an experience that will change the relationships of the people who undergo it, although to no specific pedagogical aim in this case. The notion of 'protecting' people into involvement has been turned on its head in both of these examples: people are being challenged and provoked, even in the light-hearted provocation of the street performer, into changing relationships with the material and with each other.

## Reading the audience participant

The invitation is a prime site at which to address an audience's expectations explicitly, and to draw attention to their horizons of participation, it is the point at which they can be given the view of the coming activities that you want them to hear. An overt invitation that consists of a full, clear description of the activity will help to break down anxiety as long as the activity described constructs an amenable horizon for most potential participants, but will serve only to increase their reluctance if it gives an honest picture of something they wouldn't want to do. However, this can become part of the procedure's meaning, as when Las Furas Del Baus ask for people to strip, an act clearly beyond most people's horizons. But if no-one does, the show is not spoiled, in fact it may serve to make their point about our continuing conservative attitudes to sex and our bodies more strongly:

> Like all participatory theatre, *XXX* is a challenge to its audience. And like all challenges, it is difficult to face. When *XXX* appeared in London last year, it triggered a predictable volley of yawns. Such exploitative gimmickry could never shock me or turn me on, said the critics. I bet it did both. (Benedictus 2004: 10)

In this case it seems likely that the provocation was the content as much as the participation that resulted. A lack of active participation at this point did not represent a failure of their procedure as the lack of response became a performance of the audience's inhibition.

With this sense of the audience themselves, present both as a representative body and as a group of singular individuals who become the subject matter of the performance, it is worth unpacking the different ways in which participatory performances can be read by audiences and participants. Horizons of expectation in the theatre shape how spectators read the most important semiotic equipment of theatre – the actors. The actor is available to be 'read' in a number of ways, as himself, as a specific person from another place and time, as a category of people like himself, or perhaps as a set of distinct performances of signs not attached to any particular self or category of people. The actor most often stands for a fictional (or fictionalised) other person, giving a presence, actions and words to ideas necessary to the development of a fictional narrative. This involves the audience in a double reading: the indexical signs of the present body of the performer are read as icons of something that is not present. This is a more complex process where the indexical signs, which can be read in the actor and are sometimes signs of real physiological events in his/her body, are read as standing for the presence, state and actions of another person in another time and place.

Actors also stand for categories of people like themselves, men, women, short people, tall people, black people, white people. The process here is at basis simpler, one of synecdoche: one stands for the many with no need for the double reading of fictional representation. But it becomes more complex when aspects of the fictional narrative come into play, where the actor stands for 'angry people', for example, a state partly pretended by the actor, or for 'revengers', a category largely defined by genre conventions rather than everyday social practice. Alternatively, the behaviour of actors can be read independently of any attention to their own narrative, that of a character they are playing, or of the groups of people they might stand for: as merely a set of disconnected acts, words and gestures. Many live artists and some dancers deliberately operate at this level, avoiding representation for the sake of examining actions in themselves. But the poetic, choreographic and scenic elements of a conventional play operate in this way too, though they might make connections with sets of ideas from the fiction of a play that are not actually present. It is this variety of different ways of reading a performance that is guided by interpretive communities, their horizons of interpretation and their ideological overcoding.

However, as well as these ways of reading a theatrical performance, an actor or performer is always discernable as a person in his/her own right, though this continuous individual self is disguised or denied by a variety of techniques of performance and conventions of watching. Those who know the actor or who have seen more than one performance are always able to compare, or to consider a performance as part of the greater narrative of a life, or a career. For example, watching Ian McKellen in Strindberg's *Dance of Death* might bring to mind any number of earlier stage performances, but it might also have brought to mind his knighthood, his political activism, or his appearances as Gandalf in the *Lord of the Rings* trilogy. None of these will necessarily detract from the reception of the work at hand, but the idea of him as Strindberg's malicious, pathetic and aged character will be inflected, for many spectators, by some of these dramatic and public roles. We always, to some degree, watch a performance with some attention to this current narrative of the achievement of the performance – how well the actors do with a role, who gives the most compelling performance, who makes the small errors and the fine judgements. This is a particular kind of intertextuality operating in theatre where actors, to some extent, always resemble characters they have played before, and so for some spectators produce an intertext between one play or performance and another. This is, in semiotic terms, an indexical sign relationship, the sign that the actor's body and performance stands for the actor himself, and cannot be separated from it. There are complexities that arise when the perception of the actor reflects again on the character, becoming part of the intertextual theatrical moment. Escolme comments on her own reading of Mark Rylance as Hamlet:

> My account slips from 'performer' to 'Hamlet' back to 'Rylance' here. A man on stage signalling discomfort with being before an audience cannot but denote 'performer', while the lines he speaks denote Hamlet's fictional discomfort. It is as if the presence of the audience produces the move away from the contemplation of not-existing, towards more purposeful performative speech, the justification of his perspective on his mother's marriage.
>
> Rylance's performance, then, does not merely replace Q1's simple act of communication with an internalised expression of disgust and grief to be spied upon by the audience. His is a subjectivity produced in the moment of communication with that audience and at a point where the performer's relationship with the audience is most clearly foregrounded, the moment of direct address. (Escolme 2005: 65)

Her thesis is that this double reading is part of the early modern dramaturgy, an inheritance from modes of storytelling that were closer in time than the assumptions of realistic representational theatre; but all acting traditions will suggest a horizon of expectation that allows some kind of play between the actor's identity and the roles they play.

This analysis of the way performance is read has implications for the spectator who becomes a performer in audience participation, exploring as it does the relationships between the performer and the various ways things can be read from him or her. First, there are reasons why we are more likely to interpret a performance as saying something about the person who performs, to read it as a performance that belongs to the person rather than being detached from them. It is important to the reading of a fictional character in performance that we are able to 'disattend' (Bennett 1997: 68–69) those parts of the performance that are inconsistent, much in the same way that we 'disconnect' (according to Goffman) some things that are present from a frame of interaction in everyday life because they have nothing relevant to do with it, or might even distract from its sense or tone.

> It is not that the excluded events – such as audience activity – have no semiotic value (it does make a difference if one is allowed to see the stage hands or if the entire audience is noisily eating popcorn), but that they are understood as belonging to a different level of action. (Elam in Bennett 1997: 68)

The knowledge of what to disattend comes from familiarity with whatever kind of theatrical frame is in use – the experienced spectator of an Onnagata in Kabuki knows to pay attention to the quality of gesture and the beauty of costume, and not to the evident masculinity of the performer's body or the stage hands that help him sit or rise, as they belong to a different level of action. The spectator of a naturalistic drama knows that she is entitled to gripe about inconsistencies because everything on the stage is expected to belong to the same level of action.

The audience of a participatory performance will often see the transformation of a spectator into performer, thus seeing the person as 'himself' and remaining aware of this primary role, whereas the concealment of the actor's 'real self' from the audience during the performance is a strategy still at use in most theatre practice. The audience, depending on what kind of relationship they have with each other, might know the participant before the show, might be familiar with his other everyday roles and therefore be ready to confuse or conflate them with the role of 'actor' or the actions associated with a character on stage. They might even know him intimately, and be unable to read the performance except as a significant event in his personal narrative. They will almost certainly be aware that this special role, of actor, does not normally belong to the participant, and that they would not normally be given the licence to perform; they might be less inclined to grant this licence, and its privileges, to an ordinary person, and unwilling to disconnect their actions from the rest of their lives. The participant himself, of course, might well not have much skill, and so be unable to pull off the tricks of imitation and transformation that remove great

portions of the need for disattendance. An audience participant stepping onto a stage may perhaps recall other staged performances, but will
certainly bring to mind the everyday performances they give at other
times, and so they will produce another kind of intertext for those who
know or have seen them before. This might add up to a failure of the
performance as a piece of theatre, if the action has not been 'keyed'
properly so that it is seen as connected with more mundane realities,
in other words there has not been the proper 'suspension of disbelief'.
Nicholas Ridout reminds us:

> We know who we expect to see on stage. We expect to see actors.
> This needs saying: we do not expect to see human beings, in all their
> diversity, but, as their representatives, a kind of group apart, more
> beautiful perhaps, more agile, more powerful and subtle of voice.
> (Ridout 2004: 58)

To see someone more ordinary in this position, someone we know to
be ordinary because we pass our ordinary days with them or queued to
enter the theatre with them, can be thrilling. It can also, at the same
time even, disappoint and undermine our ability to play our part in the
game of theatre.

We see the performance in the context of the performer, so complete
disattendance is no more possible than the absolute suspension of disbelief, in any kind of performance. However, this becomes more significant
in audience participation where the distance between the performer and
the act is more noticeable, and the connection of the act to the everyday
impression of the performer can be more significant. As well as being a
potential detriment to the performance, it can create interesting intertextualities, which can inform readings of the performance as related to
its context, and which might allow a person to be seen with interesting
new attributes. Or it can cause interference, as the spectator is unable
to accept this distance, and so pays attention to it in a negative way,
as evidence of the inadequacy of the performance and possibly of the
performer. In some kinds of interactive theatre the distance will be more
noticeable than others. In work with children for example, the participants might be less skilled as performers, and so will audiences be less
skilled (or less generous) as watchers, making it less likely that they will
pay attention to what is being offered as a performance, and not to what
isn't. Disattendance is also a performance by those watching, a choice
to display competence and sensitivity through paying attention to the
performance as it is intended. To display an overt lack of disattendance,

to show that we are aware of the distance between the performer and their role, is to attack the performance for its inadequacy. A significant stumbling block for interactive theatre (especially with children, and also a worry in work with adults) is the lack of respect that can be shown to participants, increasing the real and perceived risk but also altering the way a performance is read by all those present. Whatever the reasons for this disrespect – and with children it might be a matter of wanting to assert their own informal frames of behaviour wherever possible, or of giving a negative reaction to patronising or overly authoritative facilitation – it amounts to a refusal of the participatory frame.

This connection of the performer to the role, which the institution of theatre generally stages as a managed disconnection, is the source of the embarrassments, inappropriate and inopportune performances that constitute much of the risk of audience participation.

## Performativity and the public self

As I have already begun to suggest, Goffman's metaphors cannot say all that needs to be said about the ways behaviour is managed in public. He can be criticised for simplifying the matter of social agency: making it a matter of agents who act on the world, rather than being shaped and acted on by it. This is fair in respect of *The Presentation of Self in Everyday Life*, which makes little attempt to move beyond this idea of the deliberate staging of social life. In *Frame Analysis*, however, there lurks a stronger impression of the 'definition of the situation' as something that is not entirely within the scope of our control. Subsequent social theory develops concepts of how such definitions are arrived at, and how they serve to reinforce social conformity. For Judith Butler, as well as for Bourdieu, we become ourselves in the performances available to us, rather than acting on the world through performance. Some unpacking of the relationship between this assertion of a social self and the pre-given structure from which it emerges will help to put a different emphasis on what is at stake in public performance.

In Bourdieu it is the linked concepts of field, capital and habitus that describe how the social world is operable for social agents. In *Distinction: A Social Critique of the Judgement of Taste* (1984), Bourdieu uses these concepts to unpack the class-bound tastes of the French in the sixties and seventies:

Taste, the propensity and capacity to appropriate (materially or symbolically) a given class of classified, classifying objects or practices, is the generative formula of life-style, a unitary set of distinctive preferences which express the same expressive intention in the specific logic of each of the symbolic sub-spaces, furniture, clothing, language or body hexis. (Bourdieu 1984: 173)

Appropriations of objects and practices according to the acquired logic of a class are what constitute lifestyle, and it is through these formulae that '[w]here some only see "a Western starring Burt Lancaster", others "discover an early John Sturges"' (Bourdieu 1984: 28). Habitus is the facility, determined by class, culture and gender, which allows us to deploy our social capital in social situations in an informed way but, it is the degree to which this 'informed' is actually 'determined' that is the crux on which questions of social agency rest. It is, then, an invaluable concept for this examination of agency in audience participation, as it allows us to consider the habits of behaviour and interpretation that participants bring to their actions in an interactive procedure. The resources we are able to deploy are both facilitated and limited, not just by the skills and experiences we have – our various capital – but by the dispositions that we are able to take in response to the fields with which we are faced. As Maria Shevtsova says, habitus is a sometimes disconcertingly flexible term, as it has the scope to include the different logics acquired at different levels of our experience:

> The concept of habitus in Bourdieu is slippery insofar as it appears to refer to the dispositions of individual social agents, to the dispositions of social agents taken as a group (thus we could speak of a group habitus) and to the dispositions incarnated in or interiorised by the practice of a field in its distinction from another field – a distinction that is only possible because it is relational, that is always defined in respect of something else that it is not. (Shevtsova 1989: 57)

The relational quality of these concepts is an important aspect of this sociology, it is through this that the social subject can be seen to exist as a set of evolving positions, rather than as a fixed and finished entity. As Shevtstova says:

> To acknowledge the presence of subjectivity and individuation in the cultural field does not discount in the slightest its 'objective relations'. Nor does such an acknowledgement desocialize the subjectivity of the socialized agent of action. In fact, this agent is capable of individuation only because she/he is a social being, and

is differentiated only because she/he can be differentiated within the collectivity and from the objective social relations that constitute it. (1989: 47)

Although some attempts at describing subjectivity posit a transcendental self, abstracted from all events but those of the mind, later theorists consider the self to be socially constructed. Different turns of this strategy – James' 'self-feeling', Cooley's 'looking glass self', Meads' the self becoming an object to itself through interaction[8] – all point toward a self that is 'other directed'.

The theory of performativity as developed by Butler is concerned with the performative nature of gender and sexuality, which she sees as performed through each of us rather than by us and constituted before all other changes and commitments can be made. Her writing focuses on these determinations, but she has space both for the importance of the idea of the self as part of everyday practice, and for our agency in the strategic use of this practice:

> According to the understanding of identification as an enacted fantasy or incorporation, however, it is clear that coherence is desired, wished for, idealised, and that this idealisation is an effect of a corporeal signification. In other words, acts, gestures, and desire produce the effect of an internal core or substance, but produce this on the surface of the body, through the play of signifying absences that suggest, but never reveal, the organising principle of identity as a cause. Such acts, gestures and enactments, generally construed, are performative in the sense that the essence or identity that they otherwise purport to express are fabrications manufactured and sustained through corporeal signs and other discursive means. (Butler 1999: 173)

This use of acts, gestures and enactments to fabricate an identity is a fundamental strategy of everyday behaviour, for all that it may ultimately be self-deceiving. Though the idea of the performative here is very particular – the construction of an identity through gestures and acts – she acknowledges the connection between theatre and politics, and suggests how her work as an activist as well as a theorist has connected with overtly theatrical interventions such as ActUp (Butler 1999: xvii). In her theory we have an elaboration of the importance of performativity (with 'performance' as a subcategory of this interpretation of language and action), in the process of making 'character', 'self' and 'identity' both private and public. Butler says that performance in public is one place where the battle for agency can be fought, but she also shows just how difficult it is to have agency over the fundamentals of identity.

Later pragmatic social scientists (Holstein and Gubrium 2000: 21) take hold of the tendency to verbalise this fabricated identity in the form of narratives, as a methodology for both research and social work practice, in which the analysis of the way people 'story the self' tells us a much as anything about how they are taking positions, and developing dispositions to their evolving circumstance, as any other mode of enquiry, without having to burden these narratives with any greater truth than this.

These ideas: of performance as constitutive of the self, of the embodiment of ideas of the self in corporeal signs, of the narrating of the self, are very suggestive of the power of a performance that becomes attached to the narrative of a person. If, as I have suggested, audience participation has a special capacity to be taken as a representation of the person performing, it might speak about this public identity in especially powerful ways – whether it speaks truths about it or not. Audience participation is another space where we take part in the performing/becoming of the self, and the risk we perceive is a risk to this idealised substantial self, to this pragmatic self, or at least to whatever version of it we are trying to promote. This is despite the safety of the fictional space, despite the make-believe and the suspension of disbelief that we expect in our theatre: in audience participation we are lucky if the irony, the license to play or experiment, the conditions of carnival or liminality operate as they do in other kinds of theatre – either with or without audiences.

The kind of investment desired by Bolton and other practitioners of workshop drama, and some of those who invite audience participation, has a way of making it 'real', of bringing consequences. This investment is pursued by some contemporary performance practitioners, Tim Etchells for example:

> Investment forces us to know that performative actions have real consequences beyond the performance arena. That when we do these unreal things in rooms, galleries and theatre spaces the real world will change. To me that's the greatest ambition and the truth of cultural practice – things can change, things can slip, things can move, because they're pushed (deliberately), because they're knocked, by accident. All that has to happen is that the direct lines of investment get drawn – between performers and task, between witnesses and performers. (Etchells 1999: 49)

But it is, through audience participation's peculiar ability to put the person on show, through the tendency for the theatrical character to be transparent and for the everyday character underneath to show through, easier to deliberately push or accidentally knock action towards this kind of perlocutionary performative. When we volunteer we invest ourselves in a performance. The investment of a participant in a performance may not be as profound as that of a practitioner who has prepared, rehearsed and conceived a performance, but it is immediate. The practitioner's very preparation mediates, through the perception of the audience of their role as performer.

## *Know One's Fool*

Jonathan Kay's *Know One's Fool* is an ongoing body of practice, rather than a specific piece of theatre. It takes a number of forms, from small-scale solo shows, to ongoing workshops, to larger festival events where hundreds of participants are involved. To conclude this chapter I will discuss both his Glastonbury Festival shows over a number of years, and compare them to some small-scale performances at Camden People's Theatre in 2002,[9] showing how his work uses (in my terms) procedures of participation to challenge audiences to overcome their anxieties and inhibitions, and further demonstrating how the theory can be applied to interactivity that specifically addresses people's reluctance to perform in public.

He begins his theatre performances in something approximating a stand-up comedy frame, one that also has resonances of circus clowning and other pre-modern kinds of 'fooling' performance. Expectations of performances at Glastonbury are coloured by the celebratory, carnivalesque nature of the festival, where nothing serious is expected. In the 'theatre field' there is mostly street performance and circus, and in these there is rarely an expectation of a conventional actor–audience relationship. However, the clown–audience or comedian–audience relationship that Kay works from is generally still only partially interactive – either may imply heckling, singing or shouting, even some movement, but the focus still remains on the original performer: there is not a horizon of participation that contains continual and substantial participation. There are of course expectations about Kay himself, his show is famous in the festival, and people often come knowing something about what they will be asked to do, or at least that they will be asked to do something.

As I have observed, Kay does not spend much time explaining what the show will consist of, but he does establish early on that this will not be a conventional show, then launches into activity, describing how modern life encourages us to follow rules and conform to roles, and inviting us to take the opportunity to act spontaneously for a while. As the interactions develop he invites some specific activity, (singing songs, kissing – as already mentioned) sometimes in detail, sometimes directing action and the quality of action as it happens, making it clear what he wants from participants, but not giving an outline of the event as it starts. The procedure here is the unfolding of a relationship, a series of requests and demands for the indulgence of his whims, and the building of a belief that if we go along with him, we will have fun. This is participation that emphasises the fact of joining in, rather than fore-grounding any specific content, and especially not giving any attention to the skill or quality of the performance. Participants are very much on show, drawn out of their shells, behaving abnormally, and the lack of emphasis on quality or consequence plays a major role in allowing this to happen, in overcoming the element of risk in the situation.

Many of the activities of the Glastonbury 2002 show were familiar from previous festivals. Kay often uses a group movement – sometimes it has been sheep, this time it was fish – to take the audience out of the theatre tent and into the field outside. The sheep image, perhaps, undermines the sentimentality of what Kay has said before this – it can be read as a parody of the context and of the participants own herd-like following of his instructions – the crowd, on their hands and knees, 'baa' at other spectators as they move around the field. Though this may be satirical of Kay's ability to inspire a following, and of whatever aspects of festival culture or contemporary life the viewer or participant might like to make of it, the fish movement has different and less obvi-ous readings, as fish we are silent and though still frivolously character-ised, and perhaps not so degrading as the sheep; however our glass-eyed mouthing is an expression of vacancy that comes close to the sheep's image of surrender to Kay's will.

Another feature of this show helps to allay the fear of performing in such a public setting, and makes use of the aggression that this fear tends to inspire, by redirecting it. Early in the show and repeatedly throughout it, the audience are invited to shout 'fuck off' en masse, at Kay himself, at another section of the group, at passers-by not in the group, at some absent other, a 'them' who would, supposedly, want us to do or not to do something. The performance of reluctance is incorporated into the audience-performance, multiplied and magnified and brought to the surface in parody, but never entirely effaced. This loud, obscene, aggressive stance gives license to be innocent, to join in and be 'un-cool'. This is a decisive part of Kay's facilitation. Without it perceptions of his act – and the activities we are asked to join in with – could be dominated by the 'hippy' or 'new-age' associations that accrue with performances that ask for innocent, celebratory, cooperative participation.

Even in the context of this festival resistances to activities with such associations are high, and strange events are kept at arm's length. There is license here, but it is a license to drink, take drugs, immerse ourselves in the safe participatory activity of dancing, and to watch performances by other people. Festival goers rarely speak to strangers or act spontaneously, they generally engage with the entertainments in a conventional way. There have been perceptible changes in the nature of the festival over its long history, demographically, spatially, and rhetorically – there are generally older, wealthier people there, there is more room to move than in the more chaotic festivals of the eighties and early nineties, and there is commercial sponsorship. Nevertheless the festival retains some of its anti-establishment aura, its air of rebellion, even after it has achieved respectability after forty years and many changes. Kay's show encapsulates some of the contradictions of the event, between the rebellious and individualistic ethos of punk and rock, the mellow communitarianism of the festival's hippy roots, and the affirmatory hedonism of dance culture. These tensions are reconciled and reproduced many times in pop subcultures represented at the festival, and are still recognisable characterisations of its meaning.

Kay's performances in a conventional venue, when I have witnessed them, have concentrated on individual activity and have been less comfortable experiences. Though they contain similar elements and themes, there is less predictability to their structure. With a smaller audience there is more room for flexibility, for Kay to run with ideas that are offered by the audience. There are stories of whole audiences leaving the theatre and singing songs in the street,[10] reminiscent of the Glastonbury shows, but it is also common to see individuals performing ideas of their own for large parts of the performance. The procedure in the events I witnessed and participated in was: Kay enters the stage tentatively, dressed in one of his peculiar costumes, and makes his way around the performing space, treating it gingerly, exploring. He speaks some of his idiosyncratic philosophy, in his rudimentary character, the gist of which is to raise the idea of our inactivity and lack of initiative, which he, like us, cannot completely conquer. He plays the piano, asks us why we shouldn't do something very simple such as kiss the person next to us, or sing a song. Sometimes this develops into group activity, sometimes it does not. He strikes up a dialogue with someone in the audience and sooner or later invites them onto the stage to begin some act or activity. He strikes deals with the whole audience about how they will repeat their activities after the show is over. He plays the piano again and makes a final inspirational speech before leaving the stage. He meets the audience in the bar afterwards, in ordinary clothes, 'out of character'.

Again these performances are usually attended by people who know something of what to expect, or who have come before and want more. The agenda of self-realisation that is suggested in the larger festival shows is pursued more purposefully. This is manifest in the closer focus on the individual, on material that is more personal, and in a more forceful attitude to participation for all. Those who don't want to participate are sometimes isolated, in one performance in which I participated, two women who did not want to join in the communal song were surrounded by the rest of the audience and sung at, making them visibly uncomfortable. On another occasion when he asked why we should not kiss each of our neighbours, unlike with the larger Glastonbury audience, he was able to pay attention to how people went about it, and to direct the attention of the whole audience to the kissing as it went around the room, asking why people didn't want to kiss, how and where they wanted to kiss the person next to them. All of this was achieved with a smile on the face of most participants, but it clearly, and I think quite deliberately, made some anxious.

Individual acts I have witnessed have included a meeting with the Buddha, arising out of a conversation with an audience member who had met Kay before, and who apparently was looking forward to doing something more fulfilling with his life. His conversation with Kay turned to travel and religion, and when he was asked if there was something he would like to do that night, he offered that he would like to meet the Buddha. Another volunteer, after asking which school of Buddhist thought he should conform to, took the part, sat in a corner of the stage and, after a number of approaches in which Kay instructed the pilgrim to prostrate himself properly, gave gnomic answers to the questions offered. This light-hearted wish fulfilment was, however, the exception to the majority of the individual acts I have witnessed. More characteristic was the man who danced like a ballerina while we sang for him, or the woman who sang and danced a party piece for us, a music hall song with some very mild innuendo. Another element is added that is not present in the festival performance: the piano. Kay's playing is simple and sentimental, its effect is to give time for reflection, space for the spectators to attend to themselves rather than to him or to other spectators, and it adds a note of pathos to the proceedings. Where in Glastonbury we are encouraged to be frivolous and to live carelessly in the moment, the mournful tone Kay's piano interludes acknowledges the difficulty of this project, it allows us to retreat to an internal world to consider the gains and losses in taking Kay seriously.

Activities like this make the individual the centre of attention, particularly when a more personal contribution is asked for. The group activities in the smaller scale procedures will also draw more attention to individuals for how and whether they join in. It is also more difficult to escape, it is easier to walk out of a large audience in a tent, for which you haven't paid an entrance fee than it is from a small crowd in a small theatre. Though there is always a number of inconsequential acts to begin with, the show moves towards more meaningful participation by each person and by the group, though it usually has a sense of being unfulfilled in this ambition. Although Kay is more than liberal in what he allows us to do he is often very unclear as to what he expects. This combination of implied seriousness of ambition and lack of clear instruction makes for a peculiar tone to the event, in my experience (though it clearly could be very different at other times). Kay's show seems to be about what each person brings to the event and makes of it, while giving few clues to what should be profitably brought and made. There is a lingering feeling that we have failed to make the most of an opportunity, and there is also the feeling that Kay too has failed to make the most out of us. As an extension of the explicit criticism of our inertia and everyday hiding, it is effective. As an event in itself it is frustrating.

These two procedures seem to be designed to mean different things. The Glastonbury show allows festival goers to identify themselves publicly with the 'weirdness' of the theatre field; it also contains an experiential dimension in giving an opportunity to cross some inconsequential boundaries; and it is also a chance to give a performance of non-conformity that satirises itself and the event it is part of. To other festival goers participants become another strange performance – they might just as soon encounter a giant 'Terminator' robot, a family group of gorillas,[11] or Kay's crowd, singing Summer Holiday and shouting 'fuck off' at them. Participants also represent the same thing to themselves, performing a participation in the festival for their own benefit. They must confront personal fears (albeit minor ones) so they can congratulate themselves for doing so. These performatives do not, in the sense intended by Austin, create social contracts, and of course when, as he does from time to time, Kay officiates at an impromptu wedding, or naming, or the initiation of a cult, the conditions are not 'felicitous' to make these actions count. At the conclusion of the small-scale shows the performative is more specific and overt: we promise, in conclusion, to 'create our world', we 'declare' in a secular ceremony that is not entirely unserious, and agree specifically to be ready to begin our acts again should we meet outside the theatre.

There is a contrast between this approach and the careful and non-manipulative strategy taken by practitioners of interactivity in most TIE and other 'applied theatre' models. There the principles are democracy and consideration. Here they are carelessness and insistence. Kay's ideology is not based on the same class politics as Boal, but he is concerned with another kind of liberation, one which does have resonances with Boal's idea of the 'cop in the head' (Boal 1999). His technique of empowerment is very different. He makes an event that, in most of its iterations, is about the possibility of presence and liberation, but only by provocation, not by self-realisation. His is not a rehearsal for revolution, but a performance of the need for personal revolution. What he ultimately does is problematise the agency of the individual, by inviting us to do 'what we want' and leaving us to decide what that is, or giving us things to do that pastiche our lack of agency – being sheep for example. The simplicity of the surface of his events hides some complex intertextualities between the performances of the participants and the context in which they are produced. Its appearance may still seem naive, 'naff' to the sophisticated theatre goer and it is, I think, consciously so. But it is intended to address our resistances, to remove the blocks of sophistication as much as those of fear or confusion. Its success in this is limited, and Kay has a workshop practice that claims success of a different order. But the methods he uses to make an artwork out of the process of involvement are interesting because they exemplify how form and content echo each other in participatory theatre.

Kay's events exemplify how audience participation becomes a 'self-performance' because his rhetoric turns attentions back on to the participant, consciously and deliberately making the freedom to perform 'what we want' and 'ourselves' in public his theme, while challenging the learned, role-based behaviours that we might be tempted to present for him. He seems to suggest a kind of pure experience that might be achieved by throwing off these bounds, but his work puts such emphasis on performative display that it, paradoxically, produces great self-consciousness. The effect seems to be to illustrate that which he is trying to free us from, to reflexively and ironically demonstrate our impotence in the face of our inhibitions, while continuing to urge us to throw them off.

The 'meaningfulness' – the *amount* of meaning that can be carried – of an audience participation performance is not necessarily dependent upon the freedom of the participant to create it: it is possible for a narrow horizon to suggest and produce very important performances, and for a broad range to suggest and produce banal or superficial ones: when Kay creates a very open range of action in his smaller scale shows, the performances seem to say very little, when he closely directs audience-performances at Glastonbury Festival, he produces satire. Nevertheless, the experience of freedom to act in public (within whatever range of action) is meaningful in itself because it is risky. Producing performances that are both free and meaningful requires a synergy of intention and effort, of the willingness of the procedural author to open up to the unpredictable, and of the participant to be bold and take risks in a performance. This is both how audience participation can become important, and how it can do harm.

In this chapter the aesthetics of audience participation has been re-considered in the light of a major influence on the decision-making process of participants: their perception of risk in public performance. The theoretical framework as it has been established so far is largely able to accommodate this by taking an alternative perspective on the terms used so far: once again applying Bourdieu's idea of social capital, and using a more extended version of the metaphor of the marketplace, public performance can be seen as an investment of social capital in a market where good returns are not certain. This helps to explain why the creation of interactive performances can be difficult, why the tension between audience and performer arises when participation is invited, and provides another perspective on the agency of the participant who seeks to control their performance.

# 3
# Irrational Interactions

So far I have portrayed the procedure of participation as a matter of creating horizons of participation where participants can freely choose whether and how to behave, though they will do so within limits based on the resources and dispositions they bring from previous experience. I have also suggested that manipulation can take place through withholding information about the procedure, and that the perception of risk might lead a potential participant to refuse an invitation, or might create enough anxiety to make participation unattractive. But there are many other influences on a participant's state of mind at the point of invitation, which become potential tools of the procedural author. Procedures that create excitement of some kind could be considered manipulative, if that excitement means people join in who otherwise would not. Some states of mind can be said to overwhelm the conscious decision making of individuals, and make them susceptible to guidance from a crowd or from a performer. This idea of 'state of mind' is also largely misleading, as changes in the mind are often initiated and evidenced in changes in the body – and as I shall show, a clear distinction between mind and body is fallacious in the first place.

These factors need to be considered not just in terms of how they might play a part in manipulation, but also once again in terms aesthetics: how the experience of different states of mind/body are part of the art work of audience participation. The key questions for the chapter are:

- What states of mind and body play a part in accepting an invitation?
- How are they used by procedural authors, and experienced by participants?
- Is our understanding of agency, and its meaning in audience participation, altered by a consideration of mind and body state?

My discussion so far has followed Goffman's lead in modelling social interaction as a rational maximisation of benefit through strategic interaction, to describe how people make choices in response to invitations in an interactive frame. While this has been useful in developing a vocabulary and a model for my subject, it has not so far addressed directly how other, non-rational, influences on behaviour – such as affect, emotion and the embodied elements of cognition – must also play a part in interaction. All rationally motivated behaviour happens in the context of *feelings* about situations and people, and of inclinations to follow or resist suggestions that arise in the behaviour of others. One of the overall weaknesses of sociology in Goffman's mould is that it fails to account for these aspects of our behaviour. Bernard Meltzer and Jerome Manis identify the weakness of this approach in two areas:

1. Interactionism places an over-emphasis on self-consciousness; it 'plays down', ignores, or makes light of both the unconscious and emotive factors as they influence the interactive process.
2. Symbolic interactionism is guilty of an unwarranted demotion of the psychological; it has robbed human needs, motives, intentions and aspirations of their empirical and analytical reality by treating them as mere derivations and/or expressions of socially defined categories. (Meltzer and Manis 1978: 84)

This wilful under-playing of conscious and unconscious motivations, and the over-emphasis on apparently deliberate action shaped by 'socially defined categories' facilitates a useful description of the structuring of social life, but it only tells part of the story. When it frames action as 'self-conscious' it entails a proposition that conscious decision making is the entire or most important determinant of social action. And when the 'symbolic' element takes hold, the independent, individual character of the decision maker is relegated below their place in the social order. But in articulating decision making as rational and goal directed, it doesn't theorise how we perceive, interpret and rationalise situations and the goals we can achieve in them; this kind of theory is essentially interested in the structures of social life at this level of interaction, but not the full complexity of what drives and allows human subjects to create and take part in these structures. By introducing Bourdieu's theory of socially stratified influences on action I have attempted to account for some aspects of difference between people in how they are able to operate at this level of interaction, but a further elaboration, based on the 'state of mind' of individuals and groups of participants in the moment of invitation can restore the unconscious, the emotive and – to a degree – the psychological, to the picture.

In this chapter I will borrow from some approaches to perception and action, to describe some of the troublesome unconscious phenomena that can have an effect on the structured interactions that have been described so far. As in the rest of my discussion, I will be epistemologically promiscuous, moving fairly rapidly through some perspectives that might not normally be taken together, if the differences in their methods and assumptions were fully taken into account. My aim, as in earlier chapters, is to suggest the grounding for a broad-based theory of audience participation: to fully ground discrete elements of this theory would require more rigorous examination at every point. Broadly speaking what follows is drawn from theories of embodied cognition, which show how thinking – and decision making – happens throughout the body, involving affective and emotional states and processes and according to some theories directly depending on other bodies too. Considering the decision making of the audience participant using these theories suggests how some of the conceptual gaps left by symbolic interactionism might be filled, and points towards explanation of some specific, apparently intersubjective, processes such as laughter, crowd formation, and liminality, which are especially relevant to audience participation.

## Emotion in audience participation

It is self-evident that emotion plays a part in decision making in many situations of human life, and that an invitation to participate will evoke emotional responses in individuals. These responses will be informed by expectations of, dispositions towards and prior experiences of theatre and audience participation, as well as drawing on the performance that has preceded the invitation, and the style or structure of the invitation itself. Procedural authors make overt and covert use of emotional response while audience members will have both predictable and unpredictable individual responses; and – according to the theme of this book – this nexus of the authored procedure and the process of action that derives from it becomes part of the substance of the event. Any precise account of an experience of participation must articulate the feelings involved: the nervousness, excitement, anger or exhilaration that motivate or demotivate a reaction to an invitation. Everyday language serves well enough to describe how our feelings inform our decisions, but turning to the science and philosophy of cognition for more precise definitions (and distinctions, for example, between emotion and feeling) helps to develop an understanding of a more integrated relationship between the apparently rational mind, bodily reaction and emotional response, which is in operation at every stage of a theatre event, not only when we 'feel' an emotion. As Antonio Damasio argues in *Descartes Error* (2006), a bias in conventional thinking about perception and cognition, which held that mind and body were distinct entities and emotions interfered with rational analysis, has been shown to be wrong. Not only is it evident that emotions play a significant role in perception and cognition of many kinds, but also that without an emotional element thinking can break down and become ineffective, even illogical. Supported by an extensive hypothesis about the way representations of internal and external states combine to create the feelings that are essential to our sense of self and mind, Damasio proposes that:

> At their best, feelings point us in the proper direction, take us to the appropriate place in a decision-making space, where we may put the instruments of logic to good use. We are faced by uncertainty when we have to make a moral judgment, decide on the course of a personal relationship, choose some means to prevent our being penniless in old age, or plan for the life that lies ahead. Emotions and feelings, along with the covert physiological machinery underlying them, assist us with the daunting task of predicting an uncertain future and planning our actions accordingly. (Damasio 2006: xxii)

The decisions here are life-changing matters, but such decisions are made up of and expressed in the kinds of everyday negotiations mapped out by symbolic interactionism, and the dispositions towards ourselves and others that they are built on are also exhibited in the (generally) non-life-changing options presented in audience participation. The distinction, then, is not between rational/conscious and irrational/unconscious decisions, but between different combinations of emotional/mental cognition, where both responding immediately and thinking through a situation are partly made up of emotional reaction, sometimes imperceptibly in the background of a rational assessment, sometimes to the extent that conscious thought seems not to have happened at all. Damasio is at pains to point out that this is not the dominance of 'nature' over 'nurture', or of an essential humanity over context, culture and experience. Nor does he prioritise un-thought emotional response over considered action, which is where he makes use of a distinction between emotion and feeling:

> By itself, the emotional response can accomplish some useful goals: speedy concealment from a predator, for instance, or display of anger towards a competitor. The process does not stop with the bodily changes that define an emotion, however. The cycle continues, certainly in humans, and its next step is the feeling of the emotion in connection to the object that excited it, the realisation of the nexus between object and emotional body state. [...] feeling your emotional states, which is to say being conscious of emotions, offers you flexibility of response based on the particular history of your interactions with the environment. Although you need innate devices to start the ball of knowledge rolling, feelings offer you something extra. (Damasio 2006: 132–133).

Feelings, for Damasio, are emotions become conscious, recognisable and most importantly memorable and transferable to other similar situations in the future. Just as important, for my purposes, is the origin of both in the body, and their effect on the body:

> Emotion and feeling thus rely on two basic processes: (1) the view of a certain body state juxtaposed to the collection of triggering and evaluative images which caused the body state; and (2) a particular style and level of efficiency of cognitive process which accompanies the events described in (1), but is operated in parallel. (Damasio 2006: 162–163)

This is a bundle of interconnected and mutually re-enforcing phenomena – a body state that arises directly from triggering phenomena, the recognition of that state, and the 'particular style and level of efficiency of cognitive process' that shapes active responses. Though the language of predators and competitors again suggests extraordinary situations for the modern human being, Damasio asserts that this is a consistent, everyday undercurrent, or 'substrate' to our cognitive lives.

Why should this be important to an understanding of interactions in performance, if emotion is the substrate of everyday thinking, can it not be taken for granted, or merely discussed in everyday terms? Because, as has already been noted, the participant's experience reaches an important climax at the moment of decision making in response to the invitation, and knowing what this decision making consists of is therefore important; because the procedural author's work inevitably includes addressing these emotional, non-conscious processes; and because the art work, being made up of the participant's experience and its nexus with the work of the procedural author, therefore takes shape at this level of combined conscious and non-conscious response.

The 'risk assessment' outlined in the last chapter mostly as if it was a cost-benefit analysis will in some cases, momentarily at least, be determined entirely by emotion, in the way that Damasio styles it, especially if an invitation has arrived very suddenly, or with a sudden change in atmosphere or environment. Given time to think, we assimilate emotion – as feeling – into a thought process, and a conscious narrating of the situation that will attach an identifiable feeling to the emotion, and assess risks and benefits with the help of an appropriate emotional accent to our thinking.

Other theorists do not make the same distinction between emotion and feeling, Bruce McConachie, in his *Engaging Audiences: A Cognitive Approach to Spectating in the Theatre*, (2008) builds his discussion on Ciompo and Panksepp's six basic emotional systems: FEAR, RAGE, PANIC, CARE, PLAY and SEEKING (the capitalisation is McConachie's strategy for distinguishing these systems from a conventional use of these words, and I will follow it here), where less extreme or subtler variations on these basic emotions are considered part of each 'system'. These basic systems will associate with different kinds of response to stimulation from the environment or emerging situations, and they suggest broadly positive and negative responses that we can easily imagine playing a part in motivating participation: CARE, PLAY or SEEKING; or demotivating: FEAR, RAGE or PANIC. But it is conceivable that RAGE – manifesting as a kind of righteous anger – might inspire participation in which a certain point of view needs to be put across, or that variations on FEAR or PANIC might negatively inspire participants away from one kind of activity and into another, in some kind of covert invitation. Following Ciompo and Panksepp, McConachie lists the 'general operator effects' of emotions on cognition; they will:

> stimulate or, on the contrary, inhibit cognitive activities, that is they act on them as energy-regulating 'motors' or 'brakes';
> focus the attention on emotion-congruent cognitive objects, thus tending to establish an emotion-dependent hierarchy of perceiving and thinking;

> preferentially store and mobilize emotion-congruent cognitions in memory; and
>
> tend to link emotion-congruent elements and to combine them in larger cognitive entities. (McConachie 2008: 94–95).

Think of Armadillo Theatre's Mark, threatened and intimidated by Ian, inspiring CARE in an audience of young people, their attention focussed on Ian's behaviour and Mark's distress, and their thinking 'motoring' towards ways of changing the situation. Think of the emotion-congruent cognitions, based on RAGE and FEAR, at work when Yoko Ono or Marina Abramovic invite symbolic violence against their own bodies. Think of the complex of PANIC and PLAY assembled around Jonathan Kay's Glastonbury performances, as the threat of embarrassing participation becomes a celebratory transgression, inspiring 'cognitive entities' in which audience members think of themselves as more adventurous and liberated.

So emotions and feelings tell us what to prioritise in our thinking, drive us towards certain kinds of thinking in response to stimuli, and organise our thinking about stimuli in the present moment and on reflection. This much-simplified introduction to the cognitive science of emotion suggests both how decision making at a conscious level is informed by an embodied 'substrate' of emotion that then becomes a conscious feeling, and that this substrate can dictate some responses prior to conscious thought.

But there are contrasting ways of conceptualising emotions, they are: 'either a basic set of neurophysiological and anatomical substrates or recognisable and identifiable categories that are confined in particular bodies and subjects' (Reynolds in Reynolds and Reason 2012: 125); so either a set of emotions that are shared among all people, though they can evidently vary greatly in degree and precise manifestation, or a fundamentally person-specific phenomenon given by the individual character of experience combined with the culturally specific terms we have for describing and therefore learning about feelings. Without seeking to resolve disagreements of this kind, a further exploration of the science and theory of mind and what it has to say about inherent and culturally informed modes of interaction will be productive, particularly in relation to the question of the feeling of agency in deciding how to respond to an invitation.

## Embodied cognition and the enactive theory of mind

The state of mind in which we make decisions is more than a state of emotion, and to interrogate the notion of a state of mind further, it is worth pursuing a particular theory of cognition. The 'enactive' approach originated by Varela, Thompson and Rosch is appropriate as it prioritises the way our minds are embedded in our bodies and their physical and social environments: it is a theory that sees mind as a contextual, cultural and historically emergent phenomenon, as well as neurologically and evolutionarily determined. It is also, in some significant aspects, compatible with the social interactionist theory that I have used in earlier parts of my discussion. Evan Thompson, in his book *Mind in Life*, outlines the propositions that are brought together in this approach: 'The first idea is that living beings are autonomous agents that actively generate and maintain themselves, and thereby also enact or bring forth their own cognitive domains' (2010: 13).

Second, that the nervous system is an autonomous system that generates and maintains meaning and meaningful activity: both of these propositions recognise that a perceptual system has to be autonomous of the world at a basic level in order to do the work of perceiving it. Third cognition is the 'exercise of skilful know-how in situated and embodied action', bodies are in a dynamic relationship with their environment, learning and applying what is learnt. Fourth:

> a cognitive being's world is not a pre-specified, external realm, represented internally by its brain, but a relational domain enacted or brought forth by that being's autonomous agency and mode of coupling with the environment. (2010: 13)

The fifth proposition refutes earlier cognitivist and connectionist models where mind is thought of as either resembling a computer or a neural network, and to embodied dynamic models where the importance of the body was recognised, but in isolation from experience and environment: 'that experience is not an epiphenomenal side issue, but central to any understanding of the mind, and needs to be investigated in a careful phenomenological manner' (2010: 13).

This last proposition connects enactivist cognitive philosophy with continental phenomenology, a tradition with which Hans-Georg Gadamer was intimately involved, and which has things to say about aesthetics and social interaction as well as perception, philosophical and scientific method and the nature of experience. Paying attention to subjective experience is methodologically important to the enactivist position, as it avoids an explanatory gap through which the phenomenon of consciousness evades exploration by other theories of cognition – by taking first-hand experience seriously this approach does not seek to avoid the 'hard question' of what it is to have a mind. And it is important to the questions of this book, as an understanding of first-person experience is central to an understanding of audience participatory performance. Fundamental to phenomenology and to the enactivist approach is the idea of 'intentionality', which – not to be confused with the everyday concept of having intentions as goals or purposes – is the directedness of the mind towards things beyond itself. Though the idea of intentionality has been important for the discussion of mental states in much of Western philosophy, for phenomenology intentionality belongs to all mental states. The mind is constituted by its directedness towards things: not only when we want something, fear something, remember or imagine something or otherwise direct our attention towards a real or non-real object, but whenever we are conscious (and even in some unconscious states such as dreaming), we are intentionally directed towards the world. In this theory mind and world are not separate realms, which interact through sensory data and physical action, but a conjoined being-in-the-world, a consciousness of the world that emerges through its intentional directedness towards its bodily presence in the world.

As a method of investigation, phenomenology is characterised by its attention to things as they appear to us (as phenomena, as opposed to noumena – things as they are in themselves – a distinction derived from Emmanuel Kant), as they are disclosed to us by intentionality. This extends to states of mind which are not obviously 'object-directed' or amenable to a simple model of intentionality, Thompson outlines how such things as moods, pains or feelings are intentional:

> such experiences do qualify as intentional in the broader phenomenological sense of being open to what is other or having a world-involving character. Thus bodily feelings are not self-enclosed without openness to the world. On the contrary, they present things in a certain affective light or atmosphere and thereby deeply influence how we perceive and respond to things. A classic example is Sartre's discussion of feeling eye-strain and fatigue as a result of reading late into the night (1956, 332–333). The feeling first manifests itself not as an intentional object of transitive consciousness, but as a trembling of the eyes and a blurriness of the words on the page. One's body and immediate environment disclose themselves in a certain manner through this feeling. (Thompson 2010: 23)

This example serves to illustrate the holistic attitude of this approach to being-in-the-world, with its implications for perception, mental states and ultimately decision making and action that is informed by them. The human being in question (Jean-Paul Sartre, in this instance) has an experience by virtue of the disclosure of the physical object – the book and its printed words – and his first awareness of the fatigue he feels is via the manifestation of these words in this disclosure: they tremble and become blurred. The phenomenological approach to this sequence has stepped back from the obvious inference – that Sartre's eyes are tired – to address what has been disclosed and how it has been disclosed, and it reveals how body and environment are knitted together in our experience of them and of ourselves.

I don't want to propose that we should apply this approach (known as a phenomenological reduction) to all episodes of audience participation, though I shall do in some of the examples that follow. But I do want to use this brief sketch of the interdependence of body, environment and cognitive process to suggest an underpinning for various ideas about the way decision making is embedded in the complex of moment-by-moment experience.

Before moving on to some developments of this theme in relation to other bodies, I want to introduce an idea from Shaun Gallagher's *How the Body Shapes the Mind* (2005) as a way into how this situation of embeddedness is culturally constructed, and to elaborate something implied in my discussion of emotion: the idea that sometimes the body makes decisions 'before you know it'.

> The body sets the stage for action. Perhaps the claim should be a stronger one. Your body is already acting 'before you know it'. Certainly there is evidence that indicates that one's body anticipates one's conscious experience. I reach to pick up a glass. Before I am aware of it – if I ever do become explicitly aware of it – my hand shapes itself in the best way possible for purposes of picking up the glass. If I had reached for some differently shaped object, I would find that my hand had already shaped itself accordingly. (Gallagher 2005: 237)

First, the readiness of the body to fit itself to interactions with the physical world without the conscious mind having to examine and anticipate the objects in question is captured in the idea of affordance:

> things in my surroundings, such as teacups, computer keys, and door handles, have motor senses or meanings, what Gibson (1979) calls 'affordances', which elicit appropriate actions. Things in the world bring forth suitable intentional actions and motor projects from

the subject (the subject is a project of the world), but things in the world have specific motor senses or affordances only in relation to the motor skills of the subject (the world is projected by the subject). (Thompson 2010: 237)

This circuit of intentionality, where body fits environment and vice versa, is made possible by experiences of specific categories of objects and their uses. In a world without teacups, computer keys and door handles – the world of most human beings for most of human history – these affordances would not exist; and in a world where teacups are shaped and used differently, then the affordances will be different. The body is enculturated at a pre-conscious level via these affordances – and here we can hear a strong resonance with the social constructionist thinking of Bourdieu and Butler: for affordance we might read dispositions, generated by a habitus, or performatives in a citational system of gender difference. Though it is not stated explicitly in Gibson's theory that affordances apply to encounters with people as well as objects,[1] the extension is implied when Gallagher says 'Even in my encounters with others, prenoetically, before I know it, I seem to have a sense of how it is with them' (2012: 237).

The 'pre-noetic' for Gallagher is the term for this unconscious or pre-conscious occurrence, where some part of the mind-body system takes action without or before it coming to mind. It derives from Husserlian phenomenology, and the two inseparable poles of intentional experience: the 'noema' as the object, as it is disclosed, and 'noesis' as the intentionality and disclosure of the object. The prenoetic is not disclosed, or not yet disclosed, to the conscious mind. What leads Gallagher to this is experimental data indicating quite convincingly that in certain circumstances action has begun before we are aware that we have decided to act: electrical activity can be detected in the motor systems of the active part of the body before any electrical activity can be detected in the parts of the brain where conscious thought originates. For some this suggests that the sense of having initiated the action is nothing more than a useful fiction, giving the conscious mind a perspective on the actions taken by unconscious (pre-noetic) processes. It is a potentially alarming notion of what it means to be a thinking human subject, but for Gallagher, even if this delay in awareness of the initiation of action were to be proven in all cases, it would not disprove the agency of the conscious subject:

What we call free will, however, cannot be conceived as something purely subpersonal, or as something instantaneous, an event that takes place in a knife-edge moment located between being unde-cided and being decided. If that were the case it would completely dissipate in the milliseconds between brain events and our conscious awareness. Free will involves temporally extended feedback or loop-ing effects that are transformed and enhanced by the introduction of deliberative consciousness. This means that the conscious sense of agency, even if it starts out as an accessory experience generated by the brain, is itself a real force that counts in the formation of our future action. It contributes to the freedom of action, and bestows responsibility on the agent. (Gallagher 2005: 241)

And:

The 'loop' extends through and is limited by our bodily capabilities, into the surrounding environment, which is social as well as physi-cal, and feeds back through our conscious experience into the deci-sions we make. (Gallagher 2005: 242)

Agency, according to Gallagher, is extended temporally and spatially, as the 'accessory experience' generated subsequent to an action becomes part of the background mental state of actions which follow, and as the work done in creating this mental state and the physiological state associated with it is distributed across the mind, the body and the envi-ronment that the body is in. The proposition that subjectivity is not the point of origin of our actions – arrived at from an entirely different direction from the determinism that would attribute action to social structure – has been displaced by another unsettling notion, that subjec-tivity is distributed beyond the brain and the body, as intersubjectivity.

This has a number of reference points in audience participation: those moments where we consciously decide to act (to raise our hand, to shout 'stop', to step onto a stage), may have arrived pre-noetically, in conjunction with some kind of social affordance associated with a frame of interaction, an idea which, though downgraded in its impor-tance by Gallagher's argument, is still not trivial. Or the idea of the pre-noetic might help to unpack the moments where we find ourselves participating without knowing why, or surprising ourselves by stepping forward in response to an invitation. And intersubjectivity, the distribu-tion of meaningful elements of the structure of experience and agency across the body, the environment and among other people suggests that procedures of audience participation can make invitations that do more than address themselves to the individual's rational maximisation of benefit, however rational the individual might feel about the process themselves.

## Empathy and intersubjectivity in audience participation

The meaning of intersubjectivity is hotly debated in cognitive science and philosophy, with bold claims for 'extended mind' or 'embedded mind' models of the kind put forward by Gallagher. Again not presuming to take a firm position in these very challenging debates, I will outline some dimensions of the idea of intersubjectivity as it relates to social cognition – the way that we think about, and in conjunction with, other people – as a way to unpack some of the issues around audience participants' interpretation and response to invitations. Some of the issues in play are very familiar in theatre and performance studies – the role of empathy for example, has been considered important since Aristotle's *Poetics* – but drawing on cognitive science and philosophy for explanatory strategies is relatively new. The strategy I want to draw on is part of the 'enactive' approach outlined in the previous section, putting particular emphasis on the 'dynamic' elements of social interaction:

> The interaction process includes several components such as bodily resonance, affect attunement, coordination of gestures, facial and vocal expression and others. Social cognition is not a solitary task of deciphering or simulating the actions of others but emerges from the dynamical process of skilfully interacting with them. Such a view on social cognition has recently been described as 'participatory sense-making' – the process of generating and transforming meaning in the interplay between interacting individuals and the interaction process itself. (Fuchs and De Jaegher 2009: 446)

The terms used here – bodily resonance, affect attunement – are used to account for well-known phenomena that are now, in recent neurological experiments, being evidenced at the level of brain function. 'Mirror neurons' are famously found to reproduce activity in the same areas of the brain of a spectator as would be active if they were engaged in the physical movement they watch; and similar mirroring occurs when we witness other people's emotional processes. All of these effects are important to the process of becoming an audience participant, as other people will be present either as facilitators or co-participants in the vast majority of invitation procedures; and perhaps where a physically present facilitator is not involved, that very absence might be said be such a striking characteristic of an invitation as to be a key factor in the (still) social cognition in any case. I have already said something of the importance of the emotional state of the individual audience participant, as it might be addressed or generated in pre-invitation performances and in procedures of invitation, but the emotional states of the facilitating performers themselves are important too, as are those of other audience members. In some respects the simple presence of other human beings has a direct effect on cognition at the pre-noetic level.

The idea that empathy is an infection in the body by the emotional state of another person has been reinforced by empirical studies showing that when we observe another person's emotional state, it is echoed in our own body. In some theories we 'simulate' emotion as part of our unconscious assessment of ongoing interactions, and at times to the degree that it becomes consciously our own felt response to the situation (McConaghie 2008: 67–68). But Fuchs and De Jaegher view this model of simulation as overly dependent on a kind of representation of the other in the mind of the individual, and thus some kind of conscious perspectival interpretation of this representation. Their phenomenological approach is based on 'an inherent and "visible" intentionality' (Fuchs and De Jaegher 2009: 467) that is shared by people who interact in (a term taken from Merleau-Ponty) an 'intercorporeality' or 'mutual incorporation'. They use the example of the tennis player:

> I not only incorporate the ball and its trajectory but also my opponent's position, posture and movements. I feel the thrust and direction of his stroke as well as the momentum the ball receives, and with this, my own body's reaction is already being prepared. Here my lived body is also in an ambiguous state, fluctuating between the incorporated body of the other and my own embodied position. In a fluent phase of the game, even before one player strikes the ball, the other's reaction unfolds, and this already influences the first player's initial action. As this goes on reciprocally, both players are connected in a feedback/feedforward cycle, and there are no gaps of reaction time. (Fuchs and De Jaegher 2009: 474)

We can imagine corollaries of this in performance of all kinds, from music and dance to the moment-by-moment nuances added to a scripted dramatic text by actors working in close concert with each other. The aim may be cooperative rather than competitive, but the feedback/feedforward cycles by which each performer responds to the other's initiatives are of the same kind. A performer's interaction with an audience, too, though not a balanced exchange of actions of the same kind, is nevertheless a mode of intercorporeality. An audience member immersed in a performance, anticipating each word and move, and responding in synchrony with other members of the audience as a whole is in a mutual incorporation with both the performers and those sitting with them in the auditorium. And such a connection is bound to inform any response to an invitation to participate, should it follow a passage of such deep, intercorporeal involvement. These examples, however, capture interaction in moments of intensity rather than in everyday social exchange. The thesis of enactive intersubjectivity is that this is the basis of all social understanding, although we may often be thrown back on our individual resources of interpretation, when we engage with others our intentionality will tend towards this mode of cooperation. A performer who meets our gaze, extends a hand towards us, or motions towards the stage in an act of invitation, is aiming for an intercorporeal bond, and will in return feel the responses of the one or the many that they invite, whether or not they have achieved an intense mutuality in the performance leading up to this.

Empathy is not forgotten in this theory, though its importance as a representation of another's subjectivity is demoted. Mutual incorporation is, instead, seen as a decentring of intentionality, so that there is an oscillation of activity and receptivity and a shifting centre of gravity, absorbed into a dynamic whole. Empathy is the part of this process that gives us access to another's state of mind: 'In order to understand the other as other, empathy has to be balanced by alterity' (Fuchs and De Jaegher 2009: 476).

The phenomena that I will now go on to deal with in more detail all appear to depend upon embodied cognition, empathic processes, and forms of intersubjectivity: laughter and crowd behaviour appear to show agency shared across individuals; liminality describes a set of characteristics of social interaction, but its prospective attendant condition – communitas – is another phenomenon of apparently shared perception. Hypnosis is more difficult to pinpoint, and remains as controversial in itself as the notion of intersubjectivity as a whole. Intersubjectivity, it has been said, is both an epistemological dilemma and a proposition about 'how situations involving embodied interactions with others can impact on and intensify experience' (Reynolds and Reason 2012: 22) and while the impact on and intensification of experience is a central concern in audience participation, the dilemma of defining and locating subjectivity has something in common with our enquiry into the location of the art work and its originating artists.

The shared agency, which has been noted already as the proper ontology of audience participation as art work, does not in itself qualify as intersubjectivity, but a closer examination of the phenomenology of participation will reveal that the term can apply more, and explain more, than this. Giving attention to some specific phenomena that are explainable as products of intersubjective processes of perception and response provides a bridge between the possibilities of actor-audience influence and performance-audience influence, which will be a significant factor in many invitations to participate that address an audience as a group in the first instance. These group-based phenomena are also familiar elements of theatre and performance practice, and connect the idea of embodiment to a range of strategies of facilitation.

## Laughter

The limited range of behaviours available to members of a conventional theatre audience can be thought of in two categories: as conventionally constructed signals, such as applause, ovations, and shouts of approval, and involuntary reactions to the performance, such as laughter or tears. Obviously these categories are not entirely discrete – people will restrain or allow tears or laughter according to the dominant convention, and an ingrained convention may become spontaneous, even apparently involuntary in someone deeply involved in a performance. Considering laughter, for example, it is apparent that this is a kind of intersubjective behaviour, one that is not under the control of the conscious mind and that has a complex relationship with our mood, our thoughts, and our perceptions of those around us, all of which are important to theatre, interactive or otherwise.

Theories of laughter tend to be theories of what we laugh at, and why we laugh at them,[2] but not what laughter is in itself. Robert Provine (2000) has taken this other route, examining the properties of laugher as a physiological process, and from this evidence considering its function and evolution. At the most basic level he finds that laughter is stereotypical – more or less the same voiced exhalation is made by everyone, all over the world. Different cultures may write down laughter in different ways, as 'Ha Ha' or 'He He', and different individuals have different laughs, but the sound itself does not vary culturally, it is not a culturally determined code like verbal, and much non-verbal, communication: people with unusual laughs stand out, though they are mostly unable to control or change their laughter. He also finds that laughter is involuntary. This is most starkly demonstrated if we try to laugh, it is very difficult. It is possible to imitate laughter, but hard to create a genuine laugh.[3] Through studying people's laughter in everyday social interaction – away from theatres, comedy clubs, television sets – Provine gets a surprising picture of how and when people laugh. He finds that it is more often the speaker who does the most laughing, not the listener, and that laughter is mostly not to do with jokes (Provine 2000: 40), it just happens as a result of stress-free social contact. He also finds that laughter follows a pattern that prevents it from masking conversation, although the laugh may be involuntary, rarely do we laugh so much that we can't speak, and rarely do we laugh over someone else's speech (Provine 2000: 38). This indicates that laughing is not part of a simple stimulus-response routine, it is not so simple as 'hear joke – laugh', though this is the picture we are used to from stand-up comedy and comic theatre, and other 'cultures of laughter'. The conversational laugh itself, then, is an unconscious, non-verbal vocalisation that fits around conversation, and is shared by all the members of a group: it is a signal of belonging to the group.

But it is the contagiousness of laughter that is its most significant behavioural aspect. We often begin to laugh, even can't help laughing, when we hear other people laugh, a fact exploited by the producers of television comedies, who add 'laugh tracks' to encourage us to laugh along. Why does this happen? Are we subconsciously trying to join in with the group that is laughing, to make us feel socially accepted by pretending to get the joke? Provine thinks not:

> The contagious laugh response is immediate and involuntary, involving the most direct communication possible between people – brain to brain – with our intellect just going along for the ride. Contagious laughter is a compelling display of Homo Sapiens, the social mammal. It strips away our veneer of culture and challenges the shaky hypothesis that we are rational creatures in full conscious control of our behaviour. (2000: 129)

Laugh tracks edited into television programmes use the involuntary response to make us laugh, and perhaps because we are laughing we can't help but feel better, that we are in company, that what we are watching is funny. They bank on the prospect that what we are watching will actually become funnier simply because we are laughing. Provine cites neurological research showing that people's brain-function is affected when they laugh and that laughter can trigger enjoyment, as well as vice versa. He doesn't intend that we are helpless against this involuntary response – we might easily be put off by the laughter of others, either through awareness of an attempted manipulation or through an unconscious resistance – but he wants to emphasise the secondary position of the conscious mind when this effect is operating.

This contagious impulse to laugh is a kind of 'affect attunement', as noted by Fuchs and De Jaegher. We seem to be neurologically programmed to begin laughing when we hear others laughing, just as when a wolf or a dog can't help howling when it hears another howl. Provine gives an extreme example of the contagion of laughter, and of laughter that is not a response to humour: a 'laughter epidemic' in Tanzania that lasted for several years, spread from town to town and across borders and caused schools to be closed. Most of those involved were teenage girls, a group that are sometimes unjustifiably associated with hysterical behaviour, but before allowing this phenomena to be ascribed to those of weak minds, in less civilised countries, he reminds us of cults (Provine 2000: 134–136) and therapies of laughter (192) in Europe and America, which deliberately harness the contagion of non-humorous, group lauger, and its effects. As Provine says, it has to make us doubt that we are in conscious control of what we do, and I believe it is one indication that the time when we are least in control of ourselves when is we are among other people. This is reminiscent of Bakhtin's idea of Rabelaisian[4] carnival laughter, the uncultured laugh, the laugh that exists for its own sake and infects. Laughter, then, according to Provine, isn't just a way of showing amusement it is an instinctive socialising mechanism that predates speech in our evolution, and in our childhood development. Though often linked to the sharing of jokes, observations and irony – all very conscious procedures – the laugh also operates at an intersubjective, intercorporeal, level.

There are times when laughter irritates or disturbs us, but these are likely to be when we do not identify ourselves with the group or individual who is laughing. Unlike the inclusive, primal laughter of carnival, comedy revels in others' misfortune, it excludes, it humiliates, it is, as Umberto Eco says, 'always racist'.[5] We sometimes perceive laughter as directed at us, and feel threatened and excluded by laughter: as well as laughing with, we also laugh at. Again we may be using this laughter to identify ourselves as a group, but in this way by excluding those who are not in the group; we laugh at others' misfortunes because they are not our own and because they are not shared by those close to us. Again this laugh is involuntary, sometimes embarrassingly so, but where the tickle laugh shows that a touch or social interaction is stress-free, a comedic laugh shows that an apparent danger has passed, was not so dangerous, or is not a danger to one of us. Seeing someone fall, we identify danger, but also seeing that it is not us, or one that we care about, that falls, we register a lack of danger by laughing. It is a laugh of tension release and a sign that we do not care. This kind of laughter, too, helps to create and define a crowd: when we laugh at, we are identifying ourselves with the other laughers, and the victim of the misfortune that leads to our laughter as someone we care less about. When framed as theatre the formal and contextual signals (a horizon of expectation) that tell us whether we are watching comedy or drama will let us know how to receive such a spectacle of another's pain, as will the specific execution of the action, in its timing and manner of exaggeration.

Other embodied states of emotion and feeling are intersubjectively shared, but rarely as evidently as with laughter. Laughter in the theatre is the clearest signal that performers can get of how their audience feels. Applause waits for the end of the act, and the intense silence that accompanies drama can, to the anxious mind, sound like an audience that has gone to sleep. In interactive performance we have the luxury of looking into the spectator's eyes, even asking what they think while the show is still on, but in conventional theatre we must wait for sounds from the darkness of the auditorium. To hear waves of laughter rolling onto the stage is to know that your audience is having a good time, and – so long as you are performing a comedy – to know that your work is succeeding. In many of its guises the theatre is a place where we can come together to laugh. But the phenomenon of laughter tells us more than this, it can show us how audiences transform themselves from groups of individuals into crowds, and how people's responses aren't always governed by their conscious mind. While laughter at a performance event is an interaction in its own right, a participation that is generally very welcome, it is also an influence on the possibility of participation of other kinds. As well as stimulating more laughter, hearing laughter can stimulate feelings of enjoyment, and laughing oneself can do this too. Laughter as a therapy to stimulate feelings of well-being, and even to aid recovery from illness is occasionally fashionable (Provine 2000:180). but a more common expression of this phenomena is the feeling many of us will have experienced of laughing without entirely knowing why, at something we cannot objectively say is funny, but finding ourselves in a better mood anyway. An audience that has laughed together will be in 'a better mood', more likely to find things amusing, and probably more amenable to being invited to participate.

## Crowds

The contagion of laughter is one specific and highly developed element of intercorporeality as it is manifest in physical responses. As social animals our behaviour is influenced both consciously and unconsciously by other people, by what they do and say, but also simply by their presence. When we gather together in crowds certain kinds of behaviour are more likely, laughter among them, but also fighting or rioting. The study of the behaviour of people in crowds and the psychology that shapes this behaviour has tended to focus on this potential for violent, apparently primitive, action. Stephen Reicher suggests that this emphasis in the literature, beginning with Gustav le Bon in the late nineteenth century, has an unconscious ideological basis:

> one of the more remarkable features of traditional crowd psychology is that it has tended to constitute a theory without a referent. Rather than starting from a set of phenomena that are in need of explanation, a set of explanations were elaborated in order to underpin certain ideological presuppositions about the crowd – or at least the suppositions of gentleman observers who viewed the masses with alarm from the outside. To them, crowds seemed anonymous, their actions inherently destructive and random, their reasons unfathomable. (Reicher 2002)

The 'theory without a referent', here, is 'de-individuation', which proposes that under the influence of large numbers of proximate others individuals lose their sense of self, and are easily led into uncharacteristic behaviour, or even to do things normally against their own values or beliefs. While Reicher mounts a defence of crowds that take action in the interest of shared belief – using examples from political unrest from the nineteenth to late twentieth century to show that far from being phenomena of mindlessness, concerted action by crowds can be a powerfully rational response to material need. Others have used the idea of de-individuation to try to explain cooperation in acts of brutality, Stanley Milgram's experiments at Yale in 1963 being the most famous example.

Elias Canetti's view in *Crowds and Power* (1992) is a particularly vivid evocation of de-individuation, and one that is more interesting as he attributes positive effects to it as well as discussing violence. He calls it 'pack' behaviour, likening human beings to other social animals, and categorises different kinds of human crowd behaviour. His names for the main types of pack behaviour are more or less self-explanatory: the hunting pack, the war pack, and the lamenting pack; his fourth term, the increase pack, is more complex, to do with the absorption of groups into increasingly larger groups, the domination of one pack so that it integrates others. His view of their roles in the make-up of culture is not wholly relevant but his account of the point at which the individual surrenders to the pack instinct is.

> The most important occurrence within the crowd is the discharge. Before this the crowd does not actually exist; it is the discharge which creates it. This is the moment when all who belong to the crowd get rid of their differences and feel equal (Canetti 1992: 18).

And this is the moment where they become part of a larger organism that appears to make decisions with a will of its own. Until this point, he says, we are careful to avoid physical contact with others, to preserve our space and our distinction from others, we are fearful both of embarrassment in front of others and of being unduly swayed by them. This distance is a burden, and though we protect it we are also glad to be rid of it:

> During the discharge distinctions are thrown off and all feel equal. In that density, where there is scarcely any space between, and body presses against body, each man is as near the other as he is to himself; and an immense feeling of relief ensues. It is for the sake of this blessed moment, when no one is greater or better than another, that people become a crowd. (Canetti 1992: 19)

When people go to a crowded place for recreation it is usually with an expectation that they will join the crowd, not resist it. Gathering to drink alcohol and/or dance are practices of our culture that exploit this, as is watching sport, and the violence that sometimes goes with it. Canetti talks of the violent impulse of the crowd, that the crowd loves the sound of things being broken, and of the way that the destructiveness of the crowd is the seed of its manipulation in mob rule and in the making of armies, but he also cites religion as an extension of the crowd that gathers in grief, the lamenting crowd. He says that it is the urge to return to our origins as pack animals that governs our social behaviour: we have an instinctive way of reacting as a group when faced by a crisis, when threatened, hungry, faced with death, we can form a crowd and work as one animal. Canetti, a Jew who fled Vienna in 1938, writes with despair about the potential of the crowd, and the crowd to which he gives the least attention is the one that has the most positive potential: the feast crowd, the crowd of celebration. This is the crowd of carnival, the crowd celebrated by Rabelais and Bakhtin, and the crowd in which contagious laughter will play a significant part. Where violence is the malign aspect of the crowd, laughter is the benign. This kind of intersubjectivity can have a complex relationship with a person's understanding of their own experience, and with their sense of agency. People who have a diminished sense of personal initiative and personal responsibility also lose some of their inhibitions – they will do things that they normally wouldn't, whether that might be shouting and singing, or breaking windows.[6] They will also be less likely to do things that make them stand out from the crowd: crowds can bring freedom, but they can also bring conformity.

Rather than providing the basis for a coherent model for the understanding of crowd behaviour, Canetti's ideas represent the kind of fascination that crowds evoke. Contemporary researchers are less likely to construct a holistic theory like Canetti's, with its mystical evocations of our animal inheritances and their potential to undo the civilising process at a stroke, than they are to attempt to pull together ideas of states of arousal, social cognition and learned cultural behaviour, along with the embodied and enactive models of mind that have already been discussed in this chapter. An integrated theory of crowd behaviour seems some way off, but Reicher's view of a rational crowd remains an exception, with research tending to focus on the negative: crowd safety in public events and the process that leads a peaceful gathering to become a riot. Contemporary research tends to see this not as a theory without a referent, but as a set of phenomena that so far do not have a coherent explanation.

These phenomena reflect some of what happens to the crowd at a theatre. When we laugh, cheer, and applaud together we access a kind of social affordance to show that we are sharing the same reactions as those around us. But the process of apprehending a show is not so simple as receiving it entirely individually and then agreeing with those nearby. The feelings we share with others around us in relation to a show are far more reciprocal than this, we look for evidence of other people's reactions, both consciously and unconsciously, sometimes in order to declare our feelings boldly in contrast to them, but more often to validate what we feel, so that we show reactions that do not contrast markedly with what is being shown by others around us. However, the process begins prior to this, before any show has been given or received, when the crowd first gathers and even earlier. When choosing a show, buying tickets, moving towards the theatre, we are sharing behaviour with a group of strangers, aligning ourselves with a group and planning to become part of a crowd. A full auditorium is a crowd deliberately squeezed into a small space,[7] partly for the economic benefit of selling as many tickets as possible for the given space, but also for the purpose of driving people towards the intercorporeality that Canetti calls the 'discharge', towards the feelings of losing oneself, and towards a closer relationship with those around that will cause reactions to a performance to be magnified. It inclines a theatre audience in another way towards intersubjectivity.

Bill Buford describes how the suspense of a football match is intensified by the contact with other fans on the terraces, to a degree that sounds like a transformatory experience:

> As the match progressed, I found that I was developing a craving for a goal. As its promises and failures continued to be expressed through the bodies of the people pressed against me, I had a feeling akin to an appetite, increasingly more intense, of anticipation, waiting for, hoping for, wanting one of those shots to get past the Millwall goalkeeper. The business of watching the match had started to exclude other thoughts. It was involving so many aspects of my person – what I saw, smelled, said, sang, moaned, what I was feeling up and down my body – that I was becoming a different person from the one who had entered the ground: I was ceasing to be me. There wasn't one moment when I stopped noticing myself; there was only a realisation that for a period of time I hadn't been. The match had succeeded in dominating my senses and had raised me, who had never given a serious thought to the fate of Cambridge United, to a state of very heightened feeling. (Buford 1991: 169)

Buford's 'ceasing to be me' sounds distinctly like a kind of de-individuation. The numbers (even watching a relatively small team such as Cambridge United) are much larger, and the competition raises the tension enormously, but a similar transformation is conceivable in theatre crowds. All actors are familiar with the difference in playing to a full house and one that is half empty, and that it is a difference often not just of quantity but of quality too, as the crowd effect of an audience tightly packed together intensifies the feelings of that audience.

Audiences at performances in different settings come into the process of becoming a crowd at different points: an institutional audience such as a school comes with its own conflicts and solidarities, perhaps readier to become a crowd, but a crowd with a history; a congregation at a ritual performance may or may not have everyday knowledge of each other, but will have more of a common purpose and expectation, sometimes an expectation of moving into some altered mental state, as individuals or as a crowd; a theatre crowd has norms of licensed behaviour that encourage simultaneous response that will draw people into intercorporeality. The physical relationship of an audience will also affect this process: in a promenade performance an audience will often be encouraged to move as a crowd, physically enacting the process of 'becoming one' with those around, though this can be disrupted by the need to compete for a good view, or get a comfortable spot to sit.

In audience participation this can bring advantages and disadvantages. A crowd that has identified with each other and begun to share responses that approve of a performance can be more likely to give similar approval to invitations to participate, and if they have moved towards some kind of 'discharge' of their feelings of individuality may give little thought to whether or not to participate and simply follow the crowd into whatever it is doing. Alternatively a crowd that has settled into a feeling of a lack of differentiation might react badly to an invitation for individuals to participate, and this is one of the reasons that an invitation given to a large, well-established audience can be difficult, as separating oneself from the comfort of the crowd feels more distressing, like an act of violence against the larger body. A crowd can also magnify adverse reactions, either to a show as a whole or to an invitation, and a crowd that has become excited can become 'out of control'.

A number of things are implied in this everyday phrase, 'out of control'. It might refer to the pre-noetic, 'before you know it', phenomena that Gallagher proposes, and much of the shared and unconsciously directed behaviour of crowds must originate at this level. It is also indicated in the distributed agency involved in intersubjectivity, where self-control has been replaced, or at least delegated and diluted, by shared impulses. But it suggests a wildness and danger that is not necessarily what these theories refer to. Loss of control is a fearful thing, and this fear is embedded in this kind of idiom; while some trends in cognitive science tell us that conscious control may be largely illusory in any case, when we are experientially aware of giving up our self-management, it is something alarming or exhilarating. If we surrender self control to another, do we also expect them to take responsibility for our safety, and our actions? This suggests a return to the issue of informed consent.

If I have surrendered my agency to another or allowed it to dissipate among a crowd, should I be held responsible for my actions? Or alternatively, if I am about to enter into such a state, should I not be informed of the possible consequences, before I take actions that I might otherwise wish to deny responsibility for?

In the relatively trivial situation of audience participation these questions most often represent the anxieties that some people bring to events, rather than troublesome ethical issues – and as such they become part of the material of agency that is shaped by the procedural author, but as I shall show later in this chapter and the next, the ethics of control and consent can be both aesthetic material and genuine dilemma. However, my purpose in introducing the potential power of crowd phenomena is not to put a value on it, despite the charged language used by Canetti and the alarmism noted by Reicher: I do not intend that 'losing oneself' in a crowd is either a good or a bad thing, merely that it can and does happen. When it does happen, it will bring with it qualities of feeling derived from whatever physical changes it might entail, and from whatever cultural associations it has for the individual. Being among other people will influence behaviour in subtle ways, but forming such an intense bond with a crowd as to find that one's behaviour is experienced as directed from outside oneself brings an altered relationship to one's agency. This changed relationship, and its felt quality, will become part of the meaning of any audience participation that makes use of crowd phenomena.

## Liminality and communitas

However, there are cultures and practices that value the potential for de-individuation very highly. Ritual processes are sometimes portrayed as making use of intersubjectivity and de-individuation in a highly developed way, using a very focused procedural authorship to produce very intense experiences that mark moments of change in the lives of participants. In the rites of passage famously described by van Gennep (1960), and in the liminality modelled by Turner (1969) we have a particular set of procedures that use sequences of frames that mark off times and places as 'special', and mark the people who will inhabit them as special too, leading to behaviour that belongs in this time and place and nowhere else.

A liminal phase in ritual, put simply, is when the ritual participant is passing from one social status to another in a process marked by the ritual, and for a time they are considered to have neither their previous status nor the one they are about to take up, so that for a time they have no status at all. This process, according to van Gennep, has three phases: separation, margin and aggregation. In the first phase the subject is separated from society, symbolically and sometimes physically. In the second, the marginal phase, the ritual subject is at the threshold, both about to become something new and about to leave behind their previous self. According to Turner 'during the intervening "liminal" period, the characteristics of the ritual subject [...] are ambiguous; he passes through a cultural realm that has few or none of the characteristics of the past or coming state' (1969: 94). At this time the subject is to some extent free of rights and obligations, and is not subject to customary norms and ethical standards. The subject is in a special state that is often considered to have magical consequences, and in which he is expected to produce, and has license for, extraordinary behaviour: a period of liminality. After aggregation into society with new status the subject will be affected by a new set of norms, rights and obligations.

There is a possibility of confusion between the conventionally required performance of bawdy songs, cross-dressing or animalism within a ritual procedure and the spontaneous transgression of normal behaviour brought on by a feeling of liberation in the liminal phase. Turner and Van Gennep give examples of the former as a common property of liminal events, but Turner also implies that the latter may also occur as a symptom of the absence of responsibility at this time. He implies that to be given a space and time in which to be free and to be given unusual and transgressive acts to perform, is to be stimulated to further wildness. Within the liminal phase there is a glimpse of a life free of organisation and care, without obligations, rights, ethical standards and norms. The paradox is that this phase of life is fenced in by structured ritual observances, and itself may involve performance of required acts, for all that they are transgressive or liberating. It has a number of typical symbolic attachments:

> It is ritualised in many ways, but very often symbols expressive of ambiguous identity are found cross-culturally: androgynes, at once both male and female, theriomorphic figures, at once animals and men or women, angels, mermaids, centaurs, human-headed lions, and so forth, monstrous combinations of elements drawn from nature and culture. Some symbols represent both birth and death, womb and tomb, such as caverns or camps secluded from everyday eyes (Schechner and Appel 1990: 11).

Turner characterises this as a period of 'anti-structure', which contrasts to the structuring of life that we normally enforce, and notes that it has been incorporated into modern culture in a number of ways, often leaving behind its specific ritual context. For example, he sees a number of religious movements as 'liminoid' – making use of the properties of liminality – in the way they are radically egalitarian and put themselves outside the boundaries of normal society, and by the same criteria he saw hippies (a new and transgressive phenomenon at the time of his writing) the same way. Turner's distinction between liminal and liminoid is useful as his terminology has been adapted to describe a wide variety of phenomena, particularly performances, that either set themselves outside society or operate on the threshold of one category and another.

It is worth noting the difficulties in applying this model directly to theatre events. Theatre performances will not have the weight and consequence of the rites described by van Gennep and Turner: the participants will probably not be permanently transformed by the experience either in their own minds or in the eyes of society. They are not in this sense at a threshold at all, and so not taking part in a liminal activity. It is the license and liberation that come as a consequence of the liminal phase that is of interest here, not the permanent transformation of the participant. To describe all staged performance as liminoid makes some sense, as it helps to understand the special character of a stage, somewhere that has been marked off from normal space and time, and where extraordinary things happen.

A feature of liminal activity noted by Turner is a loss of the sense of self, similar to the 'discharge' described by Canetti: an altered mental state he calls 'communitas'. In communitas the ritual subject has been stripped of social status and its trappings, and grouped with a number of others in the same condition, through ritual actions and markings they have been placed outside society, and they are expected to behave in opposition to what is 'normal'. As a consequence of this they may feel less like an individual as the apparatus of individuality has been taken away, they will feel closeness to their companions enjoying a free and direct communication. Turner sometimes characterises this relationship as 'human' as opposed to 'social', and as an existential awareness of being without self. In a state of communitas people are less aware of the boundaries between them in a physical sense, of where their body ends and another begins. Turner associates communitas with marginality, with low status, as if in order to lose attachments and associate on a human level, one must become a pauper or an outsider. Liminal rituals often involve literal or figurative expulsion from the social world for a time before being re-integrated into the community: 'There is a dialectic here, for the indeterminacy of communitas gives way to the mediacy of structure, while in rites de passage men are revitalised by their experience of communitas' (Turner 1969: 120).Thus, communitas is the opposite of structure, and liminality one of the ways of facilitating it.

The twentieth century's advocates of ritual in theatre, such as Artaud, Grotowski and Brook, were attracted by the possibility of a theatre that did not depend upon words or representations, which became a vital and existential experience. Of the three types of communitas named by Turner: 'ideological' – the organisation of a subculture with its principles at the core; 'normative' – the use of the ritual process to help maintain a functioning culture; and 'existential' or 'spontaneous' communitas, it was the latter that was striven for by performers looking for the unique, magic moment in their event.

The external characteristics of liminality and communitas are, therefore, recognisable enough. But it is far from certain that they signify such an altered state in the participant. A different approach is necessary if we are to learn about the subjective experience, the internalised state of being that might correspond to Turner's communitas. Colin Turnbull, concerned with the perspective of the anthropologist, and of the deficiencies of emphasising rational and objective observation as the only model of anthropological work, insists that phenomena such as liminality must be wholeheartedly and generously experienced if they are to be understood. More than a methodological preference, his interpretation puts a much clearer emphasis on a liminal *state*. For him it is not a collection of behaviours or outward signs, or even an individual's perception of social relationships – which is how the more cautious will read Turner – but a distinct and consistent mode of being, capable of endowing extraordinary power:

> as long as we insist on taking liminality to imply a transitory in-between state of being, we are far from the truth. In our own terms it would be better seen as a timeless state of being, of 'holiness', that lies parallel to our 'normal' state of being, or is perhaps superimposed on it. Liminality is a subjective experience of the external world in which 'thisness' becomes 'thatness'. (Schechner and Appel 1990: 80)

It is in the achievement of this state among a group as well as the individual that greatest gifts are endowed upon the community, the ideal of Turner's existential communitas. Notice that it is music, communal singing, that brings the culmination of the ritual in Turnbull's example, the Molimo:

> and when ultimately the perfect sound was discovered it coincided with the discovery of the perfect mood: all disharmony, social, spiritual, mental, physical, musical [...] vanished and for a brief moment the Mbuti ideal of ekimi reigned, 'making good' everything, for in their own words whatever is, when that moment is reached is good, otherwise it would not, could not be. (Turnbull in Schechner and Appel 1990: 77)

Such a powerful experience is not to be taken for granted, and is not achieved every time a ritual of liminality is performed, although it may have evolved over millennia.

For a performance company to attempt to produce this effect may seem a worthwhile but daunting aim. Nevertheless, once again, I want to emphasise the quality of the potential phenomenon rather than its value. In Chapters 1 and 2 I made much of the connectedness of frames of performance to everyday life, and its norms and expectations, and the risks that are attendant upon giving performances in public. According to the theories of liminality and communitas, processes of detachment from everyday structure can radically alter the nature of this connectedness and remove the sense of risk associated with having a social self to protect. When one has become nothing, one has nothing to lose. As described by Schechner and Appel, and Turnbull, communitas seems like a highly particular state rather than one that could occur by degree, but given that Turner allows for varieties of liminoid phenomena that find different routes to and through status-lessness, we might expect different kinds and degrees of communitas. The subjective experience of such an alternative state of being, as well as undermining the power of social risk, will have a quality, and inflect the meaning of any participatory experience where it is manifest.

The above are not, by any means, the only irrational influences on our decision making processes: alcohol and drugs will influence our responses,[8] and our prior emotional or physical state will be very significant. Nor are these the only ways of describing these irrational impulses: there are many more, developed to a sophistication that cannot be explored here. Social psychologists write of our tendency to make decisions without carefully analysing, to follow 'heuristic cues' rather than argument when being persuaded of something:[9] a person might follow an instruction because everyone around is doing so, or because they perceive that the instruction has come from an expert. They also discuss 'audience effects' – the influence of passive spectators on the behaviour of others in everyday life, and 'co-action' effects – the influence of those who are engaged on the same tasks as each other (Argyle and Colman 1994: 103) and de-personalisation: 'The process of being dissolved, of losing the identity, personality, the "I". A mental phenomenon characterised by loss of the sense of the reality of oneself' (Watzlawick, Bavelas and Jackson 1967: 284).

## Hypnosis

> Stage hypnosis works like this. When you are hypnotised you are less inclined to be self-conscious; rather like being drunk. When you are intoxicated, should someone suggest that it would be a bit of a laugh to pretend to be a Martian, or Elvis, or a Ballerina, or whatever, you'll probably try it – why not? It's only a giggle after all. You do try it and it gets a few laughs, so you do it some more because making people laugh is good fun. That fun is intensified by your 'intoxicated' state and so you enjoy it more and so on. If the hypnotist is adept at helping you retain that lowered inhibition and maintaining a high degree of audience reaction, then the fun of being funny lasts as long as you stay in that state. (Chase 2005: 14)

This, from Jonathan Chase's 'complete instruction course in stage hypnosis', outlines how it works as entertainment rather than as a cognitive or psychological process. But stage hypnosis is a genre of popular performance that has evolved a set of routines and practices, which are based on powerful inter- and intra-subjective phenomena. It is also, obviously, a form of interactive performance, one that might suggest not only a variety of procedures and invitations, but also phenomena that might be manifest in other forms, traditions and approaches to inviting participation.

Hypnosis itself is an area of controversy among psychologists and cognitive scientists. Under hypnosis people are demonstrably able to endure pain, to increase their powers of recall, to overcome anxiety, and can be led to do things that in normal circumstances they would not; it is also a popular and successful tool in some forms of psychiatry. However, there is no agreement about what hypnosis is in psychological or cognitive terms, or how it works. Some say that the hypnotic trance is an altered state of consciousness, to which some people are susceptible and in which they are highly suggestible; some say that the trance is a variation of other altered states – daydreaming or deep involvement in a physical task for example; others deny the reality of the trance state, and believe that suggestibility is a normal, everyday phenomenon, harnessed by learned behaviours culturally specific practices of hypnosis. Again the phenomenon seems likely to be accessible to the strategies of enactive cognitive science, and suggests that the basic premises of inter-subjectivity and intercorporeality are manifested in some particularly powerful ways in some kinds of interaction:

> Our perception of others always includes a proprioceptive compo-nent that connects their bodies to our own. In more marked cases, unidirectional incorporation may even reach the degree of fascina-tion. Thus we may listen to a spellbinder, literally hanging on his every word – or on his lips, in the German expression – and feel being drawn towards him [...] This reaches an extreme in hypnosis where the subject is entirely coordinated to the hypnotist. His gaze is fixed, he is captivated by the hypnotist's appearance or performance, unable to move, or only moving in the ways the hypnotist suggests. However, a mismatch in the coordination could break the captiva-tion and bring the subject's separateness and autonomy back to his awareness. (Fuchs and De Jaegher 2009: 474)

This reference to 'fascination' recalls Freud's explanation of hypnosis, as a replacement of the 'ego idea' of the hypnotised subject with an image of an idealised other, and also suggests a trance-oriented interpretation; but they do not pursue the idea, and the benefits of a full cognitivist explanation remain to be explored.

The techniques for the induction of a hypnotic trance – or alterna-tively, the preparation for hypnotic suggestions – vary, but those used by stage hypnotists tend to address the entire audience, but only briefly, in order to select a smaller group to work with. The hypnosis that hap-pens on stage is almost always on an individual basis. Those who join in one of these acts surrender themselves to another individual, and do so voluntarily. Stage hypnotists tend to use procedures that find people who are especially suggestible – who will respond to their instructions easily and fully. This character of hypnotic trance is reminiscent of the state of absorption that might be observed in a theatre audience and similar, physiologically, to the state of people who get deeply 'involved' reading a book or watching a play, and also similar to the mental state of some performers. In this kind of state people lose track of time, forget and even become unaware of things around them.

A stage hypnotist is a procedural author working with a highly developed skill that takes these phenomena for granted, but who may also deploy other performative devices to control mood and atmosphere, to inspire confidence and compliance in participants, even to the extent of using 'stooges' to lead genuine subjects to volunteer, or as the subjects of climactic or difficult routines. An act may also, of course, be entirely faked, either by using pre-rehearsed stooges throughout or by recruiting willing subjects during the performance, secretly inviting them to 'put one over' on the rest of the audience (McGill 1996: 506).

It is possible to think of all procedural authorship as working on the suggestibility of a group of subjects, though not necessarily of all procedural authors as hypnotists. Hypnotic subjects do retain agency, despite the usual conception of being 'in the power' of the hypnotist. They respond to suggestions using the resources they have available, such as their own memories and their own imagination. The primary benefit and method of hypnosis is perhaps the removal of inhibition – surrendering to the will of the hypnotist allows a person to perform bravely, appearing to have lost their own ability to direct their actions. Stage hypnotists do not give detailed instructions to their subjects, the suggestion is often very similar to the brief given to a group of improvisers: a set of given circumstances, aims and motivations. Chase's examples of the Martian, Elvis and the ballerina imply given circumstances, which he would briefly elaborate with things to do. How the subject constructs his or her Martian, Elvis or ballerina performance, is a product of the individual's imagination. In my terminology, the hypnotist has given an invitation to enter an altered state, facilitates this, then indicated a horizon or participation, just as another procedural author would.

People who have been hypnotised will often say that they remember clearly what has happened, what they were asked to do and what they did, but that they simply saw no reason not to do it. The trance state and the hypnotist's suggestions remove the inhibitions that would normally prevent performance. It is clear that agency here is not a matter of a single, indivisible subject, able at all times to consider the wisdom and propriety of action, or to access the creative and imaginative faculties. The subject seems to have different capabilities depending on his/her interactions with others. The hypnotist appears to both take the agency from the subject by inducting them into a 'trance' (whether this is an empirically changed brain state, or a culturally sanctioned readiness to cooperate) and giving suggestions, and to give agency by using this state to give free reign to the imagination and the subject's creative impulses.

The primary process in stage hypnosis is to remove inhibition, and to make people amenable to following suggestions according to their own capabilities. Most practitioners insist that a hypnotic subject must always be willing, so rather than having their agency stolen from them by the hypnotist, they lend it for a period of time, allowing themselves to be manipulated.

There are two broad themes to draw from this in relation to audience participation: the first if we see hypnotic suggestion or processes as part of actual audience participation procedures, and the second in an analogy between hypnosis and the experience of audience participation. If suggestibility is a feature of everyday intersubjectivity, or (by the alternative model of the phenomena of trance) we are never very far from trance-like states, then it seems likely that an audience gathered to watch a performance might become open to suggestions, and/ or that something like a trance might be achieved in theatre-watching without the need for explicit hypnotic inductions. In the absence of specific empirical science to draw on about how these phenomena might be present in theatre audiences, and in view of the disagreement about the basis of the phenomena as a whole, I shall leave these questions here.

In analogy, the audience participant might appear like the hypnotic subject who delegates agency for a time, all the while having to draw on their own resources, both performative and ethical, in creating a performance. Stage hypnosis fascinates audiences because of the uncanny aspect of seeing people apparently taken out of themselves, and because of the frisson of the risk of allowing this to happen to ourselves. Much the same fascinations can be involved in any audience-participation show.

## Procedural authorship and harnessing intersubjectivity

Successful audience participation often produces these intersubjective effects; participants describe their experiences in terms that highlight the transformatory, as in Benedictus's account of *Paint Show 04*:

> I saw people lose it in there. And I think I lost it in there, too. Certainly in my first fight, as champion of the red team, I found myself surprisingly merciless towards the poor girl from the hated blue tribe. There were moments when I didn't feel completely human. (Benedictus 2004: 10)

or the communal, as in another of the same author's participations at
the Edinburgh Festival in 2004:

> There's an extra-special kind of laugh, the kind that rings out from
> the heated core of party games and food-fights, which is an unthink-
> ing response to pure, innocent abandonment. This kind of laugh
> one only gets from joining in, and I was exhausted from it after 75
> minutes of Mimirichi.

Theatre performances of many kinds employ these effects as means as
well as ends: they already exist within the network of practices that
frame behaviour in the institutions of performance, in procedures that
turn individuals into crowds, encourage a trance-like state, mark off
behaviour from that outside the theatre, and inaugurating the stage as
a place where specialised behaviour takes place. Audiences that have
reached states of heightened intersubjectivity respond more openly,
more in harmony with each other and with the performers; and invitations to participate are more likely to be accepted.

Interactive theatre that uses separate audience and performance spaces
as a starting point has some attributes that can be used to an advantage,
and others that work against interactions across this division. Musicals
that ask their audiences to sing along, for example, are helped by the
crowd-like aspect of an audience sitting in rows, but detaching oneself
from this crowd to cross the threshold of the stage is much more difficult.
In the earlier analysis of conventional theatre as consisting of a liminoid
frame on the stage, and a different, non-liminoid frame in the audience,
I suggested that this design helps to keep the audience in a position of
passivity. Logically then, in order to make the audience active, it might
be necessary to make a frame for them that has a liminoid aspect, or
a sequence of increasingly participatory frames that draw them closer
to the communitas that might be experienced by performers, to give
them a situation where they feel that extraordinary behaviour is not
only allowed but expected and easy. To attempt to create a frame for
the audience that is liminoid in precisely the same way as a stage space;
to replicate all the conventions of the performance for the audience to
participate in, would be an impossibility in most genres of contemporary
theatre, with their scripts and organised plots, but perhaps approached in
something like the walkabout improvisation of Izzo's Interactive Theatre,
or in Punchdrunk's environmental installations. In work of this kind
the physical organisation of the audience space has been altered, making it continuous with the performance space throughout. Schechner's

*Environmental Theatre* describes practices where the audience's entry to the performance space was ritualised, they were given food or drink, greeted, anointed, or asked to take off their shoes.[10] These are invitations to participate in a limited performance, to interact with performers and other spectators in a way that is risk free, or nearly, but takes the individual away from themselves, and a step towards the freedom of performance, they create an outer theatrical frame that recognises the audience in a place inside the symbolic language of the show, and a gradually expanding horizon of participation.

Creating an impression of a space of freedom can be one of the themes of a performance, as well as its technique, making the possibility of transgressive participation a challenge to the audience; in his account of Las Furas del Baus' *XXX*, Benedictus has already stepped onto the stage and had his trousers pulled down by a performer:

> Can you make it hard for us?' asked De Sade, pointing at my cock. No, I need the loo, I said. This got a laugh, but it was quite true; I'd been holding it in for the past half-hour. 'Well, you can piss here,' De Sade said, motioning hospitably across the rubber floor. (And he meant it. I can see that he really meant it.) No, I said. That's your lot. (Benedictus 2004: 10)

The sense given here is not that the performers want particular performances, or expect them, but that they want to create the impression of a limitless range of action, and so will make further invitations, whatever is offered by the participant, each more extreme than the last. The nakedness and projected film of the performers having sex that preceded this moment were potentially shocking, and potentially carnivalesque in framing the space as transgressive. Whether this was instrumental in inspiring Benedictus to cooperate and drop his trousers is not clear, but clearly it didn't broaden his horizon of participation to the limits the performers were willing to explore.

Working through a sequence of frames can also involve changing the physical relationship between members of an audience, and between audience and performers. A row of seats in a theatre typically has one arm-rest, causing neighbours to have some limited physical contact that they wouldn't have if the seat had more comfortable, separate arm-rests, and this helps to develop a crowd feeling. An audience that queues together for some time before a show goes through a procedure that taxes them a little physically, that brings them into contact with each other, physically as well as verbally, and they will enter a theatre with a different quality of anticipation to a group that walks straight to a seat, and with greater feeling of identity with each other – although this enforced community might find expression in resentment instead of excitement. The physical procedures people can be put through in the theatre are limited by their tolerance for discomfort and for humiliation, but a great variety of procedures can be conceived that will increase or decrease crowd feeling, call up feelings associated with other events, or which are meaningful in their own right. Crowds can be squashed, cosseted, soaked, singled out, chilled or warmed up, left alone to get to know each other, made to feel lost, put in the dark, or assaulted with bright lights and loud noise. All of these will have an effect on the way an audience feel about the show, about each other, and about themselves. Instead of an individual making rational choices, we see a collapsing of boundaries, and action led by impulses that come from both from within and without.

So far in my discussion of agency, I have mostly considered the individual's influence on a performance, and how that individual can be influenced in turn. Interactive events that emphasise the crowd over the individual can be very different from those that focus on the individual. Or perhaps more pertinently, those events that detach the individual from the crowd of the audience are the more radical, as they seek to undo the work that has been done in bringing people into a crowd. Theatre relies on the effect of the crowd upon people, although it may disguise the fact and celebrate the thoughtful response instead. This has implications for the analysis of interactivity, as well as for how it is controlled. If the individual is so powerfully influenced by the crowd, then their responsibility for their actions is mitigated – they are not acting entirely as themselves, but as part of a larger organism. Their agency in the process appears to be undermined. Watching in a crowd is the essence of theatre, and yet in our consideration of the reception of theatre we treat the individual as an individual, rarely with reference to how the crowd influences our thought process. My thesis is not that we are helpless in the crowd, unable to make up our own minds, but that if, as Provine has demonstrated, laughter can be stimulated by such mechanical processes, and further, can have an effect on our receptivity, we must accept that other neurological processes set in train by being in company will also have their effect on our emotional and cognitive responses to performance.

## de La Guarda's liminoid participation

I have already used De La Guarda's[11] *Villa Villa* to illustrate a number of ideas: the appearance of different 'involvement frames'; the direct control of a performance; and the manipulation of space and atmosphere to create an outer theatrical frame. I will now develop this last point, to consider whether this company successfully creates a liminoid frame for their participants, and how they make use of aspects of embodied intersubjectivity to do this, as well as to broaden the horizon of participation of their audiences. As well as my own experience of a number of visits to the show, I will use the accounts of reviewers, members of the company, and audience participants interviewed immediately after shows at the Roundhouse in London, in March 2000.

Press reviews for the London production recognised a transformative effect on the show's audiences: for example calling it 'a legal high that produces a real rush' (Spencer 1999); or noting that the cast 'create the kind of danced up delirium you get when your footie team has just lifted the Cup' (Watson 1999). Some of the comments hint at how this effect is achieved, in describing the behaviour of performers and audience: 'This is a world in which no-one talks – people growl, rant, scream and shout, but civilised behaviour is banned' (Halliburton 1999); 'There's a thrill of unbuttoned sexuality in the air, a sense of orgiastic celebration in which the constraints of language, thought and gravity itself have been gloriously suspended' (Spencer 1999). The suspension of rules, the banning of civilised behaviour, delirium, a legal high: in these comments it seems that the critics at least observed something like a liminal event.

The outer theatrical frame of the show is unusual, and designed to be unlike the usual experience of taking a seat to face a stage. The audience stand throughout, in what first appears to be a large black tent suspended inside the Roundhouse. Entering this tent is unlike entering the auditorium of a theatre, and unlike most other performance spaces; and unless you are familiar with the company's work or reputation there are no clues about where the performance is to take place. The tent is dark, the roof is close to your head, there are a lot of people very close together, there is no stage, there are no seats to point you in the direction of the performance: the architecture does not instruct you about your place. The immediate effect can be unsettling, but for many it contains allusions to spaces such as night clubs and festivals, which have participatory aesthetics and participatory practices of their own. During the opening section the performers are visible only through the roof of the tent, now transparent; when shapes and noises and colours become apparent above us, it is clear that this is the performance space – the space above our heads. This space is more radically altered again when holes appear in the roof, and the performers appear and reach down into the audience's space. The paper roof is torn back and the larger space above is revealed. This transformation is crucial. The original space is unusual in itself, but it is then disrupted and expanded. A performance space that is directly above has different boundaries to one that is in front, and while it seems unlikely that we could easily invade the performance space, as is always physically possible with a stage, the performers always seem in danger of invading our space as they defy gravity above our heads. The threat that one of the flying performers will swoop among us and steal us away is there from their first appearance through the torn ceiling, when this very thing happens, although with a 'plant'. Our desire – or fear – for this to happen 'for real' is not fulfilled until much later.

The invasiveness, threatened at the beginning, is gradually built up through the show – there are hoses trained on the dancers, which gradually begin to catch a few people in the audience, then later soak us comprehensively. The water has a levelling effect, it isn't aimed at anyone in particular, and apart from a few who shelter under the scaffolding, we are all soaked and the distinctions marked by each spectator's clothes are soon dissolved. Our sense of smell is addressed as well, there is a censer swinging over us, spreading incense, and dampness hangs in the air. More conventionally, the music is very loud, and there is dry ice periodically obscuring the view, but at all points audience members are not allowed to remain mere spectators, they are not able to reduce themselves to a gazing subjectivity, the invasiveness of the architecture of the show and its multisensory spectacle make this impossible: the outer theatrical frame locates the audience in the middle of a storm of activity. Towards the middle of the show the dancers come into the crowd and play with us, invading the audience space further, inciting us to dance with them and each other. Most of the interaction takes place at ground level, but towards the end of this section a bare-bottomed, impish dancer (male or female on different evenings) grabs people and flies them in circles above the rest of the audience.

This participatory section arrives in the middle of the event; it is its centre. It is not the conclusion of the evening, neither the outcome of a process nor a party added on as an extra; it is somewhere to get us to before carrying on with the performance. At every performance there are a number of spectators who hang back from the interactivity, taking shelter – literally – under the scaffolding from which the performers jump and swing, but most join in to some extent. As performance alone it is spectacular, accomplished, intoxicating, it shows scenarios of struggle, community, pain, ecstasy. There is a recurrent atmosphere of loss about to be regained, of joy and struggle. The imagery is of fraught though indeterminate situations – battling through storms, chasing up vertical walls, dodging flying bodies, falling repeatedly. A crucial, often repeated, image has all the dancers spiralling in a tight ball above our heads, struggling to keep together, while reaching outwards towards us. Arms, legs and bodies become one mass, each body indistinguishable from each other. If these images give resources to be used when direct participation is asked for, they suggest recklessness and physical contact more than anything more concrete.

Witnessing this performance from close proximity, with the threat of physical harm hanging, literally, over our heads, provokes a powerful kinaesthetic empathy. We frequently have to move to avoid performers moving quickly through the audience space, or swooping low over our heads. This calls on the kind of pre-noetic intentionality that would be in process moving through any everyday crowd, but with the kind of heightened sensitivity required in an unpredictable environment. Much of the performance will be happening to the audience member's body before it is disclosed to the conscious mind. And what is disclosed will be inflected by a state of arousal engineered by physical contact, bodily discomfort and potential threat.

Pichon Baldinu, one of the show's directors and original performers, describes De La Guarda's early street theatre performances[12] as 'teatro terrorista', or 'like you are throwing a bomb'.[13] The aim of *Villa Villa* is still to 'throw a bomb' into their audience but now without the brevity and disorientation of the street theatre. The aim is still to take people out of themselves, a few steps away from their normal lives, but now through celebration rather than shock. To change the way people feel now, in the same space and time as the performance, not to give them something to think about later, has become fundamental to the way they work. They aim 'to have this relationship with the audience, like something that is closer, that puts me in a closer place so that I can touch them, kiss them' and to 'place the audience and make them play on the same side you're playing, don't get them on the other side'. This interaction 'has to be something important [...] something strong and something real' it is not enough to pretend an interaction, 'to kiss somebody, you have to really kiss somebody'. Baldinu speaks about making people 'open' so that the performer can 'come inside'. These comments indicate that they are attempting to make a liminal space, a space where rules are meant to be broken, particularly rules that are rarely broken in life: (in the show) 'a woman can go and touch the arse of a guy, but a guy cannot go and touch the arse of a woman, because it's so easy, that always happens.' He observes that at the beginning of the show the audience apologise to each other for every moment of contact, but at the end they don't, and describes their new behaviour as 'natural' or, even more tellingly, 'dirty'. His use of 'dirty' seems particularly reminiscent of Turner's lowly, debased figure of communitas; and the lack of physical embarrassment at being touched recalls Canetti's 'discharge' at the point of formation of the crowd.

How participation is engineered and encouraged is something the performers are very aware of, they have rehearsed parts of the show as a participatory procedure. When talking about it they use the language of improvisation: of 'saying yes', of finding out 'what is the game', which echoes Johnstone,[14] among others. They also speak of looking into the participant's eyes, and of imitating their body language, the body language of flirtation. Imitating the audience is also a way of reminding them of their own presence, and that they have not been given the privileged position of spectator, reduced to pure gaze, that they are agents, able to affect the social world of the performance. Specific games played by performers reveal the seductive, covert, but playful quality to their invitations:

> I often allow them to, encourage them to play with me, but lead them into it. So, I'd get them, I'd make them cup their hands and then I'd actually lie down on them, and they'd take my weight and they'd suddenly realise that they were participating, and they'd move around trying to let go, but not wanting to let me drop, and that's already kind of involving them more than they want and then people clear out and then if I go to the ground then I'm immediately in a position to offer and ask for help.[15]

This is a procedural strategy for involving people, rather than a fixed procedure. As an invitation it is subtly manipulative, it acknowledges that participants may be reluctant, but asks for a very small contribution in the first place, and uses that contribution to trap the participant into feeling an obligation to continue: the overt becomes the covert. But it is the performer who makes herself vulnerable, takes a lower status than the audience rather than imposing upon them from a position of power, and calls on the empathy of the audience member at this point to make them accept the invitation and broaden their horizon of participation to include physical interaction, to the extent of sharing weight. Eye contact is important to this kind of interaction, reminiscent of Fuchs and de Jaegher's tennis players, and a kind of deep intersubjective involvement is possible in these moments, brief though they are. Some of this game will address itself to the conscious mind of the participant, who will almost certainly be able to think through the implications of the performer's sudden dependence upon them, however briefly. But as well as this the momentary changes of weight and effort needed to maintain her in a 'safe' balance will arise directly in the musculature of the participant, in a body-mind occupied in the intentionality of this physical contact. To hold another's body like this calls upon affordances between hand and head, neck, shoulders – instinctive familiarities with touching another human being, but that when disclosed to the conscious mind may seem incongruous, and perhaps uncomfortable, even as the participant's body continues to engage and interact without the need for thought or reflection.

The audience members didn't speak to me explicitly of intoxication, transportation, of being seduced, of doing the unexpected and being licensed to break the rules. Like the critics, they described the event as unlike other theatre or dance performances: they spoke about it as reminding them of a music festival, or a 'rave', the loud music particularly seems to have served to locate people's experience.

> parts of it didn't feel like a performance, it felt I was the performance, it felt like I was at a rave or, do you know what I mean, like at Glastonbury or something like that, just like not caring about, whatever, just going with the flow.[16]

One identified the crowd as 'a really clubby audience', though another seemed frustrated that there wasn't more eager participation 'I think, like, you could do with a bit more, like, party people in there.' Horizons of participation must have been coloured by perceptions of the event as belonging to these categories, at least for those who frequented such events as well as dance/theatre shows. Several referred to their anticipation of the event, many came on the recommendation of a friend, or had seen the show before, but among those who were there for the first time, surprise was equally important. This anticipation that something unusual was likely to happen would be useful in developing a liminal space, the heightening of the senses through a little fear might make people more than usually susceptible to the multisensory signals of the space. They described their feelings during the performance in ways that echo this feeling of nervous anticipation, one woman told me she felt 'excited and tense and happy all at the same time', another that she was 'a little bit scared of the performers'. But another spoke of frustration at not getting more directly involved, 'I wanted to go up with them but they didn't grab me, I was pissed'. Few of those I spoke to had participated directly in interaction with the performers, though most had danced with them briefly, and danced with each other. The interactions they described involved being 'grabbed' 'leaned on', having a hat stolen and having skin blown on or sucked; a focal point in the discussion of participation was the 'flying' of a handful of audience members, who were roped to one of the performers, and hoisted into the air with them. Some of those who had held back from participating gave reasons that were rooted in their own character: 'I'm one of those sitting on the bench type girls, you know', or in being unprepared: 'I wouldn't have minded going flying, I'd have loved that, yeah. Probably wasn't dressed appropriately, had too many clothes on, it would have suited people with t-shirts on, I've got a skirt'.

Overall, these responses don't indicate a collapse of social norms, nor of a feeling of radical interconnection between audience members, but they suggest that extraordinary experiences might have been within reach, if people were brave enough to throw themselves into the event: 'But you wanted them to do that didn't you deep down, you were kind of like avoiding their gaze, but deep down you really wanted to go up there.'

And although the performers made many references to their sense of play, suggesting that they are directly addressing what McConaghie would call a basic emotion system of PLAY, it seems that the audience's feelings were somewhat more complex. Their comments show awareness that play is being asked of them, as an activity, but the quality of PLAY as an emotional state is inflected by elements of FEAR and perhaps PANIC, while the weight sharing strategy and others like it evoke CARE very explicitly.

The performers gave indications of a different sort that some kind of liminoid frame had been created at the event, telling of being assaulted during other parts of the show, when they were flying past just above the heads of the crowd, of being grabbed and groped – sexually assaulted – 'as if they think we're superhuman or, or, because we're flying around with our knickers showing'.[17] A feeling that the performers were super- (or perhaps more accurately sub-) human seems to have allowed behaviour that would be beyond the pale in normal interaction. Or perhaps it is normal that some men would fail to respect the physical boundaries of these women, given the opportunity and anonymity of a crowd and a lack of bright light.

The company's intention to make their audience 'lose it' (to borrow Benedictus's phrase) has, then, been fulfilled to an extent, but with some occasional unintended results. The protection of performers from participants who take the freedom to interact physically caused The Performance Group to modify their work decades before this, though it seems not to be an issue for Las Furas del Baus. And though these assaults were rare, and not by any means the only interesting feature of the performance, they do highlight the bind that practitioners of audience participation put themselves in: in surrendering control one invites a degree of chaos, especially when using an overt language of chaos and abandonment in one's procedure, and when addressing, through the use of liminal frames, crowd processes and carnivalised environments, anti-structural interactions and anti-social behaviour.

## Embodiment, enculturation and meaning

Some conflict might be perceived between the conceptual apparatus of the previous chapters, and the approaches adopted in this one. Turning to cognitive science and philosophy might appear to be incompatible with social theory; but as I have observed, the basis of the enactive model of cognition and other recent developments across the field is that all cognition is encultured, or rather that culture is embodied at such a deep level as to affect even pre-noetic responses. The notion of affordance, too, might be developed in Bourdieusian terms – particularly if we think of social affordances as instances where a situation invites and draws from us certain types of action. Much as designed objects – cups, door handles – fit and call forth action from human bodies, and do so as part of a material culture, so also (and perhaps more so) types of greeting or gathering call forth the appropriate kind of active response, the response that we are disposed to because we are schooled in it, at a deeply embodied level.

However, it is more difficult to reconcile the more extravagant claims for anti-structural freedom in some readings of liminal phenomena, and a thorough interpretation of Bourdieu. Communitas appears to offer a relatively easy escape from the embodied dispositions of habitus, field and capital. To ascribe transgressing performances to acquired dispositions associated with the relevant cultural practice could integrate the approaches, but would merely restore them to a properly structural origin, and offer little to those who would seek similar results in non-traditional societies or those who see real structurelessness as the outcome of a liminal process. My scepticism about this version of liminality should not negate the importance of crowd phenomena or other situations where we might 'lose ourselves'; it is rooted in a preference for explanations that set them alongside other enculturated behaviours, as designated times where we have learnt a version of how to let go.

Rather than attempt a resolution to these conceptual difficulties, I shall turn to Carrie Noland's *Agency and Embodiment* (2009) for a view of the emergence of freedom within physical action, which does not depend upon such an easy route out of cultural habituation. Noland aims to offer some balance to what she calls an 'entrenched historical determinism' (8), through an examination of agency in everyday gesture. Such gestures are enculturated right down to the muscular and neuromuscular level, she agrees, but she insists that there is a lack of identity between gesture at a discursive level – the gesture as a sign – and as an interoceptive experience. Just as others read the performative gestures that our bodies produce, we too read them and understand their meanings, but there is the potential for dissonance between that culturally enscribed meaning and our felt experience of the gesture itself. She draws on Merleau-Ponty to examine how a smile, for example, can be understood in three ways:

> (1) as an example of motor behaviour, an attempt to solve a problem, to do something in the world (a psychological 'I can'); (2) as a 'figure,' a conventional and culturally specific sign for pleasure and approval, or, alternatively, anger and frustration; and finally (3) as a set of kinaesthetic experiences, such as clenching (of the cheek muscles and jaw), stretching (of the lips and chin), and exposure (of the teeth and gums). Merleau-Ponty's treatment of gesture is provocative because it suggests that interaction among these three levels is constant and, under certain circumstances, available to reflection. Gestures are the site of a complex negotiation of forces without which situation meanings would never appear and the history of such meanings would never evolve. (Noland 2009: 62)

The different disciplines drawn on in this chapter would understand a smile in different ways, and have different perspectives on the balance of voluntary and involuntary impulses that lead us to smile at and with other people. But what Noland draws attention to is the interplay between action, signification and sensation. Often a smile, and any other gesture, at the moment when it is called forth by a situation, will feel entirely 'natural' and suited to the affective state of the moment and the interaction; it will function as a sign and intercorporeally draw out appropriate matching gestures from others; and it will pass from memory without any need for reflection. At other times, however, a smile may feel forced, making us aware of its clenching and stretching actions, and that we are working to produce the sign that is appropriate to the moment rather than effortlessly experiencing it in passing. Or as the moment of a smile passes by, we might notice some incongruity in the situation, something less comfortable, and have cause to reflect on how the gesture was drawn from us.

My theme in these three chapters has been agency in audience participation, and the problems with understanding exactly where it lies. Noland does not provide a complete answer (and nor do Gallagher, Bourdieu, Goffman), but she does show how in the fine detail of culturally determined gesture there is the capacity for a self-awareness that does not derive entirely from the shared codification of the gesture, but from the dissonance between the gesture and the private, interoceptive experience of it. This is where she finds agency, in the resulting distance between the subject and the performative gesture, the space that allows for the repetition of gesture to be inflected with the accumulated understandings of embodied experience.

When audience participation draws action out of the bodies of participants it can create these kinds of dissonance, experienced in the moment or in reflection, which in themselves become part of the meaning of the performance event. They can also become part of the vocabulary of the individual, informing how their gestural interactions are used in the future.

# 4
# Accepting the Invitation

The questions of this chapter relate to the experience of accepting an invitation to participate, in particular the consequences that this has for the reception of a piece of participatory theatre for the audience participant, as their 'point of view' in relation to the performance alters radically at this point. The key questions are:

- What is it like to be an audience participant? And to be audience, performer and performance, simultaneously?
- What is it like to make choices at the same time as observing those choices as an audience member?
- How does the experiential aspect of participation contribute to a distinctive aesthetic character?

A piece of audience-participatory theatre will be other things as well as being audience participation. As well as containing audience participatory performance it may contain performances with conventional actor–audience relationships, and its audience participant performances will often be watched via such conventional perspectives in any case. It will have its explicit and implicit content, and it will be embedded in its traditions (even when rebelling against them), and be meaningful in their terms.

But when an invitation is offered, and even more so once an invitation is accepted, certain dynamics come into play between the participant and the performance they offer. Accepting an invitation to participate means accepting an altered social role, as we have seen, and it also means accepting some risk to social esteem, and some risk of (or opportunity for) responding unconsciously. The alteration of social role, and the roles that are played may vary enormously according to the tradition, practice and procedure of participation concerned, but what distinguishes this change of role, and the roles that emerge from such a change, is that it is a change from a simple audience role to an audience participant role. We might also call this an audience-performer role; but either way I propose that the 'audience' aspect is not extinguished in this change: when we become audience participants we remain audience members.

This is true for two reasons: first because we arrived at the event as theatre-goers and become audience members, and therefore we carry through the experiences of the event an expectation that we will 'consume', 'receive' or 'enjoy' the event as such. The institution of theatre is structured around the audience member and their consumption, reception or enjoyment of what is produced and performed, and whatever subsequently happens begins with this structure. Second, we will leave behind the role of audience participant, and leave the event restored to the role of theatre-goer, and look back on an experience organised on this premise. Whatever happens, any new relationship that emerges out of this change of role will have begun with the initial audience–performer relationship and the role of theatre-goer that extends beyond the moment of performance itself. The 'whatever happens' repeated in these two formulations is important because, as we have seen, there is at least the possibility that audience participants can 'lose themselves' in the course of an event, and thus potentially lose some sense of social role and of otherwise apparent residual identifications with the role of audience. Though 'in the moment' we might (conceivably, on rare occasions) forget the audience-ness of our experience, it is the basis of the relationships involved, and it will return in our reflections on the experience afterwards. More often, however, we are aware of being audience members even while we are also participant-performers.

This sometimes obscured, sometimes self-evident, continuing audience role brings with it some attributes. As watchers and listeners – the activities implied in the roles of spectator and audience – our point of view and point of hearing has been altered so that we now watch and listen from much greater proximity. We are closer to the action, when perhaps we are standing in among performers and other audience-performers. And we are intimately close to the action when action is produced by our own body or voice. All performance manipulates the audience's perspective on the theatrical action, whether through inherited conventions of theatre architecture and practice or through innovative audience-performer arrangements, but audience participation puts us into this peculiar relationship with action that originates within our bodies, while we remain audience members of the event as a whole.

These relationships have to be seen in their embodied aspects, because the location of perception and action within the particular body of the participant is especially important. And they have to be seen as time-based and evolving, because of the temporal presence of the participant in the moment of performance choices. The performance emerges from our own body, and is sited in our body, the same site from which we 'watch' the performance. At the same time our social self is recognisable as the source of the performance: much of the emphasis of the previous chapters has been on making choices and the action that we witness emerging from our body is the manifestation of those choices. As we have seen, a participant has at least made a choice not to refuse to participate, but has often made a choice of something to offer to the performance. Thus, the participant is simultaneously *the performer*, the one who enacts the performance through choice, *the performance* that emerges from their own body *and the audience* as they view it.

This is a complicated situation to be in, conceptually. But is this complexity a product of conceptualising it thus? Is it not in reality a simpler matter of interacting in a slightly modified frame, with a different kind of self-consciousness, or on occasion a complete lack of self-consciousness? Is it not the usual situation of the performer, whose role as audience to their own performance fades into the background while the event is under way? This chapter will show how this complexity can be a real and significant attribute of the situation of the audience participant, and that conceptualising it in this way is necessary to capture the range of different kinds of 'aesthetic distance' that can emerge in audience participation.

## Theatre audiences and feedback loops

Up to this point my argument has treated audience participants as social beings more than as audience members (as a subset of social beings). It is time to return to the situation of being an audience member. Paying attention to the institutionally derived role of 'spectator' will allow us to consider if and how that role changes when an invitation to participate is accepted, and the significance of such a change. Erica Fischer-Lichte describes how audible and visible reactions from audiences affect performance in theatre:

> Both the other spectators as well as the actors perceive and, in turn, respond to these reactions. The action on stage thus gains

or loses intensity; the actors' voices get louder and unpleasant or, alternatively, more seductive; they feel animated to invent gags, to improvise, or get distracted and miss a cue; they step closer to the lights to address the audience directly or ask them to calm down, or even to leave the theatre. The other spectators might react to their fellow spectators' responses by increasing or decreasing the extent of their participation, interest, or suspense. Their laughter grows louder, even convulsive, or is suppressed suddenly. They begin to address, argue, or insult each other. In short, whatever the actors do elicits a response from the spectators, which impacts on the entire performance. In this sense, performances are generated and determined by a self-referential and ever-changing feedback loop. Hence, performance remains unpredictable and spontaneous to a certain degree. (Fischer-Lichte 2008: 38)

She notes how in the western tradition from the end of the eighteenth century onwards audience feedback, and therefore participation in this creative looping, was gradually disciplined, until the 'performative turn' of the 1960s began to not only allow audiences to once again make themselves heard, but to self-consciously direct attention onto their presence, and their activity. This initiated a new kind of feedback loop:

The pivotal role of the audience was not only acknowledged as a pre-condition for performance but explicitly invoked as such. The feedback loop as a self-referential, autopoietic system enabling a fundamentally open, unpredictable process emerged as the defining principle of theatrical work. (Fischer-Lichte 2008: 39)

*Autopoiesis* is a term drawn from cellular biology, formulated by Humberto Maturana and Francisco Varela to address the organisational premises of living cells:

a cell produces its own components, which in turn produce it, in an ongoing circular process. The word 'autopoiesis' was coined to name this kind of continual self-production. A cell is a self-producing or autopoietic unity. (Thompson 2010: 98)

The term has since been used as part of a definition of living organisms in general, and is an important part of the enactive theory of mind discussed in the previous chapter, in which minds are seen as just such autonomous, self-producing systems. It suggests autonomy in the sense of self-generation, but not independence from the environment: evidently cells, living beings and minds have to draw on resources from their environment to do the work of producing and reproducing themselves. The implication of Fischer-Lichte's use of the term is that performance produces itself autonomously, in distinction from the creative work of the performance makers who have set it in motion: performance makers and audiences become resources which the autopoietic system of the performance draws on. Some problems with this definition of performance will be followed through later in this chapter, but for now it indicates the emphasis that Fischer-Lichte wants to place on the moment of performance itself, as its own point of origin, and the inclusion of audience members in that origin.

In Fischer-Lichte's account a feedback loop defines all theatre, but this autopoietic character arrives with the 'performative turn', with three processes consistently brought into playful experiments: role reversal, the creation of community and mutual physical contact (Fischer-Lichte 2008: 40). As examplars of role reversal she cites Marina Abramovic's *Lips of Thomas*, into which audience members intervened to bring to an end a series of acts of self-harm by the performer; the Performance Group's *Dionysus in 69* and *Commune*, and Fusco and Gomez-Pena's *Two Undiscovered Amerindians Visit the West, 1992–1994*, all well known, perhaps even canonical works; and Christoph Schlingensief's *Chance 2000 – Campaign Circus '98*, in which participants made choices in a chaotic parody of democratic process (Fischer-Lichte 2008: 40–50). In all of these, the invitation to the audience member to take an active choice-making part in the performance – what Fischer-Lichte calls role reversal – acts as a 'magnifying glass' on the feedback system of performance and their importance within it. More than this, by redistributing power to these audience participants, this technique raises the feedback loop to the level of autopoiesis.

This analysis stops short of examining the experience of the audience participant. She presents a striking articulation of the changing aesthetics of contemporary performance where this kind of involvement is invited, but her focus remains rigorously on the emergence of the work, rather on the audience member's experience of it, despite the change in quality of experience that must follow from such an invitation. Her theory positions audience participation as not just a change in the degree of creative input in the previously established feedback loops of theatre, but as a change in the *kind* of input. Her examples of audience behaviour in autopoietic feedback are of a different order to the audience behaviour in theatre that she notes in the long quotation at the beginning of this section. She calls this kind of participation 'role reversal', acknowledging that people have roles and that 'reversing' them is not trivial. To develop my own theory of the aesthetics of audience participation I will need to develop Fischer-Lichte's model of the feedback loop out of which the work of performance emerges, to show how the change in the experiential dimension of the work is significant not just to each audience member's understanding, response and contribution, but also to what kind of art work emerges.

## A new horizon

I have proposed that becoming an audience participant involves perceiving a horizon, and accepting a responsibility to act within that horizon, to make choices and to perform those choices. But we need to open out the concept of the horizon, a little further than it has been in Chapter 1. We need to take account of individual and shared perspectives, and those of participants before and during participation. And we need to pay some attention to what a horizon contains for those it appears to.

Gadamer refers to several different kinds of horizon, in his use of the term to examine the hermeneutic process of understanding: historical horizons, horizons of the present, the horizons of others. For his purposes the word designates what is perceptible from a certain point of view, and facilitates an understanding of how the historical consciousness implicit in a text (its historical horizon) must be fused with the perspective of the reader (their horizon). It is from this derivation that the term 'horizon of expectation' comes to be used in reader-response theory, and thence to find its way into the theory of theatre audiences. But Gadamer himself draws on Husserl's phenomenology, where the idea of a horizon explicates how subjectivity has a 'givenness' that works in tandem with the givenness of intentionally disclosed phenomena, as described in the previous chapter. He shows how for Husserl:

> there is such a thing as givenness that is not itself the object of intentional acts. Every experience has implicit horizons of before and after, and finally fuses with the continuum of the experiences present in the before and after to form a unified flow of experience. (Gadamer 2004: 237)

While the material world becomes real to us (is given) through our being directed towards it (intentionality), it does so in a moment that is always facing both forwards and backwards, to memories of past experience and anticipations of the future. Gadamer will go on to use terms such as 'tradition' and 'prejudice' to elaborate how a horizon facilitates the understanding of texts, but his source, Husserl, is interested in experience as an aspect of human being, more than in the hermeneutic understanding of cultural objects.

My formulation of a 'horizon of participation' depends on the relationship between an understanding of a moment of experience and its extrapolation into the possibilities for action that extend from that moment. Action depends on understanding, whether at a conscious or unconscious level, in the emergent process of mind as a meaning-making system of Varela and Thompson. The meaning of every moment of experience presses upon us to take action, even if that action might appear as refraining from action. A horizon of participation is characterised by such a pressure.

The temporality of Gadamer and Husserl's horizons applies to the horizon of participation too: it belongs to a particular moment, while at the same time facing the past and the future. And as Gadamer says, horizons are mobile and evolving. This is true for the horizon in its literal form, as although if one glances at a horizon it appears to be the static state of the border of visual perception, if one attends to the horizon for any amount of time one will inevitably see changes; and Gadamer's intention is that the horizon changes as we move through it. A horizon of participation that appears to us before accepting an invitation may appear as a fairly fixed concept, but at, and from, the moment of acceptance it is a constantly evolving perception, renewing itself moment-by-moment. Being in a horizon of participation is a fundamentally time-based (and time-pressured) state of being.

This, then, may be the strict sense of a horizon of participation: an evolving, individual understanding of the possibilities offered by an invitation. But just as Gadamer opens his term out to elaborate what is shared with others, or at other points what is owned by others and unknowable to us, a more adaptable conception of plural horizons can help to unpack the experience of participation. Additional useful aspects of horizons will include the common horizon of a work or a form of work, implicitly shared by those who have a common anticipatory understanding of its form; the anticipation of an individual of a work, informed by this common horizon; the situation of the potential individual participant, when projected by a procedural author designing a participatory event; and the shared negotiation and exploration of possibilities by all of those interacting in the relational space of the emerging work.

What does this theoretical approach to the horizon add to the detailed discussion of influences on participant choice-making presented in the last three chapters? First it offers a connection between the significance of a horizon, as an expression of expectation, experience and the influence of institutional anticipation, and the in-the-moment intentionality and affordance of embodied cognition, embedding both of these processes in a Husserlian phenomenology. Second by placing these two sets and sites of influence side by side it gives space for both cultural determination and pre-noetic, unconscious bodily response, while leaving room for 'mind' as a meaning and choice making process.

## Weather on the horizon

Martin Welton, in *Feeling Theatre* (2012), styles the prevailing *affect* within which performers do their work, and audiences receive it as a kind of 'weather'. Adding this image to the notion of the horizon of participation suggests how the unpredictable element of bodily/emotional affect has influence at a moment of invitation and afterwards. The resources offered in a pre-participatory performance, those shared resources called on in an invitation, might create an apparently well-defined common horizon; but this horizon is made clear, cloudy or even positively foggy by the affective state of the individual. A good mood and positive outlook – enhanced, of course, by an adventurous attitude to participatory art – makes the landscape of action contained by a horizon appear accessible and welcoming. A sceptical or fearful anticipation of the event, provoked or influenced by unhappy circumstances unconnected to it, makes the space of the horizon uninviting, an area of dark motives, cold encounters and hidden horrors. Alternatively the procedural author seeks to influence this internal weather, by operating on the affective state of the audience as a whole, and of participants in particular. The kinds of manipulation of states of mind and body raised in the previous chapter whip up storms among a crowd, or warm an audience to each other or to the performers, in readiness for interaction. The processes of kinaesthetic and emotional empathy, of suggestion, or of affectively stimulated anticipation will thoroughly change the experience of having a horizon.

Where this kind of affective weather is shared among an audience, or an audience and performers, whether procedurally promoted, or arrived at accidentally, we might speak of an event's atmosphere, and attempt to understand it in nuanced terms. As has been discussed in detail, the actions of performers create affect, but less has been said about how space and environment, light and sound, affect us bodily, emotionally and cognitively, and create the weather of the horizon. They too shape our mood and incline us to act or refrain from acting, and sometimes impel us to act in certain ways. Despite using a space-based metaphor in the horizon of participation, I have had little to say so far about the use of space in inviting and structuring audience participation. But as McAuley tells us (2000: 5), theatre performance is essentially char-acterised by a spatial distinction, and the appearance of one side of this distinction to those on the other side of it, that is the imaginative engagement of the audience with the scenography, is a key element of the phenomenology of spectatorship. The collapse or the transgression of this distinction does not negate the importance of space for audience participatory theatre. Participation is a bodily activity, in which the location of the body and its relationship to the organisation of space is fundamental, and the experience of audience participation is an expe-rience of changes in spatiality. It may take place within an audience space, but in this case the audience space has been re-framed, and the bodily response to this re-framing will be noticeable – when called on to participate from their seats, people sit up, or stand up, or sink back; they note the body language of those around them and assimilate themselves to it or distinguish themselves from it; presence as part of 'an audience' is suddenly marked, and a demand is made to use the language of space and bodily orientation to it, to comment on that presence.

In many cases the invitation to participate will be an invitation to enter a performance space, and therefore a transgression of the audience/performance distinction. Where this is true the moment of entry into the performance space will be particularly phenomenologi-cally charged, as the re-framing of activity, and the demand upon the choice making of the participant will be so strongly marked by this spatial invasion. Even when the 'performance' of the participation does not begin immediately, when further instructions to the volunteer are given once a participant has already taken the stage, the demand is felt, a horizon of participation is already in operation, perhaps as a first-stage re-framing of the audience's role, but nevertheless a significant altera-tion to their orientation to themselves and others at the event.

In other cases the space is an element in the horizon of participation in a less oppressive way: space can constitute an invitation in and of itself, it can help to define and suggest activity and roles to take. In an impor-tant sense the space and its contents are identical with a large portion of the horizon of participation: they are a horizon in themselves, literally and in relation to potential action. Space offers its affordances: walls define possibilities for motion, doors present opportunities for exit, furniture and props are choices made manifest, corridors demand motion. Environmental and site-specific participatory performance where audience participants are invited to wander freely make it especially obvious that the nexus of space, bodies and time stimulates motion. Activity in a space changes its character for us: waiting, moving quickly, returning to the same space again and again, exploring, hiding, will all strongly inflect the perception of a space and how it becomes part of a horizon of participation. Moving into a crowded space or moving as a crowd into a space, make different demands on us than moving into the same space alone. But in other kinds of performance too, when participants step into stage spaces, out of chairs and into school halls, into circles of audience members in the street, bodies speak through space in the way they orient themselves to it when still, and in how they move through it. Space is, therefore, a key tool for the procedural author, as it is a key part of the phenomenology of audience participation.

The horizon of participation is a spatial, embodied, time-based response to an invitation (and henceforth a commitment) to act. Accepting an invitation means moving into a horizon of participation where temporality and spatiality are reconfigured as affordances that press upon the participant, initiating and shaping responsive activity. We experience it as an atmosphere, and perceive it according to our mood, as much as we understand it in response to a performer's explicit activity.

## Gaining roles and responsibilities

I have avoided categorising or enumerating distinctive kinds of participation for the most part, to avoid appearing prescriptive about what kinds of participation are worthy of discussion, and because a list of types of participation could soon proliferate to the point of absurdity; but a useful distinction can be made between invitations to join a fictional presentation and others. A horizon of participation that requires acting of some kind has a very particular dimension to it.

The business of cooperatively presenting a fiction is highly elaborate in whatever form it takes. It entails moment-by-moment agreement about time, place, character, the relationship of characters to each other and to the people playing them, conventions of being aware of some people and not others, of being watched and denying it. But members of a theatre audience will not have to learn or have described to them this complex form – it can be taken for granted. The idea of theatrical fiction is a common shared resource. The difficulties come when someone without the benefit of rehearsal is invited to take action within this framework that either (a) effectively continues to present a consistent fiction, or (b) achieves something within the parameters of the fiction, while remaining consistent with it. In other words, the challenge might be either to perform well, or to solve a problem, or sometimes to do both.

In Chapter 1 I accounted for these two possibilities in terms of the resources that the participant can draw on from other frames of social interaction – their skills and experience in acting and or in specific circumstances. But this is only marginally helpful when thinking about what the experience of a horizon of participation of this kind is like, or what it means, when a participant takes a role. Does the participant feel something about how their prior experience is called on at the moment of invitation, and as the interaction continues? Probably a whole variety of emotions and/or reflections will be prompted: relief that there is relevant experience to draw on; anxiety that personal circumstances may come into play; excitement at the opportunity to show off; anger at the reality behind the fictional circumstances used to prompt participation; or resentment that real life has been used for this, manipulative purpose. Though the difficulty of creating a performance might be very real, the experiential character of audience participation, when a performance of fiction is involved, will be less about the un-trammelled 'immersion' in and investigation of a fiction, than it will be about the relationship of the audience participant to the performance task, and the moment to moment imperative to produce something appropriate, to satisfy the demand of the frame (in this it is very much in Goffman's territory), and to act, in both senses of the word. A closer look at this kind of horizon will help to unpack some of the complexity of the situation of being simultaneously audience and performer.

The nascent genre of 'immersive theatre' amounts to only a small corner of audience participatory theatre, and an overlapping category rather than a sub-set; not all immersive theatre is audience participatory (in my terms), and not all audience participation is immersive theatre. But the implications of the term 'immersive' and of the expectations that attach to the performances that earn the name are interesting in relation to the question of accepting invitations to participate. It is the implicit claim of immersive theatre that theatre has an inside to be immersed in. Though we might speak of immersing ourselves in other art works – in novels, films and plays – as a characteristic of a deep and effective involvement, generally something else is meant when a work is called immersive, especially in the emergent immersive theatre.

Pieces that allow audiences some combination of moving independently, exploring an environment, surrounding themselves or being surrounded by the scenography or the performance, or interacting with performers, are likely to be called immersive. The term designates audience experiences of proximity, flexibility and interaction, and regarding the physical experience the term is very appropriate – an audience inhabits and moves through the space of a performance rather than sitting outside it, much as we might move through water rather than floating on top of it. But more than this altered spatial relationship is expected of immersive theatre– both practitioners themselves in their promotional literature and critics who write about the work sometimes suggest that audiences move inside the drama in some way. We are invited to 'join in', to 'be a part of it', to 'take part'. Perhaps this should be read as the hyperbole typical of marketing any kind of leisure experience, but it begs questions about the work of the actor, the nature of dramatic fiction and the process of artistic creation. These are questions that are not to be fully resolved here, but I will attempt a brief outline of the first of the three.

An audience participant who is 'endowed' with a role in a piece of fictional theatre becomes, to some tiny extent at least, an actor. They accept an obligation to support a fictional circumstance, and to present themselves appropriately, to move forward with the fiction and move it forward. This might be a matter of very simple call and response, in which a group of children validate the actions of an actor-character from a fictional point of view, or it could be the negotiation of a complex situation in a piece of Forum Theatre – some levels of fictional framing proposed by Jonothan Neelands were cited in Chapter 2. In immersive theatre this will often be an unprepared, unscripted encounter with a performer within their scenographic environment. If the implication of immersiveness is correct, at this point the audience member is potentially most deeply inside the theatrical event, and inside the drama itself. What kind of inside is available to them at a moment like this? Answering this question is a fairly swift process of elimination: Are they inhabited by or do they inhabit the subjectivity of a fictional character, such that they perceive the events as true? No. Do they gain a thoroughgoing understanding of the fictional circumstance? No. Do they have an emotional insight into the dramatic situation? Maybe. Do they enter into the business of performing a fiction in the same way as the actors do? Again, maybe.

These tentative maybes hint at the potential awkwardness of the encounter between an in-character actor, and an audience participant who is being treated as also in-character. Sophie Nield notes her own embarrassment at being directly addressed by a character in *Reverence*, at the Southwark Playhouse: 'And as I stood there in my not-mediaeval clothes with my not-mediaeval bright green handbag, it occurred to me – who on earth is this monk supposed to think I am?' (2008: 531).

She questions not what the performer is supposed to think – and presumably the performer has some effective supposing rehearsed and ready for this kind of encounter – but what the fictional character is supposed to think, as it is just as much the audience member who has to suppose the mental state of a character as it is the actor. But more than simply confused about how to imagine the relationship between a fictional character and a role of her own conjured up on the spot, she seems troubled by how she is being asked to be present herself at this moment, in the role of spectator, by the kind of investment she is obliged to make at a moment like this.

Discussions of the emotional investment entailed in acting are often framed by the polarity of Diderot's famous essay *The Paradox of Acting*, in which he claims that it is impossible for a great performance to be given when an actor succumbs to 'sensibility', or an emotional involvement in the performance. What is paradoxical is that the appearance of being entirely swept away in the process of performance, of being entirely at one with the role and its moment is one of the most compelling facets of acting in the theatre, but that it is an impossibility; for anyone so carried away, beyond a sense of themselves and their actual circumstances, would not be able to accomplish the essential mechanical business of acting – remembering moves, lines, entrances and exits, maintaining an effective relationship with the audience, and so on. But Diderot's argument is a polemic, and as Martin Welton notes in *Feeling Theatre* (2012) – not necessarily representative of his own views – he says Diderot's text is 'mischievous', when seen in the context of his other writings on theatre (36). Diderot was at other points a 'sentimentalist' himself, an enthusiastic fan of emotional acting. As many have noted since, the nature of acting is somewhere between the poles that Diderot sets up; Henry Irving, in a preface to Diderot, said:

> It is often said that actors should not shed tears, that real tears are bad art. This is not so. If tears be produced at the actor's will and under his control, they are true art; and happy is the actor who numbers them amongst his gifts. (Irving in Diderot 1883: xx)

Actors may be immersed in something, but they are not in a literal sense inside the story of the play. For Welton, they are inside a performance's 'affective ecology', in which feelings are put to work by actors, as an important part of their work, but not in so simple a way as a reproduction of the feelings of the characters they play. Early in his chapter on 'Shows of Feeling', Welton suggests that in a simplified form, the affective ecology has two territories:

> It may appear, at first glance, that there are in fact two species of feeling at stake here; firstly, the experience of empathy of a spectator for a performer, whether they are presenting a character or not, and, secondly, of a performer who wishes to communicate a shared sense of feeling with their spectators. (Welton 2012: 25)

And while he is carefully sidestepping the idea that character-actor-spectator emotions work in a straight line from one to the other, he is highlighting the emotion work done by the professional performer, and the intention to work on the emotions of the spectator. The previous chapter approached facilitation in terms of empathy, from a different perspective, but attention here is on the participant. Their emotional work when in a performance is different of that of the actor, but they would have to be seen as requiring a third species of feeling, one that is very difficult to identify. The idea of emotional work comes from Arlie Hochschild's The *Managed Heart: Commercialization of Human Feeling*, where she describes how increasingly work puts demands on us to have, and to demonstrate that we have, appropriate feelings: to put our emotions to work. The emotional play-time of theatre is something else, but it still requires appropriate emotion work from us, at points.

> For the audience, 'vague flashes of feeling' may perhaps therefore be less to do with a psychological correspondence with either actor or character, and more to do with the opening of a connection to a broader affective ecology or atmosphere that is moved by them. (Welton 2012: 49–50)

The lack of correspondence, recognised here in (presumably) conventional audience arrangements, is perhaps even more evident when the empathy invoked between the two roles is not a vicarious engagement of one in the performed experiences of the other. But what the broader affective ecology is, is more difficult to chart. Actors are affective workers, and participants are not, in that they are not implicated in the economy of feeling in the same way; but nevertheless there is an economy of feeling at work, where their feelings matter.

While the paradox itself might be pressingly relevant to participants in immersive theatre, for other participants, the job of the actor is relevant in other ways. Acting is the task of maintaining a fiction. Modern methods of acting have also adopted techniques that use tasks at a moment-by-moment level to achieve this larger task more effectively. In Stanislavskian 'objectives' for example, the proposition is that if an actor engages in a task sincerely, especially one that involves goal-based interaction with other actors, they will be more convincing to an audience. Audience participants' tasks will be diverse, and may involve maintaining a fiction. But conceiving a horizon of participation will entail perceiving tasks, targets, goals or aims of some kind. A role defined by a frame, as conceived by Goffman, entails at least one key task: maintaining the integrity of the frame.

## Experiential learning

The experience of a fictional horizon can be understood a little better, initially, through the ideas of experiential learning, which has special manifestations in educational drama. As Neelands (1992: 6) says:

> Learning in drama results from facing the challenge of behaving realistically in a fictional situation and then being pressed by the circumstances of the fiction, as it unfolds, into finding and using appropriate vocal and active responses. It is this 'realness' of drama, in which role-players give and receive (write and read) each other's messages simultaneously, which makes drama a unique form of literacy. In conventional reading and writing activity, fictional situations are unalterable, recorded and described; students are either fixed in the role of spectator, observer or reader, or in the role of writer. In drama the same fictions are entered into and lived as a 'here and now' experience.

There are a number of echoes in this with the phenomenology of accepting an invitation to audience participation: there is the challenge of behaving appropriately; there is being pressed by circumstances as they unfold to give vocal and active responses; and there is the giving and receiving (writing and reading) of messages simultaneously. For Neelands it is the ability to enter fictional situations that is important, to treat them as if they are 'here and now', which makes educational drama so effective, rather than the challenging, pressing and giving responses. Fiction is often a factor in audience participation for adults or children, adding much the same potential for experiential learning as it would to classroom drama, but my proposal is that in audience participation demands are made in the simultaneity of performance and reception that comes with accepting an invitation and being a participant. The 'here and now' of audience participation is often complex, sometimes cripplingly so.

In classroom drama young people are given opportunities to sample experiences from other times and places, or to try out behaviour that would normally be unacceptable or risky. The focus is within the fiction not outside it with an audience, and for audience participants this can be more difficult to achieve, needing a careful procedural authorship to create a horizon of participation that downplays the importance of presentation. But participants can become invested in responding to the demands of a fiction rather than in putting on a good show. Participation in a fictional horizon will not entirely lose the benefit of experientiality as it continues to allow participants to have ownership of the events that take place in the drama. Participants who commit to the situation have more chance of surprising themselves, and of creating unique events that have grown out of their choices. A role-play that has been submitted to is a situation in which actions proceed and have consequences within the imagined world itself; the participants play their role concerned with what will happen within this imagined world, and not with the world that watches it from the outside. Committing to the situation allows the events within it to matter, and therefore to become meaningful. In the previous chapter I have accounted for some ways in which participants can 'lose themselves' in performance, and a thoroughgoing commitment to a fiction might suggest another kind of loss of self, in something like the kind of acting ridiculed by Diderot. But what is at issue here is not the kind of emotional labour needed to convince or capture the imagination of an audience, but whether and how engagement with a fictional situation is interrupted by self-consciousness.

Drama therapy is another field of practice where participatory practice is the norm, and the emphasis is almost exclusively on process rather than performance. Phil Jones, like Neelands, is concerned that the drama work puts demands on participants, but unlike Neelands he derives one of these demands from an audience function. Responding to Peter Brook's famous formulation that the most basic criteria of theatre is the meeting of an actor and a watcher Jones argues:

> against Brook proposing that the function of the audience, or witnessing, is present and crucial within Drama therapy group work, but

that it manifests itself differently and has a different function than it does in theatre. I would not say that Dramatherapy, by remaining in a closed group situation, misses the 'heat' of the central encounter, which he assigns to be the essence of theatre. Rather I would argue that it is present in a number of ways, and provides an important function in the Dramatherapeutic effect and the work of therapeutic change within a group. (Jones 1996: 110)

He uses the idea of witnessing in place of the separation of spectator/ performer roles. In dramatherapy:

- the client can function as a witness or audience to others work,
- the client can become a witness to themselves: for example by the use of doubling or role reversal, or by use of objects to represent aspects of themselves
- the client can develop the 'audience' as part of themselves towards their experience, enhancing the capabilities to engage differently with themselves and life events
- the experience of being witnessed within a dramatherapy session can be experienced as being acknowledged or supported;
- the projection of aspects of themselves or aspects of their experience on to others who are in an audience role (i.e. other group members or the drama therapist) can help the therapeutic process by enabling the client to express problematic material. (Jones 1996: 111)

Thus, there are many, possibly simultaneous, ways of witnessing, or being an audience to, dramatherapy work, and they could be applied to the reflexive reception of audience participation. These are different ways of viewing the material of experiential learning, but in the second, third and fourth point, Jones suggests how the facts of watching oneself and putting oneself on display become meaningful in another way, because they are performances appropriate to the person performing in some way. In these cases there is a real consequentiality connected to the action, hopefully a positive one, but in a therapeutic situation requiring care that traumatic experiences are not magnified or reinforced. This is a return to the problem of risk and the perception of risk, but now considering the consequentiality of the performance as important as an experience, as well as for its utilitarian effects on self-presentation. These effects are important outside the therapeutic or 'applied' performance field, they can be used to create challenging experiences for spectators at public performances. In Felix Ruckert's *Hautnah*:

> 'Do you know what I like most of all?' cooed Freund in my ear as she leaned her body over mine and suddenly the lack of comfort in my head was made flesh – should I respond? Was I expected to simply sit back and watch without responding? Had I suddenly become a participant in a new 'contact' improvisation? Was this still concert 'dance' or had it suddenly become a more traditional partner dance? She danced very close, teasing me for an answer, and I gave up – 'No, I don't know,' I stammered out.
>
> 'Dead animals,' she told me and dropped to the floor. (Kattwinkel 2003: 6)

The experience of interpreting this overt, but ambiguous, invitation is troublesome for this participant. The performance that is being offered as a resource has sexual implications, it seems to refer to other dances where women offer themselves to men, but also to 'traditional' partner dances. The participant feels the heat, and the challenge of the situation, and is embarrassed to witness himself within an image of the sexual-financial economy of the table-dancer.

## Reflexivity and witnessing

The 'meaningfulness' – the *amount* of meaning – of the performance itself is not necessarily dependent upon the freedom of the participant to create it: it is possible for a restrictive procedure to suggest and produce very important performances, and for a broad and open horizon to suggest and produce banal or superficial ones: as I have indicated, when Kay creates a very open horizon in his smaller-scale shows, the performances can seem to say very little, when he closely directs audience-performances at Glastonbury Festival, he produces satire. Nevertheless, the experience of making choices (within whatever horizon) is meaningful in itself, and can enhance the meaning of an event. Producing performances that are both free and meaningful requires a synergy of intention and effort, of the willingness of the procedural author to open up to the unpredictable, and of the participant to be bold and take risks in a performance. This is both how audience participation can do harm, and how it can become important.

Agency in this model of audience participation is the faculty of both being productive in relation to the determinations and opportunities of the horizon of participation, and of being active in controlling performatives relating to a public self. This agency also represents a kind of authorship, in that the actions produced become performances. The authors of an action are both the participant and the procedural author, but also – if context is as important as it seems to be – the society which determines citational probabilities. All authorship and all performance is citational in the way it draws on shared resources, but audience participation cites and draws attention especially to the 'self', to the person performing. It is in the citationality of audience participation that we find a way into a particular dimension of its meaning. Just like other kinds of authorship, the authorship of the participant has to be relativised: it is fundamentally contextual, rather than a matter of entirely individual initiative or agency, but though the work of these performances does not result from a singular subject, it might seem to constitute such a 'motivating identity' and in fact it will certainly be perceived as doing so in many cases.

The riskiness of participation is intimately connected with this. Whatever the meanings of the performances given, their performative values, they are experienced as a step into public performance by the participant. Though there is not necessarily a directly proportional relationship between risk and agency, there are connections between the perception of the investment of the self in a performance and its apparent risk. This might be because a participant feels un-invested and out of control, or it may be because they have invested significantly in and have agency in a performance, and fear it will reflect on them. This amounts to a kind of presence in the work, a recognition that it has reality for the individual, it is not remote. The management of risk, as we have seen, is a significant factor in audience participatory procedures, and it arises as a result of performativity, and of the possibility of misplaced performatives that reflect badly on the performer.

I have discussed how Forum Theatre has a message that is implied in its form, and how practitioners, such as Armadillo Theatre, communicate through the shape of their procedures as well as through the performances given by their actors and participants. This is true of conventional forms too, as Boal's 'Aristotle's Coercive System of Tragedy' and McGrath's *A Good Night Out*, for example, show. But in audience participation it is very difficult for this form to be invisible – we will pay close attention to the work that is done to make us participate, so that we will always be aware of our presence in the event, the way that the performers relate to us, and the differences between the participatory frame and the others in which we spend our time.

Audience participation in this sense is always metatheatrical. This is another way of finding a failing in the Armadillo Theatre workshop described at the end of Chapter 1 – the message of the form – that the students could be tricked into making poor decisions – conflicted with the message of most of their interactions – that the students had made a commitment to stopping bullying in their schools. It is also a way of seeing success in Kay's work – the unsatisfying nature of the performances draws attention to our inability to free ourselves both in the performance and in our everyday lives. Procedures of audience participation can be designed to accentuate the experiential or the performative, to play up or play down self-consciousness. The sense of reflexivity, of possible performances that will draw attention to the social self of the participant, will be a significant part of the 'weather' of the horizon.

In Punchdrunk's environmental productions (for example *The Tempest*, *Speak No More* (based on *Macbeth*), *The Masque of the Red Death*) the audience are masked and despatched separately into the derelict buildings that house the performances. Following familiar characters around, interacting with them, watching them perform scenes from the plays, and exploring their environments, spectators remain anonymous, and partially invisible. Wearing identical canvas hoods with blank plastic masks sewn in, it is easy for spectators to disattend crowds of people gathering around a scene, or alternatively to stand and watch a scene alone. When characters addressed spectators – for example, Lady Macbeth, in her madder moments, would grab people and run through corridors with them, whispering and shouting – they respond less self-consciously, hidden behind the mask, than they might if openly visible to an audience. It is possible, with these masks on, to identify people by their clothing, but communication with them is inhibited by the lack of visible facial expression and the muffling of the voice. Entering the event alone also frames the work as a solitary experience, and makes it more difficult to begin to interact with friends – it is necessary first to find them in the maze-like environment. An audience is prevented from doing what they would in another promenade performance: looking at each others' faces for reactions to the play, and laughing together with nervousness when approached by performers. The result is that a crowd does not form to the same degree, instead a string of – literally, in this case – faceless strangers mill around, each having very individual experiences. Even when a character interacts with a spectator – the actor has to do an even greater part of the work than in other actor to audience interactions, as the spectator is so restricted by the mask. The participant is hidden from view, becomes a part of the performance, but with their identity hidden far more deliberately than is usually the case through the framing devices of a participatory procedure. The process of putting participants on display is interrupted, so that a participatory performance can take place with a much more exclusive emphasis on the experiential. At times this experientiality becomes an experience of pure gaze, like the spectatorship of conventional theatre but with more voyeuristic privileges. The small eyeholes in the mask exaggerate the directedness and the disembodied feel of the gaze. We can detach ourselves from the crowd and wander, or we can engage, with a peculiar sense of licence, flirting with or stalking characters, playing at being there, while feeling that we are not. Where, in for example *Woyzeck*, Punchdrunk have constructed similar environments and set performances in them, but not given the audience masks to wear, the audience's behaviour is quite different – we speak to each other and to the characters in a very different way, with far more self-conscious laughter, and tend to spend more time talking to each other about the scenes they see. The experience is less immersive, and more self-conscious.

In other cases, rather than attempting to isolate either the experiential or the performative, one is made to inform on the other, as for example in Annie Sprinkle's 'Post Porn Modernism' (see Jones and Warr 2000: 110), in which the audience queued to inspect her cervix, and she masturbated, in the presence of a theatre full of spectators. 'In the presence of' is an important point here, these are private acts and private parts, being shared as they would in pornography, but without the anonymity that the consumer of pornography usually insists on, and with the female performer resolutely in control. Queuing to peer closely at Sprinkle's sexual organs is an experience of physical proximity and openness, but it is also an implication in a transgressive act, a demonstration of willingness to transgress, a public embarrassment, and unavoidable cause for self-examination. The transgressive and intrusive aspect of this action is magnified by its public performativity.

Paul Heritage finds Etchells' idea of witnessing apposite to a quite different context –writing about the performance of extracts from Romeo and Juliet in a juvenile prison in Brazil, he notices how the spectator becomes

> a witness of something that can only be played by those people that are in that room and that particular time. And because of this, the call that performance makes is to feel the weight of things and one's own place in them. (Heritage in Delgado and Svitch 2002: 168)

Here the issues are weighty for those performing and for those who watch – fellow inmates, service professionals, other young people who have avoided the fate of those incarcerated. Their presence in the context of the performance is enhanced by its presentational qualities. The young prisoner is inescapably visible in Romeo (as the television star is visible in the figure of Juliet). Where the performers in Forced Entertainment playfully work at the borders of their own selves, both exposing and disguising the mechanics of their artistic process, the performers in Heritage's *Romeo and Juliet* cannot help, try as they might to hide behind Shakespeare's characters, remaining present and exposed as their everyday selves. That, in these conditions, they can commit themselves to the public process is what makes this work more than an exercise in literacy.

> It is in that investment that we see the real consequences of performance that lie beyond the meaning of the play itself. Is that the moment when we are drawn to become witnesses? When the line between the performer and the task becomes so strong that we cannot resist being pushed or dragged out of our desire to be merely spectators and become the witnesses that will ensure this event has a life beyond that moment? (Heritage in Delgado and Svitch 2002: 188)

Heritage is writing about the culmination of a workshop process, not audience participation, but the features he and Etchells are noting are powerfully present in most, not just some, audience participation. Identification between spectator and participant, and the pressure on the participant to perform well are much like the 'direct lines' that Etchells seeks. Though much audience participation takes place in applied theatre, and seeks either efficacy (direct and recognisable consequences) or empowerment (development of confidence or skills), via direct lines of empathy, identification or experiential learning, these direct lines between audience participants and other spectators, exist under the surface of all audience participation. They are a formal property that audience participation brings to any style of performance, potentially allowing it to have power beyond itself because of this formal character rather than the content of its representations.

This is, then, part of the phenomenology of audience participation: the complexity of reading our own performances and their potential consequences, in conditions that are not of our making. The horizon in which we operate may derive from the resources we bring to the interactive frame of the performance, but only so far as those resources overlap with what the procedure of participation itself offers. Our inhabiting and exploring this horizon is free and flexible only so far as other participants and facilitating performers allow. The concept of informed consent was discussed briefly in Chapter 2, and here we see a mutated version of it: the audience participant who is self-aware (or self-conscious) enough to monitor how they are manipulated in the course of a procedure of audience participation may be crippled with indecision or anxiety and unable to contribute anything they would reflect on as worthwhile or a good representation of themselves. This kind of conflict can be as important to people's reluctance to participate as the straightforward risk of public embarrassment. The complexity of the audience-performer role is a threat as well as an opportunity for learning and deep experience.

## Self-awareness and self-forgetfulness

Daphna Ben Chaim's *Distance in the Theatre: the Aesthetics of Audience Response* (1981) shows how important experiments in the actor–audience relationship were to the evolution of twentieth century theatre. She charts how key figures – Brecht, Artaud and Grotowski – theorised and practiced varying degrees of psychological distance, inflected by their different attitudes to empathy and the value of involvement in dramatic fiction. She also draws attention to the dependence of this process on other, everyday, phenomena, like self-awareness:

> It should also be noted, as something clearly implicit in this concept, that distance is neither simply an on/off condition nor exclusively one of degrees but both: self-awareness for instance, either exists or does not, but the self-awareness may be induced to a greater or lesser degree. (Ben Chaim 1981: 76)

Ben Chaim is here discussing the self-awareness of the audience member, as a capacity that could be manipulated by the theatre maker, as proposed by Brecht. But from a different perspective perhaps, the self-awareness of the audience participant can be worked with. This is something different to the Brechtian proposition – that empathy and self-forgetfulness is the norm in theatre, and something to be done away with in the interests of a thoughtful and active response. As we have already seen, to make a participant forgetful of self requires much work.

Before returning to this theme, I will give some more attention to some problematics brought about by self-awareness when encountering theatrical characters – and the actors playing them. As Bert States puts it:

> Even the most unsophisticated theatregoer can detect something else in the characterisation, a superconsciousness that could be nothing other than the actor's awareness of his own self-sufficiency as he moves between the contradictory zones of the illusionary and the real, *vraisemblance* and *vrai*, seeming and being – between Hamlet and what of himself he has allowed to be displayed as Hamlet. (States 1985: 125)

The reality of the actor, as opposed to the character, is 'weakly described' (154), he says. The situation requires us – normally without too great a difficulty – to hold both of these things in our attention at once. Stanton Garner calls this a 'rival phenomenality', where the stage space discloses itself in layers, because we are able to hold these different modes in attention simultaneously. But it can get into trouble if the actors, in acknowledging the presence of the audience, muddle the separation of the two modes:

> This rival phenomenality, of course, exists within the overall act of theatrical display; in the layering and involvement of orientations, the stage, one might say, discloses itself in the mode of for-the-actor-under-the-gaze. But the authorising power of the audience's spectatorship does not eliminate the disruptive potential of the performer's own gaze or its destabilising operations within and upon the field of performance. (Garner 1994: 47)

When an actor, in character, looks directly at a spectator, this gaze – and the intersubjective response to it – can bring the presence of the actor strongly into awareness. Often this is absorbed into the complex of effects and affects of the theatrical moment, skilfully or fortuitously enhancing the experience of the actor's virtuosity, (as with Escolme's response to Mark Rylance's Hamlet, quoted in Chapter 2). I have earlier described this as a kind of intertextuality, treating the everyday 'real' persona and the performed persona of the actor as two related texts, but States' and Garner's attention is on this awareness as phenomenology, as something that is disclosed to our awareness. Intersubjectively, empathically and intercorporeally, we experience the performer, much as Fuchs and De Jaegher say that tennis players are aware of each other, experiencing their intentionality, their directedness towards the stage world, as the intentionality of the character in the dramatic setting. At the same time we are aware of their intentionality towards us as an audience, we experience their directedness towards us, and we enjoy and celebrate it. But a direct gaze can bring to consciousness more strongly – as many other surprises, interruptions or realisations might – that the body we are thus aware of is also that of an actor doing their job, directed towards the staged world and the gathered audience through a different sort of intentionality, that of a rehearsed set of actions and interactions.

But what does this duality bring to watching *participants*, as opposed to rehearsed actors? Can the authorising power of the spectatorial gaze, as Garner puts it, transform the participant into a body that we see wholeheartedly according to the rules of the staged moment? States observes that there are some kinds of performer that bring out the sense of their 'real' being more easily, animal performers particularly, but also child actors: 'Who has ever seen a child on stage without thinking "how well he acts, for a child!"' (States 1985: 31); while Nicholas Ridout, in *Stage Fright, Animals and Other Theatrical Problems* (2006) observes how these aberrant performers and performances draw attention to the nature of labour in theatre. Audiences are likely to have similar thoughts about an audience participant: 'how well he acts, for a volunteer'. Or of course something different with the same premise: 'he's not very good, but only a volunteer after all'.

This 'discrepant play of actualities' (Garner 1994: 47) only occasionally causes problems for the theatre spectator, and more often complements the peculiar pleasures of live performance; it might do so more often for the spectator of audience participation who has to make allowances. But what about the discrepancies that arise out of watching a performance while actually giving it oneself? Of course we do not actually watch these performances, or only peripherally when we do. We experience them bodily. So to unpick this we need to look more closely at embodied experience in itself, and in particular how we experience our own 'self'. This is, clearly, a complex business and a substantial field of enquiry in different fields, including psychology, neuroscience and the philosophy of mind. I shall develop some threads introduced in the previous chapter, from contemporary cognitively oriented phenomenology.

Some of the 'enactive' characteristics of first-person experience were discussed in the previous chapter, including its intentional character. Intentionality is fundamental to the sense of self, too, in that it is possible to identify a self only because of directedness towards the world. As Dan Zahavi puts it:

> Life is, as Heidegger said, world-related; it is always already living in the world and does not have to seek it out. My self is present when

I am worldly engaged; it is exactly to be found 'out there'. (Zahavi 2005: 82)

It is not that we have experiences, and afterwards attribute them to a self that is a feature of these experiences, but that the point of engagement with the world is the point of origin of both experience and the perception of being a self that can have experiences. It is possible to misidentify one of these experiences, but not possible, (it is generally accepted) to misidentify the subjectivity that is having the experience. This is a notion of self and experience at a very basic level; the social processes that produce a self (and self-understanding) of a particular, historically situated kind, or through which we narrate our sense of self, are numerous. Gallagher notes two aspects of this minimal sense of self:

> Sense of self-agency (SA): The pre-reflective experience that I am the one who is causing or generating a movement or action or thought process.
> Sense of self-ownership (SO): The pre-reflective experience that I am the one who is moving or undergoing an experience. (Gallagher 2012: 132)

To the phenomenologist, this is at the heart of what it is to have subjectivity. These are pre-reflective experiences because they occur without the need to go looking for them; to have an experience is for something to happen to us, or to cause or generate something to happen. The experiences of audience participation will move between these two modes.

When in Zecora Ura's *Hotel Medea* I put on pyjamas and get into a bunk bed, drink hot chocolate and cuddle the toy that has been given to me, I have a sense of self-agency; I experience myself causing these events. I also have self-ownership, as these things happen to me, even as I play a part in causing them to happen. When, in the same sequence, a performer tucks the bedclothes more tightly around me, or later in the performance I am pulled into motion by another participant to run away from Medea, I have only a sense of self-ownership; these things happen to me without, in this moment, my having initiated them. Most of the discussion of this book has been about the social and cognitive origin and structure of self-agency, and little has been said about the kinds of events that are experienced as only self-owned. Both of these modes of experience are intentional, we are directed towards them; in the above example I am unhappy about being tucked tightly into the bed because I would rather be watching Medea and Jason arguing in another part of the room; I feel surprise as the initiative of the other participant, led by a performer, jolts me into motion. Intentionality gives the moment and its action a quality.

At the most basic level, this is what it is to experience ourselves giving a performance, to 'watch' our performance as audience participants. And it gives some insight into what is involved when the complexity of the situation is taken into account. The horizon of participation contains social and physical affordances that draw action out of us, we choose our path from the landscape of opportunities presented to us, but we do so on the basis of the activity that is made available and called forth by this landscape. The experience of perceiving and accepting an invitation is, at basis, an experience of self-agency, but it will often contain moments when an intuition occurs that a route has been pre-planned for us, that our actions have been pre-conceived. At moments like this self-agency is inflected with something different, with a feeling that it is diluted, an intentionality based on an awareness of another's influence in shaping our actions.

When I am offered a cup of hot chocolate by an actor playing a nursemaid, I am intersubjectively involved with her to the extent that I respond carefully to her offering of the hot cup, and with an expression of my pleased surprise. These responses to the simple social affordance of her offering of the cup are also informed by my awareness of her role in the fiction, and my willingness to engage with her as a nursemaid, sooner or later adopting something of the status-role appropriate to the child that she has cast me as. But once I begin to understand that something more complex – and interesting – has been engineered, my intentionality towards this situation changes. As I realise that the role of 'child at bedtime' conflicts with my desire (and my role as audience member) to watch the dialogue between Medea and Jason, and that this conflict has been designed into the scene, my attitude towards the event changes. I become aware of the designed sequence of events – the procedural authorship – as another intersubjective presence that I can cooperate with or resist; my horizon of participation takes on different 'weather', or mood, and I view its opportunities differently. The self-agency of each moment loses something of its pre-reflective character, as the realisation of an overseeing subjectivity makes me reflect upon my choices.

Of course I have portrayed the initial level of intersubjective engagement with the invitation as having a very innocent character, as if it is not normally inflected with an awareness of manipulation. It is likely that at many if not most moments of invitation and during participatory interaction, there will be an awareness of the oddness of the situation, of a controlling intelligence beyond the action at hand, and a level of suspicion about its motives and what might ensue. Much of the time we might respond to an invitation, or experience our own self-agency, with an intentionality based on uncertainty – 'why should I do this?', 'what am I supposed to do?', 'who am I supposed to be?'. This is analogous to the gaze of the actor turning towards us, as observed by Garner, and the peculiarity of our own presence in the situation being brought to mind. In the case of participatory performance, this aware-ness leads to the pre-reflective basis of self-agency being supplemented by a reflexive awareness of our agency in negotiation with other forces, both those that are present and embodied by performers, and those that are intuited as belonging to the authorship of the procedure as a whole. This level of self-awareness can be a threat to participation, though also potentially an opportunity. It corresponds to the embarrassment felt by Ridout when addressed directly by a performer, and by Nield when she is required to play the character of 'spectator',[1] and might undermine both the quality of the experience and the inclination of the participant to respond. But this kind of puzzlement might also be a productive element of a procedure of participation, as it was in my experience of *Hotel Medea*. Participants may engage with just this 'ontological' ques-tion with a playfulness and adventure that enhances their experience. Some people find it fun, to not know who they are meant to be, and what they are meant to do, for a while; puzzles are, after all, a form of entertainment.

I would maintain that the 'innocent' level of participation, char-acterised by a straightforward experiential self-agency, is entirely possible. A person can respond openly and straightforwardly to an invitation, if their prior experience and habitus equip them with the appropriate resources, and their awareness of other agencies does not intrude too strongly. But there are other potential complications of the first-person perspective, when we consider the group processes described in the last chapter. The liminal state, which is described as a loss of constraining social status, suggests a heightened sense of self-agency as the possibilities for action are vastly extended. Or conversely the loss of definition of the sense of self associated with a state of communitas, or of crowd involvement, or of hypnosis, can be interpreted as a loss of self-agency, and an awareness only of self-ownership as initiative over action seems to originate elsewhere. There is a different sense of self-forgetfulness suggested in Gadamer's *Truth and Method*, in which an encounter with a work of art is thought of as giving oneself over, to be played by the work, rather than to have control over it:

> being outside oneself is the positive possibility of being wholly with something else. This kind of being present is a self-forgetfulness, and to be a spectator consists in giving oneself in self-forgetfulness to what one is watching. Here self-forgetfulness is anything but a private condition, for it arises from devoting one's full attention to the matter at hand, and this is the spectator's own positive accomplishment. (Gadamer 2004: 122)

Though Gadamer uses the word 'participation' at points to describe this phenomenon, he is concerned with how the apparently passive spectator – in a conventional relationship with a work of art – is in fact actively involved in this very positive surrender to the agency of the work as an event of play. Like many other ontologies of art, there is a value judgement to this: a work of art should achieve this, to qualify as such. I prefer to use it descriptively, as a potential for participatory involvement, where by surrender to the process of participation, one is played by it, and becomes something different because of it, a change that is available to reflection after the event. The irony of this is that this 'giving over' of oneself can also be seen as a kind of passivity, as a loss of agency in the midst of the event, in order to achieve its most powerful effects.

## Autopoiesis, allopoiesis, heteropoiesis

Gadamer's self-forgetful experience of an art work corresponds to the autopoiesis of performance, in Fischer-Lichte's thinking, to an emergent process that is separate from its experience, meaning and understanding, as perceived by the audience or participant. Her language makes this distinction clear, for example:

> The process of generating meaning in a performance reveals a number of significant similarities to the autopoietic feedback loop. As much as the individual participant co-determines the course of the performance and is in turn determined by it, so the perceiving subject undergoes a similar experience in its individual generation of meaning. (2008: 155)

She is quite clear that understanding, in particular, is only partly possible, and only in retrospect. The experientiality of the participant, and the moment-to-moment meaning they derive from it, she sees as contributing to the emergence of the performance, as they drive the participants' activity and contribution to the feedback loop. But a 'hermeneutic' process of interpretation she sees as of marginal importance, and the pursuit of an overall coherent understanding as a 'sisyphian task' (2008: 157). Treating these things as extrinsic to performance as autopoiesis is consistent with the strict sense of the term in cellular biology. We might look upon audiences, participants and performers as part of the environment of the autopoietic system, as with the self-sustaining process of a cell, which is: 'a thermodynamically open system, continually exchanging matter and energy with its environment' (Thompson 2010: 98). In this sense performance – as an autonomous system – continually exchanges resources with the people that contribute and respond to it.

We can see 'allopoietic' (Thompson 2008: 98) aspects of performance, where it creates things other than itself, when it creates meanings and understandings (however incomplete) that audience members take away with them; and we can see 'heteropoietic' aspects when thinking of how performance is designed and produced from outside itself, when thinking of what performance makers create and rehearse, and what is designed by a procedural author. Most thinking and writing about performance, perhaps, is concerned with the allopoietic and the heteropoietic. But awareness of performance in its autopoietic aspect is useful, especially when looking at audience participatory performance. What it is in danger of neglecting, is that for the experiencing subject performance is always also heteropoietic, having elements devised elsewhere and introduced to us, and always also allopoietic, having elements which we will take away with us and reflect upon.

The kinds of self-awareness I have discussed in this chapter contribute to both the autopoietic aspect and the allopoietic. Self-awareness can interrupt, influence or encourage input into a feedback loop. And it can be a significant part of what a person takes away from a performance, when it is retrospectively treated as a work (or event) of art. I also propose that attention to self-consciousness, in combination with attention to agency, is the key characteristic of the heteropoiesis of procedural authorship – in other words, that these are the distinctive elements of which designing and preparing for audience participation consist.

## Tim Crouch: *The Author* and *I, Malvolio*

This is a play where the actors sit among the audience, wearing their own clothes, called by their own names; where players, audience and author are lit by the same light, scrutinised by the same gaze. This is a play during which audience members have read newspapers and novels, built paper aeroplanes, performed Mexican waves, sung happy birthday to one of their own, recited poetry, slow handclapped, physically threatened actors, hummed out loud with their fingers in their ears, muttered obscenities, shouted actors down, and thrown copies of the text at the playwright. (Crouch 2011)

Thus, Tim Crouch reflects on the reception of his play, *The Author*, in which he performs as a character called Tim Crouch, who has written a controversial play with unhappy consequences for playwright, performers and at least one member of the audience. The play constructs a sophisticated relationship between performers and audience, often provoking unusual audience activity, but none of the behaviour he describes is directly invited by the play or the performers. It seems on the surface to have been a collection of uninvited gestures of resistance to the play, its content and its strategy of implicating them in the violence described (but not shown) in the play, and the culture of voyeurism it portrays. The play has received a great deal of critical attention – including a special edition of the journal *Contemporary Theatre Review*, as well as finding some notoriety. Though I will make use of some of the detailed exegesis that has built up around it to exercise some of the propositions of this chapter, I will give as much space to one of Crouch's other plays, *I, Malvolio*, which has had much less attention. *I, Malvolio* is a one-person show, again up to now performed by Crouch himself; it was commissioned by the Brighton Festival, initially for school-aged audiences. In this play there is directly invited audience participation, but not on the same scale as in the longer examples of my earlier chapters. I want, at this point, to show how brief moments of participation can play a significant part in framing audience experience of an event, as well as to explore how Crouch's strategy of metatheatrical implication – which is at work in both of these plays, in different ways – makes use of audience activity, and of the reflexive self-awareness peculiar to participatory performance.

Explicit invitations for verbal audience participation are made throughout *The Author*, but though the form of words used remains much the same, the horizon of participation offered changes drastically as the play goes on. Its opening sequence is conversational, and creates easygoing exchanges between an actor and several audience members, but it progresses so that later direct questioning is much less likely to draw responses. But while structured and invited participation fades out of the performance, the intensity of involvement, and implication, of audiences evidently increases, sometimes leading to the kind of interventions described by Crouch above.

At the start of the play 'Chris',[2] appearing as an audience member, speaks directly to the spectators sitting around him, describing his anticipation of the performance, asking names and complementing people, and sometimes drawing them into exchanges. A note in the published text describes the appropriate tone:

> There should be plenty of warm, open space in the play. The audience should be beautifully lit and cared for. When the audience is asked questions, these are direct questions that the audience are more than welcome to answer – but under no pressure to do so. (Crouch 2010: 18)

But despite this warmth there is discomfort in this relationship from the start, partly deriving from the lack of articulation of what the role of the audience will be in the performance, and partly from Chris's oversolicitous attention: 'What's your name? That's beautiful. You're beautiful! Isn't ___ beautiful? Everyone? I'll shut up. I'll stop.' (Crouch 2010: 19) The intensity builds until his 'YOU FUCKING SAY SOMETHING!!!' (23) is unlikely to draw a response. The other characters, who begin to speak only after Chris's opening conversation has reached this climax, also speak directly to the audience, only occasionally explicitly addressing each other. When they ask questions they are more likely to be interpreted as rhetorical: 'Is this okay? Is it okay if I carry on?' (24), or 'Would you like me to sing for you? Would you?' (29), though the questions are often repeated to encourage an answer.

The story told by the characters is of the impact of a play depicting sexual violence, and the research and rehearsal process in which they visit conflict zones and watch videos of the murder of hostages. The descriptions of violence are brief, though graphic, and it may be that the lack of performed violence exaggerates the audience's complicity in the use of such material as a shock tactic in the theatre: we must either allow ourselves to imagine what is described, or actively attempt not to. The effect might be further enhanced by the variations on 'Is this okay?' offered throughout the play. Each of the characters is damaged in some way by the process, but though Chris, the audience member, is physically hurt in an assault by a traumatised performer, it is the practitioners who suffer the most lasting damage; it seems that the theatre as anything but a 'safe space' from which to observe life, but more hazardous for its professionals than for audiences.

The effect is intensely reflexive and metatheatrical, as the play appears to critique theatre as an institution that is parasitic on real-life suffering, while at the same time exploiting its power to bring such suffering to life for audiences, and though this is only achieved through speech, its effect as provocation seems not to be undermined. Audience members are given a prominent role in the dramaturgy, through Chris as their representative, through their initial conversational contributions, and through the frequent textual appropriations of their approval for the continuance of the performance. And Crouch the author-performer appears as Crouch the author-character, defending the theatre's right and duty to shock and to bring the violence of the world into plain sight, and ultimately confessing to an indefensible secret indulgence in voyeuristic abuse.

As a procedure of audience participation it is unusual, generally moving from small contributions to none at all. The participation it is concerned with is really the wider issue of an audience's participation and complicity in the culture of theatre, and its potential excesses. But it is a procedure of participation, both in the way it deploys small amounts of participation to enhance its effect on most audiences, and in how it occasionally provokes performances of protest. Early in the play, the stage directions read: *'An audience member in the middle of a block gets up and leaves. They are helped to leave by an usher.'* (Crouch 2010: 22) This staging of one of the options available to audience members has often not been the only walk-out; it gives permission for one of the few acts of spectatorial disapproval conventionally allowed, helping some to take this choice for themselves. This apparently masochistic licensing of the audience to leave the show provides some immunity to accusations of manipulation: if people are clearly able to leave, then those who stay, and are made uncomfortable, have brought it upon themselves, perhaps. But the resistant performances listed by Crouch show that many people have wanted to stay, but also to demonstrate their discomfort (by humming and covering their ears), their disapproval (by slow hand-clapping), their boredom (by reading, or being mischievous with each other), or their anger (by threatening the performers). Returning to the typology of Chapter 1 we might call this uninvited participation, but clearly it is of a peculiar kind, where what is uninvited is partly expected, and mostly tolerated.

My own experience of the play was comparatively uneventful. The audience were predominantly attending as part of a symposium on the play,[3] and so likely to be both forewarned about its style and content, and as theatre students or academics not easily provoked. The collective horizon of participation was shaped by this well-schooled understanding of the games that can be played with audiences, and its 'weather' inflected by a cool tolerance. I felt a similar response to that created by Ontreorend Goed's *The Audience*: self-awareness in respect of my implication in a performance that at times felt cynical, combined with a sense that whatever I might do in response – invited or uninvited – had been anticipated in advance, and would be absorbed into the event.

*I, Malvolio* also implicates its audience and satirises theatre spectatorship, but in a much gentler way. In it Crouch plays the character:

> like a 1950's ex-military man in some undignified postwar job, trying to discipline a crowd of neds who laugh at him behind his back. And the audience recognise the character too – gone from the range of figures we are urged to respect, but still deeply present in a life-denying corner of our psyches. (McMillan 2011)

He starts the play as if just emerged from imprisonment, at the end of the plot of *Twelfth Night*, filthy, with horns on his head and a turkey wattle under his chin, and a sign saying 'turkey cock' pinned to his back. He speaks directly to the audience throughout, in some passages recounting the plot of Shakespeare's play with Malvolio's sense of the depravity of its events. But most of the text and action is concerned with his self-justification, framed by the accusation that all of the audience are as corrupt, lazy and cruel as his persecutors in Illyria. The extended and intricate rants against the crowd are partly very plausible, in the context of a piece of young people's theatre: he berates us for dropping gum, wrappers and chicken bones, for skipping church and prayer, for having scuffed shoes and top buttons undone, and for laughing behind his back; they are also peppered with the obsessions of a seventeenth century puritan, a disgust with sex, drink and indulgence, and he associates the theatre with all of these ills.

Although Malvolio takes himself entirely seriously, Crouch's text and performance engineer streams of laughter, further motivating the character's fury and despair. There is much basic visual comedy: when he turns his back and bends to pick up Olivia's letter, holes in his stained long underwear reveal a bare bum; the 'turkey cock' sign is removed by an audience member to reveal another reading 'kick me'. The verbal excess also leads to bathos and toilet humour:

> So Toby Belch, my lady's uncle, exploiting weakness in his grieving niece, enters my lady's house, treats it like a hotel, dances a caper and,

like a wild animal, for all I know, poisons the ornamental fish pond,
puts washing powder in the fountain, sticks a traffic cone on the head
of the statue of the old count my master, defecates on the lawn.
     Laugh, why don't you? (Crouch 2011: 23)

The 'kick me' sign leads to an invitation for an audience member to do
just that, one of several opportunities written into the text for Crouch
to improvise around audience participation. Written into the text as 'He
asks for "any takers?" An audience member kicks him' (19), it allows a
minute or two of unscripted activity choosing the volunteer, and advis-
ing him or her to take a good run up, to use the side of the foot not the
toe, and then to ask the audience 'Find that funny do you? That the
kind of thing you find funny?' (19). Like the 'Is this okay?' of *The Author*,
rhetorical questions of this kind run through *I, Malvolio*, reinforcing the
implication of the audience in the discomfort and persecution of the
character. Crouch makes it impossible not to find Malvolio's situation
funny, while simultaneously making his grounds for complaint very
clear.

     Through the first two-thirds of the play Malvolio gradually prepares
to hang himself, he brings on a rope with a noose tied in it, he hangs
it over whatever scaffold or beam the performance space permits, he
places a chair under the noose and stands on it. He enlists the help of
two audience members, one to hold the rope, the other to pull away the
chair. After briefing the volunteers, he pauses to recite a poem, repeatedly interrupting himself to check that they are ready, with a firm grasp
on the rope to take his weight, legs braced to be able to pull the chair
quickly when given the word.

     The complicity of these two audience members is of a different kind
to that which the audience as a whole have been drawn into, though
because of their participatory position it is more complex. Clearly,
Crouch the performer is not going to hang himself, whatever Malvolio
the character says. Yet when two young people[4] stand on stage as
instructed, appearing ready to remove the chair from under his feet or
to take his weight on the rope, they have a choice about what to do and
how to do it. They can refuse and return to their seats, refusing to cooperate with Malvolio's wish to end his life, but also refusing to work with
Crouch the performer. They can stay and perform their reluctance or
embarrassment, giving Crouch more opportunity to pause in his preparation and nag them to do the job properly. Or they can play along,
and appear eager to contribute to his demise. The ethical bind is light-
hearted, but real at the level of producing a response to the accusation

of spectatorial amorality that Malvolio (and Crouch, perhaps), has made throughout the play. These participants find themselves performing actions they cannot help but feel compromised by, one way or another, and they watch themselves giving this performance. The rest of the audience enjoy their discomfort at the same time as waiting for the outcome of Malvolio's attempt, aware that their enjoyment of this moment confirms all that he has said up to now about their cruelty and decadence.

In both of these plays Crouch constructs a relationship between performance and audience that is complex, at times blunt, at times subtle, and in which participation or the potential for participation enhances a particular kind of reflexivity in the audience experience. Though critical responses to *The Author* have been ambivalent about its strategy, and audience response evidently widely varied, Crouch is adamant about its respectful treatment of those who attend it. He has grounds: for most of the play the broad horizon of response available to audience members is very clear, what is made ambiguous through the structure of the play and the procedure of participation is what any response – private or public – can mean in relation to the depiction of violence in the theatre. *I, Malvolio* does something similar with respect to the cruelty of laughter, and though its horizon is much narrower – in the participatory moments and in the way Crouch skilfully builds and undercuts the audience's laughter – it has the potential to prompt similarly complex reflections. The characters in both plays address the audience as an audience rather than asking them to play roles in a fictional world, and the plays themselves rhetorically address us as an audience too, making us look back at ourselves and the things we choose to do in theatres generally, and in response to their specific invitations.

# 5
## Conclusion

### The procedural author

The media of theatre include, in every case, the bodily presence and active responses of audience members as individuals and as groups; but when an invitation to join the action of a performance is made and accepted, the audience participant becomes material of a different kind, more carefully shaped and manipulated, more productive of signs and affects, more complex as a site of perception and action. To unpack some of this complexity (and inevitably only some of it) I have examined the invitation itself, and described it as an authored procedure. From this proposition I have asked what aspects of the participant become manipulable material and how this happens, what kinds of resistance and embodied engagement are likely to be at stake, and what involvement in the action may feel like.

Treating this, as I have throughout, as a process that is deliberately initiated by an artist or group of artists, is one element of asserting that it has importance in aesthetic terms. People who invite participation are making art when they do so. That participation is a shared creative process, shared between theatre practitioners and the volunteers they invite into their practice, changes its character as a process of authorship, but does not fundamentally undermine it: what is authored, as well as any performance that results, is the interactional space into which the audience member can step as a participant, if they choose to.

Authorship is generally a relationship of agency with regard to an art object or a relatively defined art experience: a writer claims responsibility for a text, a painter for a painting, a performer for a performance. But procedural authorship is agency at a remove; though a procedure might be regarded as a kind of art object, it is only such a thing because it has

195

the potential to give rise to actually occurring performances. This might be exemplified through a kind of borderline case. The instructions that are the basis of some conceptual art, Fluxus scores for example, are often treated as works in themselves. Some, like these pieces from Dick Higgins's *Danger Music* series, are impossible to realise, but evocative, having a poetry in their language but also in their imaginary potential:

*Danger Music Number Nine*
(for Nam June Paik)
Volunteer to have your spine removed.
February 1962

*Danger Music Number Twelve*
Write a thousand symphonies.
March 1962
(Friedman, Smith and Sawchyn 2002: 50)

While others, like Ben Vautier's *Audience Pieces*, are viable performances too:

*Audience Piece No. 7*
   The audience is requested to come on stage one by one to sign a large book placed on a table. After signing, each is led away, one by one, to the street. This is continued until all have signed and left the theatre. Those left outside are not permitted to return.
1965
(Friedman, Smith and Sawchyn 2002: 108)

An impossible procedure is not a work of procedural authorship in the sense we have been concerned with; it has no iterations, no actual processes of performance arise from it, for all that it will work on the imagination of the reader. The same might be said of a procedure that is never put to an audience, so that its invitation is never made. I take this firm stance with the concept of procedural authorship, not as part of a manifesto for audience participation as a privileged practice, but because it draws attention to what is in common across the work of practitioners who choose to invite participation: that they work with audience members as their material. This peculiar authorship is realised when a practitioner takes the risk of making an invitation, and opens the conversation out of which the action of participation will arise.

## The aesthetic theory

Framing the thesis of this book as an aesthetics of audience participation has been motivated by a desire to treat its particular practices and experiences as equivalent to the other, non-participatory elements of theatre performance. In other words I have attempted to treat audience participation as art, and to explore what is entailed when we do so. My main strategy has been to think of the audience participant, their actions, and their experiences first as performances, and second as the material or the media that are manipulated by the procedural author as an artist. To ground these ideas more securely, it is helpful to explore the idea of the material of art a little further, and to unpack a bit more of what aesthetics has to offer the understanding of performance.

As Koren says, the words 'aesthetics' and 'the aesthetic' are used in conflicting and confusing ways: to name a field of philosophy, an approach to the theory of art, the properties of art works and everyday objects, and many other things besides. The words present puzzles in themselves when we try to discern what they refer to at any given point, and substantial conceptual problems when we have located their point of reference in a particular discourse. Halsall, Jansen and O'Connor, introducing *Rediscovering Aesthetics*, acknowledge the problem of the term they have chosen: '[d]ue to its polysemy, aesthetics can appear like an arbitrary placeholder for a wide range of incommensurable issues' (2009: 2). Clarifying the senses of the words that I will deal with, and the associated issues, will help at this stage. First I will briefly set out some ideas of the ontology of art that underpin the approach I have taken in the book; second I will introduce a theory that develops ideas of media and material; and third I will return to the problem of politics in art, which features strongly in most accounts of participatory practice but which has mostly been neglected in this discussion, for all that politically inflected social theory has played a major role in the development of the ideas. In each of these issues, the question of what is particular and proper to art, as opposed to other non-art realms of life, returns in different ways.

In the last chapter I briefly introduced Gadamer's ontology of the work of art, in which an art experience provoked by a work leads to a kind of truth event. This is a valuable concept for understanding art as a highly subjective experience, in the most rigorous sense, as an event that occurs at the level of subjectivity. However it sets dauntingly high standards for a definition of art, which are unhelpful to an enquiry such as this that has addressed many kinds of event, which do not have ambitions of this sort, as well as those that may try, and fail, to reach so high. Many other varieties of aesthetic theory are concerned with the ontology of art at this level: what art ought to be, what its potential is, what should be looked for to distinguish true art from mere entertainment. The ontology of an art work that suits my purposes needs to be broader and more open minded. It is part suggested in the assumption running through this book, employed to define audience participation as a set of practices that depend on an institutional assumption about audiences. Just as, for us to recognise an audience (and whether an audience is 'participating'), it is necessary to know something about the theatre, it is necessary in a broader sense to have experience of the category of art to be able to recognise a work of art. This is the 'art world' hypothesis put forward by Arthur Danto (1964), and implied in a different way in Bourdieu's discussion of art and culture. It asserts, essentially, that a work of art is such a thing because it is named as such by a network of institutions and their associated practices and practitioners.

For much of the past fifty years or more, 'aesthetics' as an approach to the key problems of art – including theatre and performance, along with fine art, literature, music and other forms – has been out of fashion. It has been associated with conservative and elitist values: a fixation on beauty that is inherently sexist, the privilege of western high art, and the importance of the 'disinterestedness' of art, that it is apolitical. This traditional aesthetics, associated with Emmanuel Kant above all, is based on an idea of the autonomy of art, and the possibility of distinguishing genuine works of beauty and genius from both inferior works and things that should not properly be called art works at all.

## Making special

Nevertheless, when we treat something differently because it is part of a socially-constructed art world, that different treatment means something. By marking off cultural space in which to attend to forms of life – objects, appearances, actions and bodies, or events via the narrative practices that make use of all of these forms – we allow them to appear to us differently.

Ellen Dissanayake's ethological approach tackles the institutional character of art from a different direction, by considering why such practices are ubiquitous in human culture, despite their many differences in their varied contexts. In *Homo Aestheticus: Where Art Comes From and Why* (1995), she seeks an explanation in art's adaptive benefits, as a predisposition towards behaviour of a definable type. Dissanayake's attention is not on the explanations offered for the place of art in any society or by any philosophical or aesthetic tradition, nor is it on the meaning of any piece of art. Instead it is on what is evidently generalisable at a species level, and meaningful in terms of species survival: in other words, if 'art' is a propensity that belongs to all people, and is not reducible to another phenomenon (sexuality, say, or play), then it will have emerged and survived because our lives as individuals and groups are more productive and durable because of it. If this assumption holds true, then 'art' as an adaptive benefit becomes a need, and a behaviour that will find its place whatever the human context. Dissanayake compares this predisposition to animal behaviour – the pack behaviour of wolves, for example – that is also compulsive, species-wide but not self-evidently beneficial to the individual animal:

> Recognising art as a biological need can give us not only a way to better understand art, but by understanding art as a natural part of us, we can understand ourselves to be part of nature. [...] Art can be considered as a behaviour (a 'need', fulfilment of which feels good) like play, like food sharing, like howling, that is, something humans do because it helps them to survive, and to survive better than they would without it. (Dissanayake 1995: 34)

This may seem like an odd approach to turn to in relation to audience participation – and it is not chosen because I want to show that audience participation is any more a 'natural' need or a species-wide behaviour than any other way of engaging with performance, but because it is helpfully reductive. Dissanayake's thesis that art consists of the 'making special' of objects or activities is reductive. It can be applied to works that are simply decorative or that are provocative and political; to performances that belong to ritual or high art traditions; to body art, conceptual art, social dance, storytelling, advertising and theatre. By locating an essential nature of art in this core criteria this approach does not reduce their other values out of existence: whatever else has accumulated around a tradition or a practice in its culturally and contextually specific history remains meaningful, in whatever terms are appropriate to it. And whatever else can be achieved by an artist, an art work, or by the engagement of an audience or spectator also survives this reduction: making special gives a place for many kinds of activity and all their various outcomes, because across all of its various manifestations, it offers something valuable at a very basic level.

The benefits that human beings have derived from art (and according to Dissanayake have done since the emergence of homo-sapiens as a species, potentially even earlier) derive from a pleasurable sense of mastery over objects and circumstances. This mastery arises in its most fundamental form in patterning and elaborating, in the making of tools, the decoration of the body, and ceremony and ritual; it requires control over these materials, and the feeling of this control becomes reassuring, 'a means of working out anxiety and attempting to influence the outcome of uncertain events or feared possibilities' (Dissanayake 1995: 89). This mastery over feelings relating to uncertain situations is evolutionarily important because:

> the appropriation from nature of the means of subsistence often includes psychological or emotional along with technological components; the 'nature' that requires cultural control includes human behaviour and feeling as well as the physical environment. Where materialist thought is inadequate, I believe, is in not acknowledging that means of enhancement (i.e., the control of human behaviour and emotion [...]) are frequently if not always intrinsic to the control of the means of production. (Dissanayake 1995: 9)

Though symbolism and representation may derive from a different behavioural source, and have uses in other systems such as ritual, belief and play, they overlap with the need to make things special, and give rise to the complexes of art making behaviour in different traditions and forms. For Dissanayake the satisfying sense of mastery drives the pleasure to be had from listening to well told stories as well as telling them, wearing elaborate clothes and body decorations, as well as making them, and, in post-traditional and technological societies, the accumulation and replaying of recorded music, via record-collections, ring-tones and radio stations.

But this is not directly relevant to the discussion of audience participation, I include it to put Dissanayake's 'making special' into its proper context. What is relevant is that this model of art escapes the binaries of author and audience, and the priority of the self-expression of the artist that dominates the western tradition of aesthetics. The identification of art as a behaviour does not depend on levels of quality, kinds of engagement or arguments for autonomy, it also acknowledges that much of what is important to art as it is made and experienced depends upon the practice, institution and situation through which it is identified to the groups of people involved. Making special reduces art to its most basic behaviour, but it does not say that this is all there is to it.

It also puts the manipulation of everyday, non-art material at the heart of art behaviour, and is very liberal about what kind of material can be thus manipulated: giving scope to describe not just the bodies and voices of participants as material, but also their relations with action via agency and point-of-view. As I have already suggested, accepting an invitation puts a participant in a position of having to respond, and thence having to view their own response as part of a work of art. When we consider the way the artist shapes these dimensions of experience – patterns them and elaborates them – then we must acknowledge that they have been 'made special' in a deliberate way, and have become aesthetic material at the most basic level.

## Patterning and elaborating participation

Dissanayake notes the capacity that facilitates the pleasure derived from a thing that has been made special, as 'sensitivity to changes in tempo, dynamics, size, quality, and so forth' (Dissanayake 1995: 180), which is exploited differently by the different art forms. With patterning and elaboration as a foundation, she cites Leonard Bernstein's observation of how the shaping of music is analogous to the shaping of poetry, with techniques comparable to antithesis, alliteration, anaphora, chiasmus (192), and W.B. Stanford on how Greek drama can be described in terms of 'crescendos and diminuendos, accelerandos and rallentandos, scherzo movements and maestoso movements, recurrent motifs and ingenious variations' (128). All of these operate not only on change and contrast, but also repetition, and work on the expectations of audience members, as patterns are established, elaborated and then altered. Patterning of this kind, whatever the medium, entails a kind of stimulation:

> The brain is prepared for or 'expects' certain prototypical features once a pattern is suggested or given. Emotion results from delayed and manipulated gratification of expectation, provided that deviations from the anticipated pattern are not so small as to be predictable and boring or so large as to be incomprehensible and confusing. (Dissanayake 1995: 162)

If an audience participant has become aesthetic material, then analogous, if not identical, features should be observable in the attributes that are thus brought into play. At the level of vocal and physical action, there are often patterns and variations. Obviously when music or dance is involved, bodies are put to work according to the dictates of the form in a more general sense: when in Kneehigh's *Midnight's Pumpkin*,[1] (a version of Cinderella) the whole audience is invited to take the stage to join in the choreography of the Prince's ball, the patterning and elaboration of their movement is that of social dance, with an added frisson because of its setting. More importantly, sometimes it is the invitation itself that has a pattern: panto's call and response games are based on repetition, as is the interjection of 'stop!' in a Forum Theatre event. Whenever there is turn taking, or a formula for invitation that is repeated, and accepted by a series of participants, there is a repetition and variation involved. The audience – at Jonathan Kay's *Know One's Fool*, for example, or at Las Furas Del Baus' *XXX* – that sees others take the stage before them and waits nervously to be singled out, experiences each successive moment of potential embarrassment as a crescendo of anticipation, leading to a climax when actually invited, or either disappointment or relief when left alone. The rhythm of 'you say something', 'is this alright?' and 'shall I go on?' running through *The Author*, punctuates the other verbal patterns of the spoken text, and also sets out a series of opportunities to respond, each with a different inflection as the discomfort builds.

In other realms of experience, aesthetic manipulation is as much a matter of contrast and combination, in Yuriko Saito's *Everyday Aesthetics*, she observes that in the Japanese tradition: 'The activity of eating [...] is not just a matter of consumption, but also of making aesthetic choices concerning the best order for elucidating each ingredient's taste and texture' (Saito 2007: 231).

The contrast between the agencies available to audience participants and audience members is fundamental, and is perhaps where the most subtle range and shades of feeling are manifested. The contrasts of openness and closure, frustration, exhilarating freedom and entrapment of Armadillo's workshop, or the gradual but powerful erosion of spatial and social differentiation in *Villa Villa*, work because they heighten the sensation of self-agency, or its absence, by bringing the participant into contact with many variations of it.

## The aesthetic regime

In my introduction, I proposed that this book is an 'aesthetics' of participation in the sense that it would defer political and ethical questions pending a discussion of the character of participation as an artistic material, because questions and claims of that kind have tended to dominate discussion of participation at the expense of close attention to the substance of the work as it happens. I also promised to return to politics, better equipped to make informed judgements about it; it is time to make good that promise. Jacques Rancière's argument in *The Emancipated Spectator* was used as an example of a polemic in which assumptions are made about participatory performance in order to justify a certain perspective of the possibility of artistic efficacy. Returning to Rancière at this point I will articulate how the thesis of that essay fits into his overall conceptualisation of aesthetics, showing how an alternative perspective can integrate participation into his view of political art, and as a complement to this introducing a more precise formulation of 'the aesthetic' than has been outlined in this chapter so far.

The foundation of Rancière's approach to aesthetics is his conception of the historical character of art as a system of 'practices, forms of visibility and modes of intelligibility' that allow us to recognise works of art. The prevalent system he identifies as the 'aesthetic regime', which in western culture superseded 'ethical' and 'representative' regimes of art (Rancière 2009b: 28–29). The origin of this regime coincides with the Enlightenment, when Baumgarten and Kant first began to formulate the judgements evoked by art as having a distinct character based on the art work's autonomy from concerns for the good or the agreeable, and subsequently the romantics' (particularly Schiller's) celebration of the potential for art to create a new life-in-common, in other words to have good effects. For Rancière the character of this regime is this paradox of simultaneous connection and disconnection. As Claire Bishop (2012: 27) describes it, this regime is: 'predicated precisely on a tension and confusion between autonomy (the desire for art to be at one remove from means-ends relationships) and heteronomy (that is, the blurring of art and life)'.

Although philosophical aesthetics has sought and failed to square this circle ever since, and art practice has from time to time sought to escape the paradox by either renouncing all claims for effect (as high modernism did) or seeking to collapse the distinction between art and life (as DADA and futurism did, in some forms), it continues to hold sway, even over those forms of art that would deny it. Rather than being crippled by this paradox, Rancière says, art derives its power from its 'productive contradiction' (Bishop 2012: 29). Having faith in both art's independence from worldly concerns, and its promise to make the world a better place, creates spaces and opportunities for alternative ways of feeling and understanding to arise.

He is very sceptical, however, of art practice ('critical art', Rancière 2009b: 45–60, 2009a, 25–50) that intends a direct connection between its political aims and effects. Imagining that art works as a tool of this kind reproduces the unequal 'distribution of the sensible' in which there are people who are equipped to know and understand in a certain way, and others who have to be led into understanding, as their place in society determines their perceptive abilities. This is the basis of his critique of the manipulation of aesthetic distance in *The Emancipated Spectator*, where the conventional, stultifying practice of education and the political theatre practitioners he identifies with it, reproduce such a distribution because of (and in spite of) their ambition to share their knowledge.

Instrumentalising art in this way misses the potential of its ambiguous, paradoxical nature, attending only to its heteronomous, worldly connections. To think through how art has effects that are not predictable, and therefore do not re-institute the relative power of the artist, he puts the emphasis on autonomy in the process of response, which is possible precisely because there is no direct connection between cause and effect. He calls the process of response 'aisthesis', and notes an 'aethetic cut' between poiesis and aisthesis,[2] and the belief that art can bridge this gap is what leads to the stultifying and anti-emancipatory critical art he abhors. The potential effect of aisthesis, when it is allowed to take its own course, is reminiscent of Gadamer's 'truth event' in art, though with a particular emphasis on the shifting of sensory worlds, on 'sensibility' as the organisation of what is perceptible, that is important to Rancière's theorisation of aesthetics as a political phenomenon:

> Aesthetic experience has a political effect to the extent that the loss of destination it presupposes disrupts the way in which bodies fit their functions and destinations. What it produces is not rhetorical persuasion about what must be done. Nor is it the framing of a collective body. It is a multiplication of connections and disconnections that reframe the relation between bodies, the world they live in and the way in which they are equipped to adapt to it. It is a multiplicity of folds and gaps in the fabric of common experience that change the cartography of the perceptible, the thinkable and the feasible. (Rancière 2009a: 72)

I would say that rhetorical persuasion and the framing of a collective body are still political outcomes of many art events, which may be enhanced by effects that are powerfully manipulated in art practice: the patterning and elaboration of media that grabs and holds attention and makes a message more accessible and compelling, the gathering of bodies and voices that engages suggestibility and group identification. But in Rancière's terms these are not *aesthetic* effects.

The imagery of 'folds and gaps' used in this passage suggests changes in detail and nuance rather than grand transformations. The reference to 'the relation between bodies, the world they live in and the way in which they are equipped to adapt to it' also suggests Bourdieu's language of embodiment and disposition, of the relation of habitus to field and capital. But Rancière is famously opposed to Bourdieu's work, seeing in the analysis of the structural exclusion of some classes from cultures of education and art an attitude that reifies this exclusion. Rancière's work addresses the persistent inequalities of access, through his idea of the 'distribution of the sensible', (2004: 12–19) but insists upon the potential of the dispossessed to escape their allotted place in the economy of perceptions, however unpredictably or fleetingly. Any theory or policy based on the rigidity of inequality, and the responsibility of those in possession of knowledge and power to share what they have with those who do not have it, is destined, in his thinking, to reproduce and perpetuate inequality. Change in the distribution of the sensible will come from below, and its unpredictability is the essence of politics for Rancière.

To fully unpack the conflict between these two is a project for another place, and would entail situating their work in the development of progressive theory in France since 1968. Both are relevant to the project of this book, and so is the point at which they disagree. Bourdieu is the theorist par excellence of the connectedness of art. For him all art is political because it directly reflects and reproduces the class structure of society: its claims to autonomy only serve to disguise this connectedness. His terms have been used in my argument primarily to articulate how connectedness – of participants as situated social beings – runs through audience participation at every point, but by combining it with Goffman's notions around framing I hope to have kept in mind that these connections can simultaneously be bracketed off: not entirely denied, but held in abeyance temporarily by the learned associations of the practice at hand. The different manifestations of bodily and social connectedness, and practices of disconnection, described in the preceding chapters are perhaps too diverse to pull together too neatly, but what Rancière offers is a theory which re-reads the role of autonomy in aesthetics, giving it a political character. What he does not recognise is that the kind of autonomy he observes can happen in audience participation, and I would assert that this can be better understood because of what has gone before in this book.

For Rancière the spectator remains a spectator. The autonomy of the art work is located in the autonomy of the one experiencing it. This is the crux of whether a participatory spectator can be an emancipated spectator in Rancière's terms. What I have shown is that a participant can be a spectator to their own actions in a variety of ways, re-encountering themselves in 'the forest of things and signs'. It is in the sheer variety of experiential relationships to participatory action that we find a kind of autonomy, in the potential for any of them to become an encounter with oneself, facilitated by the distance that can open up when subjectivity has become an aesthetic material.

The inclusion of the participant in the work cannot entail a direct effect – though practitioners may attempt such direct effects and even appear to achieve them. A procedure of invitation can move you and manipulate you physically, but it cannot assume how you will experience this movement. It can emotionally manipulate you, or work on your psychological capacity for suggestion, but must allow that after the event you will do what you choose with the experience. In different guises the argument of this book has always been about heteronomy and autonomy, about the continuity of the participant's social being, and how it is connected to and marked off from an altered version of itself in performance. The practices of audience participation temporarily re-shape our social being, make it special, intensify it or bring its contours into focus, expose folds and gaps in its surfaces and depths, and perhaps, on occasion, allow us to perceive ourselves anew.

# Notes

## Introduction

1. For an interesting borderline example of this we might look to Shannon Jackson's account of artist Paul Chan's production of *Waiting for Godot in New Orleans*, in which Chan – an artist with connections and credentials in the fine art establishment appropriated the form of the theatre for a specifically situated project. (Jackson 2011: 210–238)
2. My point of reference is the essay of that title, first published in Artforum in 2007, and later reproduced in a volume of essays under the same title.
3. Helen Freshwater, in Theatre and Audience, says that 'Although Rancière's challenge to the ingrained connection between passivity and spectatorship is invaluable, his reading of theatre practice – limited as it is to Antonin Artaud and Bertolt Brecht – presumes a determinism among directors and drama-turges which has in many ways passed. In fact, a plethora of theatrical work now foregrounds the need for active interpretation on the part of the specta-tor, as it requires observers to make their own decisions about the significance of actions or symbolic material' (2009:16).
4. This proposition about political subjectivisation, and about politics and democracy in general, runs through most of Rancière's work, for example, in the essays collected as *Dissensus* (2010), and is helpfully unpacked by Todd May (2008) and Nick Hewlett (2010).

## 1  Process and Procedure

1. The 'gaps' or 'blanks' that are a crucial feature of literary text were theorised by Wolfgang Iser (1974: 58): 'with a literary text we can only picture things which are not there; the written part of the text gives us the knowledge, but it is the unwritten part that gives us the opportunity to picture things; indeed without the elements of indeterminacy, the gaps in the texts, we should not be able to use our imagination.' What we have in the opportu-nity to imaginatively picture when watching performance is quite differ-ent, as Susan Bennett (1997) has observed, nevertheless there are elements 'unwritten' that stimulate rich and varied responses.
2. For an early articulation of the techniques and priorities of TIE, which also includes a perceptive typology of participatory strategies, see O'Toole (1976).
3. *Grounded*, by Eileen Murphy, toured schools in the North West of England in 1991 and 1994, directed initially by Murphy, and by Joe Sumsion for the second tour.
4. De La Guarda's *Villa Villa* opened in London in May 1999, and ran for a year, though a version of the same show had visited London two years previously as part of the London International Festival of Theatre. From their origins in the Argentinean avant-garde and the international festival circuit, they

became something like an international franchise – at one time with shows running simultaneously in London, New York and Las Vegas.

5. Chapter 3 'Keys and Keyings' and Chapter 5 'The Theatrical Frame', of *Frame Analysis* contain much more complex analyses of make-believe situations and their special manifestations in the theatre: to be very brief about it, Goffman shows how the definition of a situation can allow the transcription of other situations that are defined very differently, but re-organised to conform with the conventions of the 'outer' frame, the one that has not been transcribed.

6. The relevance of Goffman's reference to hypnotic suggestion will become more apparent in Chapter 3, but his purpose is to suggest that the performance a person can give of something they apparently have no experience of can be surprisingly complete. Whether the performance of a 'compulsive crime' would be convincing to a habitual criminal or someone else with real experience of the matter is another thing, the performance might be drawing on resources that are remote from the real thing, from films, television or literature.

7. *Dance Bear Dance* was performed at the Shunt Arches, Bethnal Green, from September 2002 to May 2003.

8. 'Something Beautiful' was toured to schools in the South of England through the mid-nineties, it had two characters played by actors, and a number of supporting roles played by volunteers, usually invited on stage by less devious means. The acting area was a carpet in a figure of eight shape, marked like a road, with students seated all around it and in the loops of the eight, so that bringing a student onto the stage only took a moment. My own involvement was limited to one tour, and this way of making an invitation was my own, rather than the company's. Keith Johnstone in *Impro for Storytellers*, comes out against covert invitations: '"anyone seen improvisation before? Good, come up on stage." Never "hook" unwitting volunteers this way' (2000: 371), as he is against all actions that might humiliate or manipulate volunteers.

9. Jay Sankey feels that this is explained by an evident lack of respect for the audience on the part of the performer, resulting in a reciprocal lack of respect from the audience, the effect is a display of disrespect for the frame, as well as the performer: 'Some comics seem a little disrespectful of the crowd, other comics seem unsure of their own abilities, and still other comics deliver material about sensitive subjects in an overly cavalier fashion. Any and all of these things can diminish the crowd's primary respect for the performer, virtually inviting hecklers.' (Sankey 1998: 175, original emphasis)

10. This play toured schools and other venues in South East London in early 2002, to audiences of 11 to 13 year olds, the performance I saw was at Deptford Albany in March of that year.

11. Goffman notes an interaction between habitus and capital that can be expected in theatrical performance, if not in audience participation: 'An individual who plays Hamlet must learn the part, but he need not be taught theatrical English unless he is a high school Prince; presumably his occupational role as a professional actor guarantees that he already knows how to speak in that manner and can bring this capacity (alas) to any character he is obliged to project' (1986: 290–291).

12. Susan Bennett discusses the idea of disattendance and its importance to the theatre event, (1997: 68), as does Goffman (1975: 144).
13. Kitchen was first performed in Berlin in 2007 and toured to London's Soho Theatre in July 2008.
14. This standard Forum Theatre rule allows an audience member to stop an intervention that they consider unrealistic in the given circumstances, by shouting 'that's magic!' (See for example Cohen-Cruz and Schutzman 1994: 226.)

## 2   Risk and Rational Action

1. There is a danger of 'losing face' by giving a bad performance, but also of gaining esteem by giving a good one. Risk in these performances can also be a chance to gain. Ideas such as Bourdieu's 'cultural capital' can also help to elaborate on the continuities and the perduring self that have been taken from *Frame Analysis* to show how a performance is an investment. As in other areas of risk in our lives, our financial dealings, and personal relationships and so on, we take risks in performance when we see a possible benefit, and can weigh it rationally against the possible loss. Nicholson, writing about trust in classroom drama, acknowledges this: 'the participants' willingness to involve themselves in (dramatic) action is dependent on measuring the perceived advantages and disadvantages of entering into that particular relationship of situation' (Nicholson 2002: 88).
2. *Invitation* was performed at Siobhan Davies Dance Studios and Central School of Speech and Drama in 2010.
3. *Internal* was first performed in Hasselt, Belgium in 2007, and toured internationally until 2011.
4. This kind of behaviour by facilitators is unusual, especially in the applied theatres, where the tendency is usually to be helpful, respectful, and gentle with participants. It is possible, however, it happens deliberately in stand-up comedy, where volunteers can be derided, and in Jonathan Kay's work; it could also happen accidentally, if an observation was meant constructively but perceived critically.
5. This incident, and the ethics of inviting this kind of socially risky performance, is explored in my article: 'Navigating the Ethics of Audience Participation' (White 2006).
6. See Weindling 2001, for an account of the derivation of the principles of research ethics in the war crimes trials of the 1940s; the Nuremburg Code is now seen as the basis of medical practice ethics internationally, but originates in a response to the abuse of subjects in medical research in Nazi Germany.
7. The misreading I refer to here is simply that the need for undergraduate and postgraduate students to observe research ethics in their work was applied to performance practice that was not research in the relevant sense.
8. Holstein and Gubrium 2000: 21 and 24 respectively. Cooley's idea of the 'looking glass self', a characterisation of self-perception as constructed through seeing ourselves as others see us, is manifest in some or the strategies of experimental social psychology, for example, in confronting phobic people with the object of their fear, demonstrating different reactions

when a mirror is present, and they can watch their behaviour. See Deaux, Wrightsman and Dane, 1993.

9. My examples will be taken from different events, but particularly from the 2002 festival, and small shows at Camden People's Theatre and Hoxton Hall in the same year.

10. Have you ever seen a field of human fish? Two lanes of traffic stopped by a crowd singing "Baby you can drive my car"? Remarkable things can happen during a Jonathan Kay performance.' Hoxton Hall (2002)

11. These were two of many 'walkabout' performances at Glastonbury 2002.

## 3   Irrational Interactions

1. The term has some currency, especially in studies of computer mediated interaction – see for example, Bradner, Kellogg and Erikson (1999).

2. For example, Bergson (1935).

3. Provine thinks that laughter originates in tickling, the laugh-response to being tickled is especially involuntary and though many of us, especially adults, don't like to be tickled we may still laugh in spite of ourselves. Tickling children socialises them, teaches them to accept contact with those in the family and the social group – as is the case with chimpanzees. The laugh in reaction to tickling demonstrates that we know it is a non-threatening touch. Laughing in the wider context shows that social contact is welcome and pleasurable. In fact laughter has a role in making social contact pleasurable – studies have shown that laughter even works as a pain killer.

4. 'It is, first of all, a festive laughter. Therefore it is not an individual reaction to some isolated "comic" event. Carnival laughter is the laughter of all the people. Second, it is universal in scope; it is directed at all and everyone, including the carnival's participants. The entire world is seen in its droll aspect, in its gay relativity. Third, this laughter is ambivalent: it is gay, triumphant, and at the same time mocking, deriding. It asserts and denies, it buries and revives. Such is the laughter of carnival.' (Bakhtin 1984: 11–12)

5. 'Comedy is always racist: only the others, the Barbarians, are supposed to pay.' Eco, Umberto. 'Frames of Comic Freedom' in Sebeok (1984: 2).

6. Canetti tells of how crowds love destruction, especially the destruction of representational images – statues – and the easily broken boundary markers of houses – their doors and windows (Canetti, 1992: 20). Bill Buford gives an account that echoes this: 'The sound of the shattering windscreen – I realise now – had been a powerful stimulant, physical and intrusive, and it had been the range of sounds, of things breaking and crashing, coming from somewhere in the darkness, unidentifiable, that was increasing steadily the strength of feeling of everyone around me. It was also what was making me so uneasy. The evening had been a series of stimulants, assaults on the senses, that succeeded, each time, in raising the pitch of excitement'. (Buford 1991: 91)

7. These spaces vary in size and configuration, some, like the replica Shakespeare's Globe, appear designed to increase the contact between spectators, others, like newer cinemas, to give us more individual space. The single arm-rest between two seats in most theatres is probably a function

of pressure to increase audience size, but it has the effect of making us rub shoulders (and elbows) with fellow audience members. 'Every crowd has a threshold; all crowds are initially held in place by boundaries of some kind. There are rules that say: this much, but no more. A march has a route and a destination. A picket line is precisely itself: an arrangement of points that cannot be crossed. A political rally: there is the politician, the rally's event, at its centre. A parade, a protest, a procession: there is the police escort, the pavement the street the overwhelming fact of the surrounding property. The crowd can be here, but not there. There is form in the experience that tends towards abandon. I have described the relentless physicalness of the terraces and how they concentrate the spectator experience: that of existing so intensely in the present that it is possible to disappear into the power of numbers – the strength of them, the emotion of belonging to them.' (Buford 1991: 192)

8. Reynolds in Duncombe (2002) and Measham, Aldridge and Parker (2001: 112): 'The setting: the club, the dance floor, the posing and posturing, the buzz of anticipation and excitement and, most of all, the music are all available to drinkers and abstainers; but with tablets and powders the fusion and enhancement of the experience and endurance therein are uniquely amplified.'

9. 'social psychologists have provided theories of argument-based persuasion and have conducted extensive research to test these models. The earlier theories emphasised the systematic processing of message content, whereas later theories added the assumption that people are often not sufficiently motivated to engage in message-relevant thinking and therefore base their decision to accept or reject a persuasive message on heuristic cues or other peripheral processes.' (Argyle and Colman 1994: 16)

10. Some of these tactics are described in Schechner's *Environmental Theatre* (1994). The techniques are based on a performance space which was continuous with the audience space. Welfare State International describes the use of food to involve people in an event (see Sue Fox in Coult and Kershaw, 1990: 126–137).

11. *Villa Villa* opened in London in May 1999, and ran for a year, though a version of the same show had visited London two years previously as part of the London International Festival of Theatre. From their origins in the Argentinean avant-garde (the group's name can be translated as 'avant-garde') and the festival circuit, they became something like an international franchise – at one time with shows running simultaneously in London, New York and Las Vegas.

12. These took place soon after the collapse of Argentina's military government in the eighties, and were designed to shock passers-by and to remind them of the oppression they had tolerated during the years of dictatorship. They were often short interventions into everyday street life, for example, the firing of a starter pistol as a cue for the performers to fall down, en masse, on a street crossing, pause for a few moments; or a man on a stretcher being carried through a shopping arcade surrounded by 'secret police', but carrying a pig's head on his lap.

13. This interview with Pichon Baldinu took place on March 2000, the text is available from the author on request.

14. See, for example, the games 'Blind Offers' and 'Yes, but...' in Johnstone (1981: 101–104).
15. Interviews with performers took place at the Roundhouse, Camden, London in March 2000, in the afternoon before a performance. Interview texts are available on request.
16. They were recorded in the bar at the venue after an evening performance on the same day as the interviews with performers. All interviewees had stayed in the venue after the performance, and were drinking, all were in groups of three or more. The text is available from the author on request.
17. Another female performer spoke of audience members being 'very aggressive, getting big clumps of soggy paper and very violently and aggressively, you know squashing it and pressing it into your face'.

## 4  Accepting the Invitation

1. 'Someone is making claims on me and it's not entirely clear who. On the one hand, I feel obliged as a responsible and professional theatre-goer to comply with the contract I am being offered. Look for look is the deal. To turn my eyes away from his would be rude, and what's more, a betrayal of my own principles (those Brechtian principles of my youth). [...] But who exactly is it making this claim on me? Is it Samuel West or is it Richard II? When the ethical claim of the face-to-face encounter is deployed in this way, I feel I am entitled to know. And I am embarrassed because the utter foolishness of the theatrical contract I have been going on with overwhelms me.' (Ridout 2006: 87)
2. The characters of the play take the names of the performers. In the published text this includes Chris Goode, Vic Llewellyn, and Esther Smith, as well as Crouch himself. In the original performances Goode's role was played by Adrian Howells.
3. *The Author and the Audience* took place at the University of Leeds on November 6th 2010 among its outcomes was the special edition of *Contemporary Theatre Review*, 21:4.
4. The play is sometimes performed for adults, with a slightly modified script. For younger audiences this sequence can be challenging, despite its black humour, as Lyn Gardner notes after discussion with Crouch:

> And the 11+ version? The thong was replaced by trunks, the buttocks took a back seat, and no one mentioned cock unless it was firmly prefaced with 'turkey'. But, other than that, Crouch tells me, the text remained exactly the same. To the point, in fact, where one girl started sobbing into her dad's shoulder at the sight of Malvolio with a noose in his hand [...] Had Crouch pushed it too far? When I spoke to him afterwards, he didn't reckon so, arguing that the world is full of adult things, and children deal with them every day – guided by sympathetic, supportive adults, on hand to help them make sense of it all. Crouch's work for children presents the adult world, and the guide too. So, on stage, when the girl started crying, Crouch was able to step out of character, smile, and say: 'It's alright, it's OK, I'm not really going to go through with this.' (Gardner 2009)

## Conclusion

1. *Midnight's Pumpkin* was at Battersea Arts Centre in December 2012 and January 2013.
2. Rancière has little to say specifically about aisthesis in everyday life, or the different character of sensory responses to art and to nature. He does indicate, however, that opportunity for discovering a different sensorium is relatively easy to find; he quotes a passage on the life of a joiner in nineteenth century France, from Gabriel Gauny's *Le Tocsin des Travailleurs*, to describe how such moments can arise:

> Believing himself as home, he loves the arrangement of a room, so long as he has not finished laying the floor. If the window opens out onto a garden of commands a view of a picturesque horizon, he stops his arms and glides in imagination toward the spacious view to enjoy it better than the [owners] of the neighbouring residences. (2009a: 71)

# Bibliography

Ansorge, Peter. *Disrupting the Spectacle*. London: Pitman, 1975.

Argyle, Michael and Andrew Colman. *Social Psychology*. New York: Longman, 1994.

Armstrong, Isobel. *The Radical Aesthetic*. London: Wiley-Blackwell, 2000.

Babbage, Frances. *Augusto Boal*. Abingdon: Routledge, 2004.

Bakhtin, Mikhail, (trans. H. Iswolsky). *Rabelais and His World*. Bloomington: Indiana University Press, 1984.

Barker, Martin. 'Performing Opposition: Modern Theatre and the Scandalised Audience and Audience Participation: Essays on Inclusion and Performance (Review)', *Participations* 1:2, (May 2004), (online version).

Beck, Lewis White. *The Actor and the Spectator*. New York: Yale University Press, 1975.

Bell, Clive. *Art*. London: Dodo Press, 2007.

Ben Chaim, Daphna. *Distance in the Theatre, The Aesthetics of Audience Response*. Ann Arbor: University of Michigan Press, 1981.

Benedictus, Leo. 'Don't Just Sit There', *The Guardian* 12th August 2004. Available from: http://www.guardian.co.uk/culture/2004/aug/12/edinburgh04. edinburghfestival4. Accessed 8 April 2013.

Bennett, Susan. *Theatre Audiences*. London: Routledge, 1997.

Bergson, Henri. *Laughter*. London: Macmillan, 1935.

Bishop, Claire. *Artificial Hells*. London: Verso, 2012.

Bishop, Claire. *Participation*. London: Whitechapel Gallery/MIT Press, 2006.

Bishop, Claire. 'Antagonism and Relational Aesthetics', *October 110*, (Fall 2004), 51–79.

Blackadder, Neil. *Performing Opposition: Modern Theatre and the Scandalised Audience*. Westport, CT: Praeger Publishers, 2003.

Boal, Augusto. *The Theatre of the Oppressed*. London: Pluto Press, 1979.

Boal, Augusto. *Games for Actors and Non-Actors*. London: Routledge, 1992.

Boal, Augusto. *Games for Actors and Non-Actors* (2nd Edition). London: Routledge, 2002.

Boal, Augusto. *The Rainbow of Desire: The Boal Method of Theatre and Therapy*. London: Routledge, 1999.

Boal, Augusto. *Legislative Theatre*. London: Routledge, 1998.

Boal, Augusto. *Hamlet and the Baker's Son*. London: Routledge, 2001.

Bolton, Gavin. *New Perspectives on Classroom Drama*. London: Simon and Schuster, 1992.

Bourriaud, Pierre. *Relational Aesthetics*. London: Les Presse Du Reel, 1998.

Bourdieu, Pierre. *Outline of A Theory of Practice*. Cambridge: Cambridge University Press, 1977.

Bourdieu, Pierre. *Distinction: A Social Critique of the Judgement of Taste*. London: Routledge, 1984.

Bourdieu, Pierre. *The Field of Cultural Production*. Cambridge: Polity, 1993.

Bourdieu, Pierre and Loic Wacquant. *An Invitation to Reflexive Sociology*. Chicago: University of Chicago Press, 1992.

Bourriaud, Nicholas, *Relational Aesthetics*. Paris: Les Press du Reel, 2002.

Bradner, Erin, Wendy Kellogg and Thomas Erikson 'The Adoption and Use of "BABBLE": A Field Study of Chat in the Workplace', in Bodker, S., M. Kyng and K. Schmidt (eds.). *Proceedings of the Sixth European Conference on Computer-Supported Cooperative Work*. Copenhagen, Denmark: Kluwer, 1999.

Brantley, Ben. 'Surviving an Epic Night of Being Everything and Nothing', *New York Times*. 27th July 2010. Available from: http://theater.nytimes.com/2010/07/28/theater/28bumbum.html?_r=0. Accessed 8 April 2013.

Buford, Bill. *Among the Thugs*. London: Secker and Warburg, 1991.

Butler, Judith. *Gender Trouble: Feminism and the Subversion of Identity*. London: Routledge, 1999.

Byam, L. Dale, *Community in Motion: Theatre for Development in Africa*. Westport: Bergin & Garvey, 1999.

Byram, Martin. *Theatre for Development: A Guide to Training*. Amhurst: Center for International Education, University of Massachusetts, 1985.

Canetti, Elias. *Crowds and Power*. London: Penguin, 1992.

Case, Sue-Ellen. (ed.), *Performing Feminisms*. London: Johns Hopkins University Press, 1990.

Cavell, Marcia. *Becoming a Subject*. Oxford: Oxford University Press, 2006.

Chase, Jonathan. *Deeper and Deeper: The Secrets of Stage Hypnosis*. Falmouth: Academy of Hypnotic Arts, 2005.

Cohen-Cruz, Jan. *Engaging Performance*. London: Routledge, 2010.

Cohen-Cruz, Jan and Mady Schutzman. *Playing Boal: Theatre, Therapy, Activism*. London: Routledge, 1994.

Coult, Tony and Baz Kershaw. *Engineers of the Imagination*. London: Methuen, 1990.

Craig, Sandy. *Dreams and Deconstructions*. London: Amber Lane Press, 1980.

Crouch, Tim. *The Author*. London: Oberon Books, 2010.

Crouch, Tim. *I, Shakespeare*. London: Oberon Books, 2011.

Crouch, Tim. 'Death of The Author: How Did my Play Fare in LA?' *The Guardian*, 7 March 2011. Available from: http://www.guardian.co.uk/stage/2011/mar/07/tim-crouch-the-author-la-tour. Accessed 19 April 2013.

Damasio, Antonio. *Descartes' Error*. London: Vintage, 2006.

Danto, Arthur. 'The Artworld', *The Journal of Philosophy*, 61:9 (1964): 571–584.

de Certeau, Michel. *The Practice of Everyday Life*. London: University of California Press, 1988.

Deaux, Kay, Lawrence Wrightsman and Fancis Dane. *Social Psychology in the 90's*. Pacific Grove, CA: Brooks/Cole Publishing Company, 1993.

Delgado, Maria M. and Caridad Svich (eds.). *Theatre in Crisis? Performance Manifestos for a New Century*. Manchester: Manchester University Press, 2002.

Deleuze, Gilles and Felix Guattari. *A Thousand Plateaus*. London: Athlone, 1988.

Dennett, Daniel. *Freedom Evolves*. London: Penguin, 2004.

Dewey, John. *Art as Experience*. London: Pedigree, 1980.

Diderot, Denis. *The Paradox of Acting*. London: Chatto and Windus, 1883.

Dissanayake, Ellen. *Homo Aestheticus: Where Art Comes From and Why*. Seattle: University of Washington Press, 1995.

Double, Oliver. *Stand Up! On the Art of Being a Comedian*. London: Methuen Drama, 1997.

Duncombe, Stephen. *Cultural Resistance Reader*. London: Verso, 2002.

Dwyer, Paul. 'Making Bodies Talk in Forum Theatre', *Research in Drama Education* 9:2, (2004): 199–210.

Eagleton, Terry. *The Ideology of the Aesthetic*. London, Wiley-Blackwell, 1990.

Eco, Umberto. *The Role of the Reader*. Bloomington: Indiana University Press, 1979.

Engelberts, Matthijs. '"Alive and Present": Theatresports and Contemporary Live Performance', *Theatre Research International*, 29:2, (2004): 155–173.

Escolme, Bridget. *Talking to the Audience. Shakespeare, Performance, Self*. Abingdon, UK: Routledge, 2005.

Etchells, Tim. *Certain Fragments. Contemporary Performance and Forced Entertainment*. London: Routledge, 1999.

Fischer-Lichte, Erica. *The Transformative Power of Performance: A New Aesthetics*. London, Routledge, 2008.

Freshwater, Helen. *Theatre and Audience*. London: Palgrave Macmillan, 2009.

Freud, Sigmund, (trans. James Strachey). *Group Psychology and the Analysis of the Ego*. New York: W. W. Norton, 1959.

Friedman, Ken, Owen Smith and Lauren Sawchyn. *The Fluxus Performance Workbook*. Performance Research e-publication 2002. Available from: http://www.deluxxe.com/beat/fluxusworkbook.pdf. Accessed 1 December 2012.

Fuchs, Thomas and Hanne De Jaegher. 'Enactive Intersubjectivity: Participatory Sense-making and Mutual Incorporation', *Phenomenology and the Cognitive Sciences*, 6:4 (2009): 485–507.

Gadamer, Hans-Georg. *Truth and Method*. London & New York: Continuum, 2004.

Gallagher, Shaun. *How the Body Shapes the Mind*. Oxford: Oxford University Press, 2005.

Gallagher, Shaun. *Phenomenology*. London: Palgrave Macmillan, 2012.

Gardner, Lyn. 'Tim Crouch Proves that there's Nothing Childish about Theatre for Kids', Guardian Theatre Blog. 17 May 2009. Available from http://www.guardian.co.uk/stage/theatreblog/2010/may/17/grown-up-theatre-children. Accessed 19 April 2013.

Garner, Stanton. *Bodied Spaces: Phenomenology and Performance in Contemporary Drama*. London: Cornell University Press, 1994.

Giddens, A. *An Introduction to Sociology*. New York: Norton, 1996.

Gilbert, Helen. *Postcolonial Plays*. London: Routledge, 2001.

Goffman, Erving. *The Presentation of Self in Everyday Life*. Harmondsworth: Pelican, 1969.

Goffman, Erving. *Strategic Interaction*. Oxford: Blackwell, 1970.

Goffman, Erving. *Interaction Ritual*. Harmondsworth: Allen Lane, 1972.

Goffman, Erving. *Frame Analysis*. Harmondsworth: Penguin, 1986.

Goldberg, Rose Lee. *Performance Art – From Futurism to the Present*. London: Thames & Hudson, 1979.

Haedicke, Susan C. and Tobin Nellhaus (eds.). *Performing Democracy. International Perspectives on Urban Community-Based Performance*. Ann Arbor: University of Michigan Press, 2001.

Hahlo, Richard and Peter Reynolds. *Dramatic Events – How to Run a Successful Workshop*. London: Faber and Faber, 2000.

Halliburton, Rachel. 'Circus: Who Needs a Safety Net', *The Independent* 20th May 1999. Available from: http://www.independent.co.uk/arts-entertainment/circus-who-needs-a-safety-net-1094713.html. Accessed 8 April 2013.

Halsall, Francis, Julia Jansen and Tony O'Connor. *Rediscovering Aesthetics: Transdisciplinary Voices from Art History, Philosophy, and Art Practice*. Stanford, CA: Stanford University Press, 2009.

Hays, Sharon. 'Structure and Agency and the Sticky Problem of Culture', *Sociological Theory*, 12:1 (March 1994), 57–72.

Hewlett, Nick. *Badiou, Balibar, Ranciere: Re-thinking Emancipation*. 2010.

Holstein, James A. and Jaber F. Gubrium. *The Self We Live By: Narrative Identity in a Postmodern World*. New York: Oxford University Press, 2000.

Holub, Robert. *Reception Theory: A Critical Introduction*. London: Routledge, 1984.

Hoxton Hall (2002) Promotional website: http://www.hoxtonhall.co.uk/Jonathan%20Kay.htm. Accessed 1 August 2002.

Iser, Wolfgang. *The Implied Reader*. Baltimore, MD: Johns Hopkins University Press, 1974.

Izzo, Gary. *The Art of Play: The New Genre of Interactive Theatre*. New York: Greenwood Press, 1997.

Izzo, Gary. *Acting Interactive Theatre: The Handbook*. New York: Greenwood Press, 1998.

Jackson, Antony. 'Positioning the Audience: Inter-Active Strategies and the Aesthetic in Educational Theatre', *Theatre Research International* 22:1, (Spring 1997): 48–60.

Jackson, Antony. *Theatre, Education and the Making of Meanings: Art or Instrument?* Manchester: Manchester University Press, 2007.

Jackson, Shannon. *Social Works – Performing Art, Supporting Publics*. London: Routledge, 2011.

Jauss, Hans-Robert. *Towards an Aesthetic of Reception*. Minneapolis: University of Minnesota Press, 1982.

Jenkins, Richard. *Pierre Bourdieu*. London: Routledge, 1992.

Johnstone, Keith. *Impro, Improvisation and the Theatre*. London: Methuen, 1981.

Johnstone, Keith. *Impro for Storytellers*. London: Routledge, 2000.

Jones, Amelia and Tracy Warr. *The Artist's Body (Themes and Movements)*. London: Phaidon Press, 2000.

Jones, Phil. *Drama as Therapy: Theatre as Living*. London: Routledge, 1996

Kaprow, Alan. *Essays on the Blurring of Art and Life*. Berkeley: University of California Press, 1993.

Kattwinkel, Susan. *Audience Participation: Essays on Inclusion in Performance*. Westport, CT: Praeger Publishers, 2003.

Kershaw, Baz. *The Politics of Performance*. London: Routledge, 1992.

Kershaw, Baz. *The Radical in Performance*. London: Routledge, 1999.

Kester, Grant. *Conversation Pieces*. London: University of California Press, 2004.

Kirby, Michael. *Happenings: An Illustrated Anthology*. Toronto: Clarke, Irwin and Company, 1965.

Koren, Leonard. *Which Aesthetics Do You Mean?: Ten Definitions*. Point Reyes, CA: Imperfect Publishing 2010.

Kostelanetz, Richard. *On Innovative Performance(s): Three Decades of Recollections on Alternative Theatre*. New York: McFarland, 1994.

Liepe-Levinson, Katherine. 'Striptease: Desire, Mimetic Jeopardy and Performing Spectators', *The Drama Review*, 42:2, (Summer 1998): 9–37.

Machon, Josephine. *(Syn)aesthetics*. Basingstoke: Palgrave, 2009.

Mason, Bim. *Street Theatre and Other Outdoor Performance*. London: Routledge, 1992.

May, Todd. *The Political Thought of Jacques Ranciere*. Edinburgh: University of Edinburgh Press, 2008.

McAuley, Gay. *Space in Performance. Making Meaning in the Theatre*. Ann Arbor: University of Michigan Press, 2000.

McConachie, Bruce. *Engaging Audiences: A Cognitive Approach to Spectating in the Theatre*. London: Palgrave Macmillan, 2008.

McConachie, Bruce and F. Elixabeth Hart (eds.). *Performance and Cognition: Theatre Studies and the Cognitive Turn*. London: Routledge, 2010.

McGill, Ormond. *The New Encyclopedia of Stage Hypnosis*. Carmarthen, UK: Crown House Pub Limited, 1996.

McMillan, Joyce. 'Theatre Reviews: I, Malvolio', 22 August 2009. Available at: http://www.edinburgh-festivals.com/viewreview.aspx?id=3023. Accessed 19 April 2012.

Mda, Zakes. *When People Play People*. London: Zed Books, 1993.

Measham, Fiona, Judith Aldridge and Howard Parker. *Dancing on Drugs*. London: Free Association Books, 2001.

Meltzer, Bernard N. and Jerome B. Manis. *Symbolic Interaction*. London: Alleyn & Bacon, 1978.

Murray, Janet. *Hamlet on the Holodeck – The Future of Narrative in Cyberspace*. Cambridge, MA: The MIT Press, 1999.

Neelands, Jonothan. *Learning Through Imagined Experience*. London: Hodder and Stoughton, 1992.

Neelands, Jonothan. *Beginning Drama 11–14*. London: David Fulton Publishers, 1998.

Nicholson, Helen. 'The Politics of Trust', *Research in Drama Education*, 7:1, (2002): 81–91.

Noland, Carrie. *Agency and Embodiment: Performing Gestures/Producing Culture*. Cambridge, MA: Harvard University Press, 2009.

Ono, Yoko. *Have You Seen the Horizon Lately?* Oxford: Museum of Modern Art, 1997.

O'Toole, John. *Theatre in Education: New Objectives for Theatre, New Techniques in Education*. Sevenoaks: Hodder and Stoughton, 1976.

O'Toole, John. *The Process of Drama*. London: Routledge, 1992.

Phillips, Tom. 'Ontreorend Goed: Internal', *Recreation Ground*, 17th December 2010. Available at http://recreationground.blogspot.co.uk/2010/12/ontroerend-goed-internal.html. Accessed 8 April 2013.

Provine, Robert. *Laughter: A Scientific Investigation*. London: Faber and Faber, 2000.

Punchdrunk. http:www.punchdrunk.com, 2010. Accessed 1 March 2011.

Rancière, Jacques. *The Politics of Aesthetics*. London: Continuum, 2004.

Rancière, Jacques. *The Emancipated Spectator*. London: Verso 2009a.

Rancière, Jacques. *Aesthetics and its Discontents*. Cambridge: Polity 2009b.

Rancière, Jacques. *Dissensus: On Politics and Aesthetics*. London: Continuum, 2010.

Reicher, Stephen. 'The Psychology of Crowd Dynamics', in Hogg and Tindale (eds.) *Blackwell Handbook of Social Psychology: Group Process*. London: Blackwell, 2002: 182–208.

Reynolds, Dee and Matthew Reason. *Kinaesthetic Empathy in Creative and Cultural Practices*. Bristol: Intellect 2012.

Ridout, Nicholas. *Stage Fright, Animals and Other Theatrical Problems*. London: Cambridge University Press, 2004.

Riggins, Stephen (ed.). *Beyond Goffman: Studies in Communication, Institution and Social Interaction*. New York: Mouton de Gruyter, 1990.

Rozik, Eli. *Fictional Thinking: A Poetics and Rhetoric of Fictional Creativity in Theatre*. Eastbourne: Sussex University Press, 2009.

Saito, Yuriko. *Everyday Aesthetics*. Oxford: Oxford University Press, 2007.

Salhi, Kamal, (ed.). *African Theatre for Development: Art for Self-Determination*. Exeter, UK: Intellect, 1998.

Sankey, Jay. *Zen and the Art of Stand-Up Comedy*. London and New York: Routledge, 1998.

Sartre, Jean-Paul. *Being and Nothingness*, trans. Hazel Barnes. New York: Philosophical Library, 1956.

Schechner, Richard. *Environmental Theatre*. New York: Applause, 1994.

Schechner, Richard. *Performance Theory*. London: Routledge, 1988.

Schechner, Richard and Willa Appel. *By Means of Performance: Intercultural Studies of Theatre and Ritual*. Cambridge: University of Cambridge Press, 1990.

Sebeok, Thomas (ed.). *Carnival*. New York: Mouton, 1984.

Shevtsova, Maria. 'The Sociology of the Theatre (1, 2 and 3)', *New Theatre Quarterly*. 5:17, 18 &19, (February, May and August 1989).

Smith, Peter and Sonya Sharp. *School Bullying: Insights and Perspectives*. London: Routledge, 1994.

Spencer, Charles. 'Thrilling High Sends Shivers Down the Spine', *The Telegraph*, 24th May 1999. Available at http://www.telegraph.co.uk/culture/4717504/Thrilling-high-send-shivers-down-the-spine.html. Accessed 8 April 2013.

States, Bert. *Great Reckonings in Little Rooms: On the Phenomenology of the Theater*. Berkeley: University of California Press, 1985.

Thompson, Evan. *Mind in Life: Biology, Phenomenology, and the Science of Mind*. Cambridge, MA: Harvard University Press, 2010.

Thompson, James. *Applied Theatre: Bewilderment and Beyond*. Oxford: Peter Lang, 2003.

Thompson, James. *Performance Affects: Applied Theatre and the Ends of Effect*. Basingstoke: Palgrave Macmillan, 2009.

Turner, Victor. *The Ritual Process*. London: Routledge, 1969.

Turner, Victor. *From – Ritual to Theatre, The Human Seriousness of Play*. New York: PAJ Publications, 1982.

Turner, Victor. *The Anthropology of Performance*. New York: PAJ Publications, 1987.

Turner, Victor. *Dramas, Fields and Metaphors*. Ithaca: Cornell University Press, 1974.

van Gennep, Arnold. *The Rites of Passage*. Ann Arbor: University of Chicago Press, 1960.

Watson, Keith. 'C'mon Join the Joy Ride', *The Guardian*, 22nd May 1999. Available at http://www.guardian.co.uk/books/1999/may/22/books.guardianreview11. Accessed 8 April 2013.

Watzlawick, Paul Janet Beavin Bavelas and Don Jackson. *Pragmatics of Human Communication*. London: W. W. Norton & Co., 1967.

Way, Brian. *Audience Participation: Theatre for Young People*. New York: W. H. Baker Co., 1980.

Weindling, Paul. 'The Origins of Informed Consent: The International Scientific Commission on Medical War Crimes, and the Nuremberg Code', *Bulletin of the History of Medicine* 75:1, (Spring 2001): 37–71.

Welton, Martin. *Feeling Theatre*. New York: Palgrave Macmillan, 2012.

White, Gareth. 'Navigating the Ethics of Audience Participation', *Applied Theatre Researcher* 7, (2006).

Winston, Joe. *Beauty and Education*. London: Routledge, 2010.

Wolff, Janet. *The Aesthetics of Uncertainty*. Chichester: Columbia University Press, 2008.

Zahavi, Dan. *Subjectivity and Selfhood: Investigating the First-Person Perspective*. Cambridge, MA: MIT Press, 2005.

# Index

Printed and bound by CPI Group (UK) Ltd, Croydon, CR0 4YY